Writing Changes: Alphabetic Text and Multimodal Composition

I0869111

Writing Changes: Alphabetic Text and Multimodal Composition

Edited by

Pegeen Reichert Powell

Modern Language Association of America
New York 2020

Printed in the United States of America

Library of Congress Cataloging-in-Publication Data

Names: Powell, Pegeen Reichert, 1970– editor.
Title: Writing changes : alphabetic text and multimodal composition / edited by Pegeen Reichert Powell.
Description: New York : The Modern Language Association of America, 2020. | Includes bibliographical references. | Summary: "Examines the relationship of multimodality and writing in composition studies, including considerations of composition as social practice and of changes to the conception of writing in relation to new social media and to writing program administration"—Provided by publisher.
Identifiers: LCCN 2019054104 (print) | LCCN 2019054105 (ebook) | ISBN 9781603294737 (hardcover) | ISBN 9781603294744 (paperback) | ISBN 9781603294751 (EPUB) | ISBN 9781603294768 (Kindle)
Subjects: LCSH: English language—Rhetoric—Study and teaching—Technological innovations. | English language—Composition and exercises—Computer-assisted instruction. | Writing centers—Administration.
Classification: LCC PE1404 .W696 2020 (print) | LCC PE1404 (ebook) | DDC 808/.042071—dc23
LC record available at https://lccn.loc.gov/2019054104
LC ebook record available at https://lccn.loc.gov/2019054105

Published by The Modern Language Association of America
85 Broad Street, suite 500, New York, New York 10004-2434
www.mla.org

Contents

Introduction: Writing Changes: Beyond the Binary of Writing versus Multimodality

Pegeen Reichert Powell

Writing Changes is a book about multimodality; it is words on a page about how we use music, video, image, and gesture to communicate. The apparent discrepancy between medium and message is a good place to begin. This discrepancy might be considered problematic, a sign that the field of composition studies, or the academy more generally, is too slow to respond to the world outside our walls. Or it might be considered reactionary, an assertion of the dominance, or even superiority, of writing over other modes of communication.

On the one hand, one of the key arguments of *Writing Changes* is that, in fact, there is no discrepancy. The discrepancy between medium and message can only be a discrepancy if alphabetic text and multimodality are understood as competing propositions, and much of the work of this collection attempts to advance the understanding that this just isn't the case—that the conversation about medium and message isn't a matter of writing (or print or alphabetic text) versus multimodality. Rather, this collection argues that such a binary is unproductive and misleading.

On the other hand, though, it is too facile to claim simply that there is no discrepancy between writing and multimodality. In fact, the perception that authors must choose between words and images when they compose, or that instructors must give up time teaching writing to make room in their syllabi for discussions of multimodal composing, shapes much of the discourse in our field surrounding multimodality.

The specious persistence of this binary comes in part from a story we tell ourselves as a field about multimodality and composition studies. The story is built around other related binaries: the book is the past and digital genres are the future; writing is passé and other modes are contemporary. In some versions of that story, the plot involves revolution, colonization, and a romance in peril. The WIDE Research Center Collective writes of our historical "romance with print conventions and theories," a romance that has run its course in the context of changes that, as Gunther Kress argues, "are vast enough to warrant the term 'revolution'" (6). Yet the revolution is incomplete: according to Jonathan Alexander and Jacqueline Rhodes, still today, "some composition instruction often colonizes multimedia with more text- and print-driven aims" (24–25).

The characterization of composition studies as both suitor and colonizer in this story notwithstanding, it is a story that many in the field are familiar with. Jason Palmeri refers to this trope as the "multimodal progress narrative":

> In the past few years, advocates of the "multimodal turn" in composition have been telling a very persuasive and influential narrative about the past, present, and future of composition studies—a narrative about how and why we must move beyond our historic focus on alphabetic literacy. . . . Over and over again, we encounter the same refrain: alphabetic literacy is our past; multimodal composing is our future. (4–5)

John Trimbur and Karen Press, summarizing this same trope in composition scholarship and identifying a range of related binaries, explain, "Multimodality . . . was understood as a matter of historical periodization. It signified an epochal shift from print to digital, page to screen, the logic of writing to the logic of the image, offering terms to divide multimodal text design in the new millennium from the older monomodal word-based, black-and-white alphabetic past of print culture" (19). In this narrative we have created for our field, writing is ceding dominance to image, to connectivity, to multiple modes, to design—and the new era is better, especially for student writers.

In this introduction, I identify some of the assumptions about both writing and multimodality that tend to reinforce the persistent binaries that underlie the multimodal progress narrative. In doing so, I lay the groundwork for the essays that follow, and, more broadly, attempt to loosen the hold this either-or construction has on our collective sense of what we can and should do in the classroom and who we are as a field.

Assumptions about Writing

Perhaps the most entrenched and unexamined assumption in the field's current discourse about multimodality is that writing is monomodal. This claim is rarely made overtly, but it is evident in the construction of arguments about multimodality. For example, Alexander and Rhodes, in their CCCC 2015 best book of the year, *On Multimodality: New Media in Composition Studies*, articulate their position this way: "We worry that the richness of multimedia, and the diversity of rhetorical affordances germane to the many dimensions of new and multimedia, may become lost as we incorporate these media into our classrooms and make them do the work of 'writing'" (17). Here, writing is unmodified, set apart in scare quotes from the "richness" and "diversity" and "many dimensions" of multimedia. The plentitude of the first half of the sentence becomes "lost" by the end of the sentence when you get to writing, isolated, and by implication, monomodal.

The assumption that writing is monomodal has been built into the discourse about multimodality in our field from the beginning. Arguably the most influential scholar when it comes to the uptake of multimodality across disciplines, including our own, is Gunther Kress. In his early work, he was especially interested in the role of image in the communication practices of young children and in educational texts (Bazalgette and Buckingham 96). Addressing our field in "Gains and Losses: New Forms of Texts, Knowledge, and Learning," published in *Computers and Composition* in 2005, he focuses on image: "[I]t seems evident to many commentators that writing is giving way, is being displaced by image in many instances of communication where previously it held sway" (5). The focus on image in Kress's work contributes to the assumption that monomodality is possible; pieces like "Gains and Losses" posit one mode, image, against another, writing. Moreover, in Kress's piece, and throughout the research and teaching about multimodality in our field and others, image, holding the promise and possibility of what's new, is conflated with multimodality more broadly. The focus in "Gains and Losses" is on image versus writing, but the larger argument is about multimodality, so it becomes multimodality versus writing. This conflation of image with multimodality more broadly comes, at least in part, from necessity: academic publishers are able to reproduce images for the purposes of analysis and theory-building about multimodality, but it has been impossible—

or at least inconceivable—to do the same with sound, moving image, gesture, and so on, in academic journals and books in print. Textbook authors and publishers, likewise, have relied on image as a stand-in for considerations of multimodality (see Sarat-St. Peter and Allan, this collection). In the construction of image versus writing, where image holds all the richness and potential of multimodality more generally, writing is the limited, monomodal other.

In many ways, we see lurking under the writing-multimodality binary some of the same long-disputed assumptions about writing that underlie the literacy-orality binary, but this time these characteristics are understood as limitations; writing is too closely associated with academic or school genres, it relies too much on linearity, it is too rational:

> We as a field are often charged with confirming students' abilities to "write" in "standard" English. . . . How often must the free-form creativity of brainstorming and prewriting eventually give way to the composed text that presents its arguments in a complex (one hopes) but nonetheless rational, straightforward manner? Excess, often characterized as the extraneous, the "off-topic," must be trimmed to produce shapely texts that argue points, consider counterarguments, and reach reasonable, rational conclusions. New and multimedia, however, often (not always, granted, but often) play with excess, with the dis-composed, with possibilities of communication and rhetorical affects and effects that take us far beyond the reasonable, the rational, the composed. (Alexander and Rhodes 24)

In Alexander and Rhodes's characterization of the binary of writing-multimodality, the good stuff must "give way" and "be trimmed" in written texts, whereas multimedia can "take us far beyond" those limitations. (See also Horner, this collection, for his similar analysis about the limitations of writing.)

If pressed, presumably most authors and teachers would acknowledge that writing is not, in fact, a limited, monomodal other. Indeed, they might point out, "all texts are multimodal" (more about this commonplace later). But the figure of writing disappears altogether in this commonplace. The effect of this disappearance for some teachers and scholars in our field is a feeling that they need to eschew all considerations of multimodality in an attempt to keep writing in their sights at all. Even if not entirely invisible in the discourse about multimodality, writing, at best, remains "uninterrogated" (see Rule, this collection). What this collection seeks to do is recognize and interrogate the disciplinary expertise and pedagogical practices associated with writing that are inherent, if hidden, in the claim that all texts are multimodal—for example, to recognize the potential of the ur-genre of composition studies, the essay, in digital and online communication as Joseph Harris does in his essay in this collection, or to identify the rhetorical concepts and pedagogical principles that have long been a part of writing instruction that should be brought to bear on teaching search engine optimization, as Jenna Pack Sheffield does in her essay.

Assumptions about Multimodality

If the most persistent assumption about writing is that it is monomodal, perhaps the most persistent assumption about multimodality is that we know what it is. However, scholars in various fields who use *multimodality* to describe their theoretical or methodological projects share the conceptual problem that if *all* communication events and artifacts draw on more than one semiotic resource, and they always have, then to say that one is studying or teaching multimodality is casting a wide, unwieldy net. As an object of study, multimodality, by definition, is all communication across all time. Thus, the theories, methodologies, and pedagogies that deal with multimodality necessarily remain tentative and inconsistent about purview and purpose, although this isn't always acknowledged in the scholarship.

Carey Jewitt, in her introduction to *The Routledge Handbook of Multimodal Analysis*, admits that "[m]ultimodal analysis is an intensive research process both in relation to time and labour. Multimodal research can be applied to take a detailed look at 'big' issues and questions through specific instances. Nonetheless the scale of multimodal research can restrict the potential of multimodality to comment beyond the specific to the general" (27). Therefore, when scholars, teachers, or textbook authors introduce ideas about the affordances of different modes or provide instruction about designing pages, drawing on analytical frameworks and concepts from multimodal scholarship as part of their instruction, they risk codifying claims that have been tested only in specific instances or a limited corpus.

Moreover, Jewitt acknowledges that multimodality "can seem rather impressionistic in its analysis. How do you know that this gesture means this or this image means that?" (26). David Machin, in the same handbook, elaborates: trying to make sense of a multimodal text, we bring what we know about the historical and cultural context and extratextual references to our analysis, what critics refer to as "post hoc analysis" (188). Machin warns, "[W]e must be careful that our concepts are not simply being imposed afterwards organised around our already existing understandings and need to impose our own frameworks" (189). In post hoc analysis, our theoretical concepts about the way various modes operate do not derive inherently from the modes themselves but from our understanding of the way they operate in specific texts. For example, analysts might make claims about how images or words work in a movie poster by pointing to the role of those images or words in meaning-making, but they might fail to recognize the extent to which their claims about the affordances of these modes are informed by personal prior knowledge about the genre of movie posters or the historical and cultural context of the particular movie. (For further examples, see Machin 188–189.) In short, we may not know as much as we assume we do about multimodality itself.

Complicating the effort to construct theories and methodologies about multimodality is the way that language metaphors, as well as what we know about the way language works, have largely driven how scholars have theorized the ways that other modes work (see Scollon and Scollon 171). As Cary Bazalgette and David Buckingham argue, the "linguistic turn" in the social sciences in the 1970s turned everything into a text "that could be analysed and explained in linguistic terms: from popular culture to fashion to food, and from politics to the operations of the unconscious mind, it was all about language. And these languages could all be understood as logical systems, with their own codes and conventions and forms of grammar and syntax" (97). It is no wonder, then, that when scholars began to turn their attention to multimodality, this framework was imposed on these new theoretical and methodological questions. For example, we see this framework in the title and argument of Kress and Theo van Leeuwen's influential *Reading Images: The Grammar of Visual Design*. They draw the parallel between language and images explicitly in their introduction: "Like linguistic structures, visual structures point to particular interpretations of experience and forms of social interaction" (2). Their reliance on the notions of "visual literacy" and "visual language" in this book indicate the pervasiveness of the language metaphor in their approach to studying images. However, some scholars are questioning the efficacy of bringing linguistic concepts and frameworks to bear on the study of other modes and the analysis of the relations among modes: "Is it . . . necessarily a good move to try to explain one phenomenon by use of a framework developed to describe and understand another?" (Machin 181).

We see this, too, in our field's tendency to use *literacy* and *writing* as metaphors to talk about communication practices more generally. Anne Frances Wysocki and Johndan Johnson-Eilola, in their 1999 piece "Blinded by the Letter: Why Are We Using Literacy as a Metaphor for Everything Else?," and more recently Lisa Dush, in her 2015 article "When Writing Becomes Content," interrogate literacy and writing, respectively, as metaphors. Dush, following Wysocki and Johnson-Eilola, calls for us to pay attention to the implications of these metaphors, but she argues, "Writing is, of course, so essential to our field's identity that it is difficult to see its attendant bundles" (179).

One of the implications of the language metaphors driving the scholarship on multimodality is that modality is assumed to be a characteristic of texts, constitutive of a given text in the same way that grammar or syntax might be considered constitutive of a sentence. Bruce Horner, in his essay in this collection, argues that instead of seeing modality as constitutive of a text, "modality is more appropriately, usefully understood as social practice." As Horner points out, seeing modality as a feature of a text contributes to the most persuasive assumption that underlies the binary of writing versus multimodality, that multimodality is automatically positive: "The presumption that modalities are attributes of specific kinds of text objects effectively treats modalities as countable—*modalities* rather than *modality*. . . . It stands to reason, then, that, if modality is countable, more would be better and less, worse."

We see this more-is-better assumption in the quotation cited above from Alexander and Rhodes: multimodality is rich, diverse, full of possibility. Trimbur and Press address the point that multimodality, the very term itself, is positive because of the "positive valence attached to the prefix 'multi-.' Since at least the 1980s, terms such as 'multicultural,' 'multilingual,' 'multimedia,' and 'multiliteracies' seemed, understandably enough, to be ethically and politically preferable to their singular, apparently regressive versions such as 'monocultural' and 'monolingual,' less restrictive, and more open to differences" (22–23). If we assume we know what multimodality is, and that it is a characteristic of texts, perhaps the most persuasive assumption underlying the progress narrative and the writing-versus-modality binary is that multimodality is unequivocally positive.

Beyond the Binary

Recognizing the faulty (if persistent) assumptions that reinforce the binary between writing and multimodality is an important intellectual exercise, just in terms of establishing more veracious claims about what we're doing as scholars of composition. But unpacking these assumptions is also important because, to the extent that they sustain the binary, they prevent us from moving forward. If writing and multimodality are established as competing propositions, then teachers and researchers are compelled to make an impossible choice. The progress narrative insists that as a field we must get past writing, leave it behind, but this is neither feasible nor desirable. At the same time, denying the changes in communication practices or framing the changes as a threat to or break from disciplinary expertise with writing limits how we understand, respond to, and contribute thoughtfully to those changes. Ultimately, the binary and the assumptions that feed it create an intellectual stalemate.

The oft repeated claim that all texts are multimodal, or all writing is multimodal, is an attempt to deconstruct the binary and avoid the impossible choice it presents. In her essay in this collection, "Beyond Page Design: Writing as Multimodal Embodied Meaning," Hannah Rule cites several instances of the assertion that all texts are multimodal. While not disagreeing with the claim itself, Rule wonders if

> Seeing writing and multimodality in this way—with multimodality as always already a condition, if on the literal periphery, of traditional alphabetic texts— . . . could be, too, a kind of strategy. Claiming that writing is already multimodal urges us to accept that multimodality isn't something additional to teach, but just another dimension of what we already do.

The claim that all texts are multimodal is a strategy for urging teachers and researchers to embrace the progress inherent in multimodality. However, this phrase moves too quickly past the unproductive and persistent binary at the center of the progress narrative, between writing and multimodality, a tension that is still felt by many in the field. The claim that all texts are multimodal conveniently collapses this binary into a truism that is difficult to argue with (especially when accompanied by the explication of the visual and design elements inherent in the traditional print essay). However, the assumptions about writing and multimodality that I discuss above remain obscured, and unquestioned, in this commonplace. I can think of no other assertion that we would make about all texts. "All texts are multimodal," I argue, is a too-easy response to the changes in our communication practices brought on by digital technologies and platforms. It is a response that arises at a particular moment in our field's trajectory, an attempt to fit our historical focus on writing and print into a new vision for the field.

Trimbur and Press explain, "multimodality is new as a *term*, a *conceptual terrain* that surfaced at a particular historical conjuncture, goaded by the need to understand dramatic changes in the means of communication. There is nothing new, however, about multimodality as a practice of text production" (21). They are making a distinction between the "conceptual terrain" of multimodality, a relatively new phenomenon, and the practices that have always comprised communication. This distinction is a more useful response to the changes brought on by digital technologies and new platforms than the facile claim that all texts are multimodal. Likewise, Bruce Horner, Cynthia Selfe, and Tim Lockridge, in *Translinguality, Transmodality, and Difference: Exploring Dispositions and Change in Language and Learning*, argue for "a distinction between specific material practices, on the one hand, and, on the other, beliefs about/dispositions towards those practices." This distinction is important for getting past the false choice between writing and multimodality.

Teasing out specific material practices from the "beliefs about/dispositions towards those practices" helps us recognize, for example, that despite the pervasive and persuasive *belief* that writing with alphabetic text is monomodal, in fact, monomodality as a *practice* is impossible. (Ron Scollon and Suzie Wong Scollon assert that "no mode of communication operates in a monomodal fashion" [170].) When Horner, in his essay in this collection, refers to the "ritual acknowledgments that all texts are multimodal," his use of the term *ritual* is telling: the incantation that "all texts are multimodal" is itself an expression of a *belief* about multimodality, rather than an assertion about the complex *practices* inherent in communication. In this phrase, texts—not practices—are described as multimodal. In fact, this happens in many theories and analytical frameworks surrounding multimodality. As Paul Prior argues about Kress's influential "Gains and Losses" and *Literacy and the New Media Age*, "[D]istributed practices of production, interpretation and use tend to be relocated, as obligatory elements, inside texts themselves." He continues, "I do not believe that we can account for multimodality and affordances without a focus on the whole of practice—on artifacts, activity, and people alike" (28–29).

Therefore, maintaining the distinction between practices and beliefs allows us to ask about the role of writing, as material and social practice, in composition studies, in an era characterized by rapidly changing technologies and platforms, as a practice woven within and located alongside countless other material and social practices. Practices are messy and contradictory, so it's no wonder that there isn't a single path forward charted in these pages. This project was, from the beginning, conceived as a collection of arguments and ideas to allow for some of those contradictions to emerge. The essays in this book embrace some of the inconsistent practices at work in the field or in individual programs. For example, Denise Paster and Alan J. Reid explore how a digital, multimodal badging system can reinforce what some might consider to be traditional writing practices, and Stephanie Vie reports on the uneven adoption of social media writing in composition studies as a whole. And the tensions can be felt across essays as well: Claire Lutkewitte, Star Medzerian Vanguri, and Vie outline a productive understanding of "style" (one of the five rhetorical canons, and so not exactly new) that points toward rich approaches for assessing a variety of texts being produced today in our composition classrooms, but Rory Lee notes in his survey of undergraduate writing and rhetoric programs that assessment is one of the most daunting obstacles for teachers who want to embrace multimodal practices and one reason instructors cite for not doing so.

To the extent that we can tolerate messiness and contradictions in our material and social practices, this collection—as a reflection of the field of composition studies as a whole—might be able to get past the writing-multimodality binary, recognizing that it never was and never can be writing versus multimodality when we consider how humans communicate and therefore how we might teach students to produce texts of their own. The pedagogical space we occupy when we focus on the production of student work provides us with the opportunity to recognize the "haphazard and improvised nature of much human communication, as well as its emotional dimensions," which Bazalgette and Buckingham argue that multimodal theory in general ignores (98). We can begin to imagine how we might intervene in the material and social practices themselves, and some essays here point to specific ways that might happen.

However, I would argue that the binary itself has never been about the practices in the first place but about disciplinarity more generally. Alexander and Rhodes's *On Multimodality: New Media in Composition Studies* is significant because Alexander and Rhodes no longer find it necessary to argue for the importance of teaching with multiple modes; instead, they "want to take stock of how our field is changing and to chart its potential trajectories" (17). They determine that "composition studies has found itself at a crossroads" (3). While they do not explicate this metaphor, it is clear that the choice is for the field to continue on the road of writing or to take a new direction toward multimodality, and the image of a crossroads communicates the implied binary.

Perhaps paradoxically, the question of who we are as a field, and in fact the very nature of disciplinarity, has been at the center of composition studies for decades. It is striking the number of prominent scholars in composition studies (listed here in alphabetical order) who have taken up the question of disciplinarity: James Berlin, Robert Connors, Sharon Crowley, Maxine Hairston, Joseph Harris, Susan Miller, Stephen North, Louise Wetherbee Phelps, among others. In spite of (or perhaps because of) this impressive body of scholarship raising questions of disciplinarity, our hold on disciplinarity remains tentative and we see deliberate efforts to redress this situation. The prominent pedagogical approach of *writing about writing*, first and most forcefully articulated by Douglas Downs and Elizabeth Wardle, is explicitly about disciplinarity. Downs and Wardle argue that through this approach, "we will raise awareness not only about the existence of our discipline, but about what we do as a discipline—what we study and think about." They continue, with an admission about our provisionary status as a discipline, that teaching "writing about writing" will "lead us further toward full disciplinarity" (578). (Derek Owens and Tara Roeder, in their essay in this collection, survey the way the field of composition studies has turned to *writing studies* as a way to stake a claim in the institution.) Likewise, the growing body of work about threshold concepts is arguably the most recent claim to disciplinarity. In her introduction to *Naming What We Know: Threshold Concepts of Writing Studies*, Kathleen Blake Yancey sets the context for this compendium of disciplinary concepts with the claim, "What seems to be missing, since the beginning of the field and even in this late age of print, is any consensus in the field on what we might call the content of composition: the questions, kinds of evidence, and materials that define disciplines and would thus define us as well" (xviii).

It is no wonder that without such a consensus—even as *Naming What We Know* attempts to work toward one—multimodality as a set of beliefs might expose some raw questions about who we are as composition professionals and where we're headed. To be clear, digital technologies and online platforms do multiply the practices that constitute human communication and thus what we might teach. However, the persistence of the writing-multimodality binary in our discourse, in the progress narrative we tell ourselves about the field, may be less about communication practices and more about the lack of a disciplinary center—or, at the very least, that at the center is simply a question of identity. To claim that we're at a crossroads, as Alexander and Rhodes do, assumes too much about the ground beneath our feet in the first place.

Writing, as social and material practice, with all the inherent messiness and contradictions and affective dimensions, is inevitable, just as all the other social and material practices that constitute human communication are inevitable, and the relations among these various practices will be layered and complex as well. What we can begin to do, without resorting to or appealing to the writing-versus-multimodality binary, is to be mindful about what practices are valued and rewarded in various contexts and to allow for shifting priorities across various writing and teaching situations. We can pause to consider what assumptions are shaping our beliefs about these practices. In his reflection on the field of composition studies in the postprocess, postpedagogy era, *After Pedagogy: The Experience of Teaching*, Paul Lynch argues that to focus on practices themselves does not mean throwing up our hands at the possibility of disciplinary expertise. Rather, "the question is how we bring rigor to the expression and experience of contingency." He imagines a conversation "in which teachers attempt to articulate practical wisdom, to imaginatively bureaucratize" (137). This era of rapidly changing technologies and everyday communication happening at lightning speed is certainly one of contingency, but the goal of this collection is to bring some rigor to that experience so that we can indeed move forward, even as the ground beneath us continues to shift.

Collection Overview

This collection is organized into four parts. Each part examines modality through social and pedagogical practices that influence the evolution of composition studies and multimodality's role in the composition classroom. The essays in the first two parts, "Modality as Social Practice" and "Modality in Texts and in the Classroom," interrogate the notion of modality and survey historical and contemporary communication practices to expand the definition of multimodal composition. In the final two parts, "Modality and Writing Program Administration" and "Modality and Disciplinarity," the essays more broadly explore student and faculty engagement with and attitudes toward writing and technology to describe how multimodality might affect composition programs as our communication practices evolve.

Modality as Social Practice

The essays in the opening part begin by complicating and enriching our understanding of modality itself and challenging the perceived dichotomy between multimodality and monomodality. In "Modality as Social Practice in Written Language," Bruce Horner argues that rather than think of modality as "a distinguishing attribute of texts," it is "more appropriately, usefully understood as social practice." In "Something Borrowed, Something New: Multimodal Composition through the Reclamation of Vernacular Literacies," Sara Cooper looks at the vernacular literacy practices of women and other underrepresented groups through their "letters, postcards, recipes, diaries—of the sort kept in an attic or a shoebox under the bed." In so doing, she studies modality as social practice, much as Horner suggests. Hannah J. Rule challenges the dichotomy between monomodality and multimodality in the next essay, "Beyond Page Design: Writing as Multimodal Embodied Meaning," by studying how our perception of this dichotomy is shaped by the psychological theories surrounding our teaching. Specifically, whereas Howard Gardner's theory of multiple intelligences might perpetuate the belief that communicating with words is different than communicating with other modes, the work of the neurolinguist Benjamin Bergen and the philosopher Mark Johnson, for example, can help us conceptualize the "dynamic multimodality within the linguistic." In the last essay in this part, "Translating Modalities: Interactions between Digital and Alphabetic Modes in Professional Translation Work," Laura Gonzales considers translation practices as a site "for studying the interactions between alphabetic and digitally mediated modalities in situated cultural-rhetorical contexts." Thus, she illustrates modality as social practice and she also considers the "embodied modalities" involved in translation work.

Modality in Texts and in the Classroom

The richer understanding of modality advanced in part 1 lays the groundwork for part 2, which demonstrates that the forms and practices that constitute our work in the composition classroom are relevant beyond alphabetic text and multimodal composing. In the first three essays in this part, the authors discuss how old or familiar forms and practices associated with alphabetic text can and should inform the work of multimodal composition. In "The Places of Writing on the Multimodal Page," Matthew Davis and Alex Mueller argue that the history of the medieval manuscript page is an important resource for understanding the textual activity of digital writing, and that "the knowledge of this history compels us to orient our reading and writing pedagogy newly to the page. . . ." Next, Joseph Harris moves from the page to the essay in "The Essay as Form in a Digital Age." Drawing on T. W. Adorno's "The Essay as Form," Harris argues that "the Internet may now offer more congenial spaces for the essay than does much of the academy" and so as instructors we can rely on "the affordances of the Web to reinvigorate how we teach a form of writing, the critical essay, that has long been part of a dissenting tradition of work in the academy." The next essay, "Styling the Multimodal Classroom: Addressing the Labor of Assessment through the Rhetorical Lexicon of Style," takes up the renewed interest in the rhetorical canon of style. In this essay, Claire Lutkewitte, Star Medzerian Vanguri, and Stephanie Vie argue that the lexicon of style is an important resource for teaching and assessing multimodal composition, as it "addresses the concerns of faculty members who seek assessment tools that can be applied to all texts."

The last essays in this part look at digital and multimodal practices, genres, and media that can influence how we understand and teach alphabetic text, emphasizing the ways that writing is intrinsic to, rather than separate from, new media and digital communication. In "Search Engine Optimization and Its Significance for Alphabetic Composing in Writing Pedagogy," Jenna Pack Sheffield argues that search engine optimization (SEO)—producing text that improves the ranking of a Web site—is becoming increasingly important for writers in the twenty-first century. As a new writing convention, SEO requires unique strategies but also draws on elements of familiar writing pedagogy, such as audience, invention, and ethos. Brenta Blevins explicates the ways that alphabetic writing is intrinsic to producing and circulating new media such as augmented reality in "Of Writing and the Future: Augmented Reality Composition." In so doing, she challenges the binary between writing and multimodality but also between process and product. Part 2 of this collection, then, offers rich possibilities that arise from understanding that writing is intrinsic to, not opposed to or threatened by, multimodality and digital composition.

Modality and Writing Program Administration

The essays in part 3 step back and take stock of where we are now in terms of communicating this more productive understanding of the relation between alphabetic text and multimodal composing. Perhaps it's not surprising, given the rapid pace of change in recent years, that, as the essays in this part purport, our field unevenly embraces the argument that challenges the binary between writing and multimodality. In "Positioning Writing: An Analysis of Textbook Arguments about Multimodality," Hilary A. Sarat-St. Peter and Elizabeth G. Allan analyze popular textbooks that support multimodal composing to reveal the textbooks' arguments about alphabetic text. Recognizing that students and instructors may ignore, endorse, or resist these arguments, the analysis of these textbooks nonetheless offers a glimpse at the relation between alphabetic text and multimodal composing in the field, and how that relation has evolved over approximately ten years. In "*Facebook* Posts, *Twitter* Hashtags, and *Snapchat* Stories: Changing Conceptions of Writing in a Social Media Landscape," Stephanie Vie's data about faculty attitudes toward and uses of social media leads her to conclude that "institutional context is crucial and that faculty members' own orientations toward technology in general and social media specifically play key roles" in the varying ways that social media writing practices are recognized and rewarded in their classrooms.

Part 3 moves from textbooks and faculty attitudes to a writing program initiative with Denise P. Paster and Alan J. Reid's "The *Coastal Composition Commons*: Considering Flexibility, Delivery, and Valuation in a Badging Initiative." Paster and Reid study the gap between digital and multimodal infrastructure in writing programs and the traditional print texts still expected of students. Their example is an online badging system that encourages students to earn badges for achieving various writing skills. While the badging system itself is entirely digital and multimodal, students earn the badges by submitting texts that are predominantly print-based. The final essay in this part, "Making the Case: Implementing Multimodality in Undergraduate Major Programs in Writing and Rhetoric," draws on case studies of undergraduate writing majors at three different institutions, illustrating the uneven adoption of multimodal pedagogies. In this essay, Rory Lee investigates the circumstances that might promote and constrain more alphabetic writing or more multimodal activity in these majors.

Modality and Disciplinarity

In part 4, two essays broaden the lens and lay out arguments about disciplinarity in the context of ongoing changes in our communication practices. In "Following Directions, Responding to Shifts, Shaking Foundations: Multimodal Composition within and across Writing Programs," Beth Brunk-Chavez asks how the changes in communication practices and the inclusion of multimodality might prompt significant changes across our programs and institutions. Derek Owens and Tara Roeder argue that instead of dubbing our field *writing studies*, the label *composition and design* better captures what we as an interdisciplinary field ought to do in the twenty-first century. In "Reclaiming Composition: A Twenty-First-Century Interdisciplinary Imperative," Owens and Roeder claim that this nomenclature calls for a "shift in attitude and acceptance" toward different compositional strategies, technologies, and forms and challenges our sense of disciplinarity. These final essays resist the dichotomy between alphabetic text and multimodal composing, even while they offer different visions of the field. Taken together, and in the context of the volume as a whole, these essays lay out the challenges and the possibilities we face as writing changes in the twenty-first century.

Works Cited

Alexander, Jonathan, and Jacqueline Rhodes. *On Multimodality: New Media in Composition Studies*. Conference on College Composition and Communication / National Council of Teachers of English, 2014.

Bazalgette, Cary, and David Buckingham. "Literacy, Media and Multimodality: A Critical Response." *Literacy*, vol. 47, no. 2, July 2013, pp. 95–102.

Downs, Douglas, and Elizabeth Wardle. "Teaching about Writing, Righting Misconceptions: (Re)envisioning 'First-Year Composition' as 'Introduction to Writing Studies.'" *College Composition and Communication*, vol. 58, no. 4, June 2007, pp. 552–84. *JSTOR*, www.jstor.org/stable/i20456960.

Dush, Lisa. "When Writing Becomes Content." *College Composition and Communication*, vol. 67, no. 2, Dec. 2015, pp. 173–96, www.ncte.org/library/NCTEFiles/Resources/Journals/CCC/0672-dec2015/CCC0672When.pdf.

Horner, Bruce, et al. *Translinguality, Transmodality, and Difference: Exploring Dispositions and Change in Language and Learning*. Enculturation/Intermezzo, 2015, intermezzo.enculturation.net/01/ttd-horner-selfe-lockridge/index.htm.

Jewitt, Carey. "An Introduction to Multimodality." *The Routledge Handbook of Multimodal Analysis*, edited by Jewitt, Routledge, 2009, pp. 14–27.

Kress, Gunther. "Gains and Losses: New Forms of Texts, Knowledge, and Learning." *Computers and Composition*, vol. 22, no. 1, Dec. 2005, pp. 5–22.

Kress, Gunther, and Theo van Leeuwen. *Reading Images: The Grammar of Visual Design*. 2nd ed., Routledge, 2006.

Lynch, Paul. *After Pedagogy: The Experience of Teaching*. NCTE, 2013.

Machin, David. "Multimodality and Theories of the Visual." *The Routledge Handbook of Multimodal Analysis*, edited by Carey Jewitt, Routledge, 2009, pp. 181–90.

Palmeri, Jason. *Remixing Composition: A History of Multimodal Writing Pedagogy*. Southern Illinois UP / NCTE, 2012.

Prior, Paul. "Moving Multimodality beyond the Binaries: A Response to Gunther Kress' 'Gains and Losses.'" *Computers and Composition*, vol. 22, no. 1, Dec. 2005, pp. 23–30.

Scollon, Ron, and Suzie Wong Scollon. "Multimodality and Language: A Retrospective and Prospective View." *The Routledge Handbook of Multimodal Analysis*, edited by Carey Jewitt, Routledge, 2009, pp. 170–80.

Trimbur, John, and Karen Press. "When Was Multimodality? Modality and the Rhetoric of Transparency." *Multimodality in Writing: The State of the Art in Theory, Methodology and Pedagogy*, edited by Arlene Archer and Esther Breuer, Brill, 2015, pp. 19–42.

The WIDE Research Center Collective. "Why Teach Digital Writing?" *Kairos*, vol. 10, no. 1, Fall 2005, kairos.technorhetoric.net/10.1/coverweb/wide/collective_bio.html.

Wysocki, Anne Frances, and Johndan Johnson-Eilola. "Blinded by the Letter: Why Are We Using Literacy as a Metaphor for Everything Else?" *Passions, Pedagogies, and 21st Century Technologies*, edited by Gail E. Hawisher and Cynthia L. Selfe, Utah State UP / NCTE, 1999, pp. 349–68.

Yancey, Kathleen Blake. "Coming to Terms: Composition/Rhetoric, Threshold Concepts, and a Disciplinary Core." *Naming What We Know: Threshold Concepts of Writing Studies*, edited by Linda Adler-Kassner and Elizabeth Wardle, Utah State UP, 2015, pp. xvii–xxxi.

Part One

Modality as Social Practice

Modality as Social Practice in Written Language

Bruce Horner

In conjoining alphabetic text and multimodal composition, this collection poses the question of the relation of one to the other. That question itself presupposes a distinction between the two—that alphabetic text and multimodal composition are somehow different. It is that presupposition that then raises the question of what the relation between these two might be. But I will argue that we need, instead, to pose the question of modality. That is, rather than assuming that alphabetic text and multimodal composition are distinct, we can ask how we might best understand modality, and what understandings of modality have led us to assume a distinction between something called alphabetic text and something called multimodal composition that has raised the question of their relation to one another.

Admittedly, this might seem to reverse the course of scholarship on multimodality, or at the very least to ignore large swaths of that scholarship—to take us back to matters that have long been settled. But there is use in unsettling such matters, if only to better grasp how we have come to where we are, and what course we might be heading toward. And in light of the curious alignments that have emerged between neoliberalist discourse and the course on which much scholarship on multimodality appears to be bent (more on this later), it would seem to be appropriate to at least consider thinking about how we have been thinking about, well, alphabetic text and multimodal composition.

My argument is that while modality is ordinarily understood as a distinguishing attribute of texts—as in the distinction between "alphabetic" and "multimodal" compositions—modality is more appropriately, usefully understood as social practice. Admittedly, this runs against prevailing understandings of modality. But those prevailing understandings underlie the alignments of mainstream scholarly discourse on multimodality and neoliberal discourse, and hence are worth running against. Following a review of strands of mainstream discourse on multimodality (and alphabetic text) to explicate such alignments, I outline my proposed alternative conception of modality as social practice. I argue that conceiving of modality as social practice can account for significant differences in the effects experienced by those engaging with what is ordinarily identified as a particular modality (as well as the experience of seemingly identical effects among those engaging with what are identified as quite different modalities). This alternative conception of modality as social practice, I argue, suggests a pedagogy that investigates students' different and changing experiences of and with modality to both identify and potentially revise traditions of social practice with modality.

Modality and Text Objects

Modality is predominantly understood as an attribute of text objects—the physical medium of the text object in question and, in consequence it is assumed, the sense by which it is perceived: sound/hearing, image/sight. More broadly, modality is implicated by the genre of the text object: film versus symphony versus painting versus novel. While it is granted that genres may and do deploy multiple media and modes, modalities are understood as part of what constitutes and defines such genres. As Gunther Kress, for example, puts it, "[T]extual objects are [now] more clearly seen to be . . . constituted by a number of modes" ("Multimodality" 184). It makes sense to speak of multimodal as a trait distinguishing a particular kind of composition only if we believe texts can be defined in terms of the modalities that constitute them.

The presumption that modalities are attributes of specific kinds of text objects effectively treats modalities as countable—*modalities* rather than *modality*. In fact, use of *modality* as a noncount noun is uncommon (unlike *multimodality*). Instead, there are *modes* and *modalities*. It stands to reason, then, that, if modality is countable, more would be better and less, worse. Thus monomodality has become the unmentionable other to multimodality (and hence the ritual acknowledgements that all texts are multimodal).

The treatment of modality as a matter of discrete, countable modalities also contributes to the framing of modality as a matter of choices and resources. It is within that framing that having or using more modalities comes to be understood as better—at least within the ideology of neoliberalism and its posited rational, individual consumer subject. We can see such framing, for example, in Kathleen Yanccy's argument that compositions are made "not *only* in words" (my emphasis), in Pippa Stein's observation that multimodal texts "allow for the expression of a *much fuller* range of human emotion and experience" (95; my emphasis), in Cynthia Selfe's call for a "more capacious choice" of "openness to multiple modalities of rhetorical expression" ("Response" 606–07), and in Jonathan Alexander and Jacqueline Rhodes's call for exploring "the *richness* of multimedia" (17; my emphasis; see also 19).[1]

Arguments defining multimodality as a matter of offering more tend to conflate that "more" with what is different, better, and new. We can see this conflation in Glynda A. Hull and Mark Evan Nelson's insistence that

> multimodal composing . . . is not *simply* an additive art whereby images, words, and music, by virtue of being juxtaposed, *increase* the meaning-making potential of a text. Rather, . . . a multimodal text can create a *different* system of signification, one that transcends the collective contribution of its constituent part. . . . *Multimodality can afford*, not just a *new* way to make meaning, but a *different* kind of meaning. (225; emphases added)

As I've argued elsewhere (Horner), and as the arguments cited above illustrate, the identification of multimodality with what is different, with the good, and with the new leads to treating multimodality as a break from the past, the status quo, and the dominant, which are then conflated with print text, identified with being "narrow" and "exclusionary" (Selfe, "Response" 610) and by which Western societies remain "dominated" (Hull and Nelson 225). At the same time, reassuringly, multimodality is offered not as a replacement for alphabetic print text but, instead, as enriching possibilities—a means of moving *beyond* the "limits of language" (Stein 95). As Kathy Ann Mills puts it in her "Review of the 'Digital Turn,'" "There is a shared recognition that reading and writing practices using words on paper-based text formats are necessary, but not sufficient, for communicating across the multiple platforms of meaning-making in society" (251, citing Kress). And as Hull and Nelson suggest, "[T]he new media that afford multimodal composing might helpfully be viewed not as a threat to or impoverishment of the print-based canon or traditional means of composing, but rather as an opportunity to contribute a newly invigorated literate tradition and to enrich our available means of signification" (226). Or, as Selfe assures us, "we need to pay attention to *both* writing *and* . . . other composing modalities" ("Movement" 618).

For my purposes here, what is crucial in such tellings is the presumption of a specific, fixed definition of alphabetic print text (a.k.a. "writing") as distinct from what is termed multimodality, seen as something additional. It's commonly acknowledged that multimodality did not begin with the rise of digital technologies, even that predigital multimodality is often identified only with mixtures of text and other media, e.g., pictures, graphs, or music. That is to say, alphabetic print text, a.k.a. "writing," comes to be seen as the monomodal other to multimodality, hence the distinction and calls for studying the relation between alphabetic text and multimodal composition (cf. Kress, "Gains" 11).

Tellingly, the difference of multimodality identified with the new, the better, the enriching, and even the liberating is understood to be brought about by means of technologies, which, through slippage, are conflated with modes (images/vision, sounds/hearing). But to avert a sense of technological determinism, the notion of *affordances* is typically invoked; these tools do not produce but are said to afford specific effects—making them available. But what is afforded is understood to be an outcome of the technology or mode itself: what it affords and whether or not users choose to purchase what it affords.[2]

Multimodality as Commodity

There is a parallel here to neoliberalist inflections of multilingualism. Against a Fordist insistence on universal conformity to a single standard—say, global Standard English—to enable the friction-free exchange of goods, knowledge, and services, neoliberalism encourages linguistic diversity for the markets it ostensibly opens for exploitation. As Daniel Dor explains, "In this new state of affairs, the forces of economic globalization do not have a vested interest in the global spread of English. They have a short-term interest in penetrating local markets through local languages and a long-term interest in turning these languages into commodified tools of communication" (98; cf. also Kubota; Flores). Hence Visa claims that "It's Fluent in Every Language," and MasterCard counters, "Any time, Anywhere, Any Language" (qtd. in Ganahl 24). Difference, enrichment, and novelty—here in language—become terms of affordance.

What neoliberalist inflections of multilingualism and dominant arguments on multimodality share is a commodification, whether of language or mode. That is to say, in either case, a specific abstraction from communicative practice—language, mode—is then treated as itself having the effects that are, in fact, contingent on the concrete labor of practitioners—composers, listeners, viewers, readers, writers. Commodification by definition occludes the contribution of concrete labor to the production and realization of any use value from the commodified entity. To counter this requires, then, that we recognize that labor and relocate and redefine modality and effects ordinarily attributed to modality in and with the labor of those communicative practices.[3]

But instead, in dominant representations of communicative practices, specific effects are attributed to specific abstracted "modes" as themselves the agents of those effects (or affordances). So, for example, Alexander and Rhodes invoke "the power of images"—apparently all by themselves—"to create rhetorical possibilities . . . [that] communicate powerfully in ways that a composed [alphabetic print] text cannot" (25), and Hull and Nelson, drawing on Kress, assert that "[p]ictures . . . do not convey meaning in the same way that language does, and as such, their meaning-making affordances are different" (229).

Such attributions abstract and select from the range of possible results of different social practices (Prior 26–28). We can see evidence of that process of abstraction and selection in the quite different characterizations of what is ostensibly the same mode. So, for example, Kress sees writing as in danger of losing its privileged position by "the increasing prominence—dominance even—of the visual in many areas of public communication" ("Multimodality" 182), while Cynthia Selfe identifies print writing *with* the visual and in need of supplement by attention to the aural ("Movement" 621–23). The fact is that both (and neither) are correct: in specific practices with print writing, the aural, the visual, and other senses can predominate. That is not to say that there are not dominant practices with print writing, but it is to acknowledge that the dominance of such practices is a social historical phenomenon rather than a consequence of the inherent affordances of specific abstracted modes (cf. Jewitt et al. 82, discussed below).

For example, as John Trimbur explains, the sense of alphabetic print text as being no more than words on the page is a consequence of schooling: "For ourselves and our students, when we learned to read and write in school, we also learned to occupy certain subject positions as readers and writers and to orient our language practices in certain bounded ways toward written texts," ways that treated the texts as nothing more than words on the page, to be understood without attention to matters like paper texture, coloring, layout, and so on (74). Of course, what has been learned at school is never the sum of what anyone actually does, always and everywhere, with written texts. Rather, what is learned is an ideology of monomodality: a set of beliefs about texts, meanings, and valuations of these (Trimbur and Press 21).

It is thus possible to accept the seeming monomodality of alphabetic print text, on the one hand, while also recognizing that this effect of monomodality is the consequence not of alphabetic print text per se as one of its defining characteristics but, rather, of the ideological practice of monomodality, which renders such texts effectively monomodal, despite the inherent multimodality of all texts that Kress and others have acknowledged (if subsequently ignored). As Trimbur and Karen Press put it, "[T]he very idea of monomodality needs to be examined as an ideological claim and a rhetorical effect rather than an 'unquestioned' depiction of print texts" (Trimbur and Press 21).

Ironically, dominant arguments for multimodality perpetuate the ideology of monomodality in their ascriptions of monomodality to alphabetic print text. So, for example, when Hull and Nelson raise the question of "the relationship between multimodality and unimodal texts, such as academic essays" (252), that question assumes the unimodality of academic essays, leading to a skewed understanding of the relation between multimodality and such texts. Likewise, when Alexander and Rhodes argue against defenses of multimodality as equivalent to "writing"—insisting that "not *everything* is writing" (17)—they ascribe specific characteristics to writing (i.e., alphabetic print text) beyond which, they claim, other media can take us: "[W]e would do well," they argue (citing Kress), to remind ourselves that the "'distinct logics' and 'different affordances' of various media and modes are not reducible to one another," for to ignore this keeps ourselves and our students from understanding "the richness of multimedia" that "play with excess, with the dis-composed, with possibilities of communication and rhetorical affects and effects that take us far beyond the reasonable, the rational, the composed" (17, 24). But without discounting the possibilities that specific practices with multimedia might play in just such ways, it's unclear why writing itself must be, as Alexander and Rhodes claim, "rational," "straightforward," and "composed" in which authors "argue points, consider counterarguments, and reach reasonable, rational conclusions" (24).

This excludes from consideration, for example, the well-documented fact that at least some writers' writing is not rational, straightforward, and "composed" but, instead, plays with excess and with the discomposed, and pursues "rhetorical affects and effects that take us far beyond the reasonable, the rational, the composed." I'm thinking here not so much of, say, Whitman's "Leaves of Grass" or Ginsberg's "Howl" or erotica or other poetry or fiction, or not only of such writing, but work such as wisdom literature, *The Diamond Sutra*, the book of Revelation, political slogans and manifestos, presidents' tweets, surrealist writings, personal letters and emails and SMS "texts," as well as forests of texts that pretend to be but are not at all composed, straightforward, or rational (leaving aside my own writing).

Ironically, ascriptions of unimodality and a particular kind of communication to alphabetic print text align advocates of multimodality with, first, the ideology of autonomous literacy and, second, opponents of digital composition. The ideology of autonomous literacy, Brian Street has taught us, holds that literacy is an internally uniform monolith with autonomous effects on individuals and whole cultures, i.e., that literacy—treated as a noncount noun—changes cognition in specific and profound ways and thus has powerful effects not only on individuals' life chances but the character (and even possibility) of civilizations (*Literacy*). Typically the literacy so invoked is an essayist, even academic essayist, literacy conflated with alphabetic print text tout court. Latter-day proponents of this ideology of autonomous literacy, while opposing digital forms of communication for what they deem to be their intellectually damaging effects, nonetheless are in agreement with advocates of multimodality in claiming that it is alphabetic print text that makes possible (affords) the composition of rational argument and straightforward thinking (see, for example, Carr).

Here it is worth recalling that Street's critique of the ideology of autonomous literacy holds that what that ideology occludes are the social practices with literacy (rendering *literacy* plural, as *literacies*). It is those practices, rather than the abstracted medium ostensibly deployed in all and every instance of literacy practice, that are responsible for the kinds of effects that might otherwise, mistakenly, be attributed to literacy per se. It is this same insight that leads Street to call for an ideological model of multimodality, in parallel with his ideological model of literacy ("Future" 31–33). That is, rather than ascribing specific effects to abstracted modalities (or combinations thereof), which renders the question of multimodality a purely technical matter (as in technicism), an ideological model of multimodality—including ideologies of alphabetic print text—attends to the interplay of practices with and ideological beliefs about modality/ies (see Street, "New Literacy Studies" 27–28; Lea 108–10).

Ideologies of Multimodality

The *new* in literacy studies, Street reminds us, refers not to new forms of literacy but to new ways of understanding literacy as, in fact, ideological social practices ("New Literacy Studies" 28). From a pedagogical standpoint especially, what is important is the interplay between practices and ideologies of those practices. We can benefit here from what Louis-Jean Calvet has to say about that interplay, albeit in terms of language practices and beliefs. Calvet has made the point that beliefs about language—representations—act on language practices (241). So, on the one hand, "the notion of a *language* is an abstraction that rests on the regularity of a certain number of facts, of features, in the products of speakers and in their *practices*." Thus languages "exist only in and through their speakers, and they are reinvented, renewed and transformed in every interaction, each time that we speak" (7). On the other hand, Calvet notes, "Coexisting with these practices there are *representations*—what people think about languages and the way they are spoken—representations that act on practices and are one of the factors of change. They produce in particular *security/insecurity* and this leads speakers to types of *behaviour* that transform practices" (241). Thus it is that "*the invention of a language* and consequently the *way it is named* constitute an intervention in and modify the ecolinguistic niche" (248). The same may be said of modality: on the one hand, following Calvet, modalities are abstractions that rest on the regularity of a certain number of facts, of features, in the products of composers and in their *practices*, and, therefore, modalities exist only in and through their composers, and they are reinvented, renewed, and transformed in every interaction. On the other hand, also following Calvet, representations of modality/ies—what people think about modality/ies—act on practices and are one of the factors of change. And, following Calvet again, *the invention of a modality* and consequently the *way it is named* constitute an intervention in and modify the eco(communicative) niche.

The prevailing ideology of modality ascribes to alphabetic print text a particular value, legitimacy, and modal character: just "the words on the page," as Trimbur puts it, so that rational, reasoned argument, and nothing but, is presented—or so it is assumed, occluding the implicitly or explicitly unreasonable and irrational in alphabetic print text. Trimbur is critiquing what he terms the "rhetoric of deproduction" associated with the tradition of academic essayist literacy, by which the material social location of texts is erased, leaving, ideally, transparent reasoning and empirical evidence alone to persuade readers of the texts' truth value. From the perspective of modality I'm advancing, the ascription of monomodality to alphabetic print text—a monomodality that is itself associated with the "composed," the "rational," and "reasoned argument"—attests and contributes to that rhetoric of deproduction in the significance it assigns to the conventional modal characteristics of alphabetic print text: dense, small, plain-style black font on white or off-white durable but nonglossy paper, sans images, in hard bound or stiff paperback books or journals bound with somber-colored covers.

This is what Stephen Bernhardt identifies as at the "non-visually-informative" end of a continuum of texts ranging from highly visually informative (e.g., advertisements) to non-visually-informative (e.g., academic journal articles). Instead, we can recognize the latter not as non-visually-informative but, rather, as deploying visuality (and kinesthetically and even olfactorily perceived characteristics) to communicate a different kind of information than other texts—albeit a kind of information that has come to be understood—represented as nonvisual. While Bernhardt argues that "a preoccupation with conventional essay format allows little attention to visual features" (77), it's more the case that conventional essays rely heavily on visual features and learned practices in reading those features in particular ways—say, as unimportant, immaterial. Leaving aside the fact that my depiction of alphabetic print text is at best a caricature based on professional academic journals of specific disciplines at particular historical periods, even as caricature, it brings out the multimodal character of what has been instead identified as monomodal: colors, textures, page size, bindings, smells, weight, and the arrangement of all these. Further, my depiction suggests that persuasion accomplished through such texts has as much to do with readers' learned responses to their particular modal features—again, the font size and type and color, the feel and smell and weight of the pages and bound volume, the cover, and so on—as it has to do with any presentation of reasoned argument. Suresh Canagarajah's study of the poor reception granted to manuscripts submitted to academic journals that fail to meet "nondiscursive requirements"—e.g., manuscripts having yellowed rather than starch-white paper, pale typescript rather than sharp laser print—demonstrates precisely the significance of such modal features. The ostensible singularity of the modality of such academic texts is thus itself a learned perception of what is manifestly multimodal. Just as white is typically seen not as a color at all, so particular configurations of ink and paper have come to be viewed—seen, perceived—as transparent (invisible), im-material, disembodied arguments rather than material, physical objects with material, social histories, the products of practices.

There is a telling parallel here in studies of representations of Western classical music. Western classical chamber music (e.g., string quartets) especially, though not exclusively, has long been studied, understood, represented, and officially heard as no more than a set of relations of pitch and duration—the "corporealization of the intelligence that is in sounds" (a.k.a. "absolute" music—music without verbal text or program).[4] Correspondingly, the modal characteristics of performances of such music—typically, performers remaining seated while performing, wearing "formal," dark-colored clothing (black pants or skirts and shoes, white tops, black jackets), and rarely engaging "directly" with audience members, who likewise remain seated and quiet throughout the performances, applauding only at the conclusion of each composition's performance, with no whistling or shouting—have been understood, represented, as in line with "privileging" perceptions of music as no more or less than such corporealizations of intelligence in sound. These characteristics are said to push all other perceptions to the background, denying (or disciplining) the body (see Leppert 25).

But rather than seeing these features as evidence of the monomodality of "this kind of music" (the phrase itself a reduction of the full experience in the same way "language" reduces the full panoply of what any communicative effort entails), it is more accurate to say that the experience of chamber music includes these modal features as key components, as it were, of social historical conventions for "transcending" the material social realm; i.e., such transcendence is associated with performers wearing dark clothing, remaining seated, playing string instruments, etc., and audience members remaining largely still—being attentive through bodily deportment different from, but no less or more attentive than, say, jazz performance audience members' embodiment of being attentive through snapping fingers, nodding heads, clapping and shouting accolades after solos, etc. Such listening practices—what listeners listen for and how they manifest their listening—have been learned as part of what Leon Botstein refers to as competing versions of musical literacy in which concertgoers have been schooled, formally and informally.[5]

Writing Modality as Social Practice

To counter the limitations of ideological notions of Western classical chamber music (and other music) as immaterial and absolute in its purity from the social historical realm, musicologists have devised the neologism *musicking*, by which is meant the full panoply of practices and media of participation in events ascribed to be musical, including the practices of listeners as well as performers, composers, music publishers, concert hall architects, instruments and instrument makers, concert hall janitors, and so on (see Small). That is, rather than treating music as the text-object (i.e., the score as visible manifestation of the transcendent, timeless "work of art"), with effects attributed to specific features of that text-object (the organization of pitch and duration), "musicking" treats music as social practice, and thereby the outcome of the labor of multiple participants in any given experience identified as musical, including practices of listening. This means, too, that features not conventionally identified as constituents of the music and its experience can come back into focus and consideration, such as those described above: the musicians' (and the audience members') bodies, clothing, gestures, etc. Raymond Williams notes that practical consciousness and experience inevitably exceed official representations of experience (*Marxism* 130–31). To return to alphabetic print text, we might say that students' practical consciousness and experience of the full modality of alphabetic print texts—including the most resolutely "academic" of these—can be tapped to undermine the "rhetoric of deproduction" and return to significance the visual, aural, olfactory, kinesthetic, etc., character of the practices of reading and writing such texts: as Trimbur argues, "We need to teach them how to re-materialize the circumstances of text production and use" (85).

Trimbur is concerned especially with the rhetoric of deproduction operating in the formal features and institutional practices of school textbooks as well as with the practices schools encourage readers to take up in their engagements with textbooks. But we can extend his notion of rematerialization to address the materiality and modality entailed in the production, reception, circulation, and use of all kinds of texts, alphabetic print texts included. That process of rematerialization can begin with attention to what is experienced and noticed but falls outside the boundaries of what, officially, students (and the rest of us) have come to know as what's important in alphabetic print texts (i.e., the words on the page as timeless, immaterial entities), and can bring into conscious articulation those officially sanctioned concerns. For example, as Anne Frances Wysocki suggests, students "need to question how they have come to understand the spaces of pages so that they can, if need be, use different spaces, potentially powerful spaces that . . . have been rendered unavailable by naturalized, unquestioned practice" (57).

While it is also possible to bring unofficial characteristics of alphabetic print text into relief through comparisons to other kinds of text-objects—e.g., Web sites, films, *YouTube* videos—the risk in doing so is that our acquired predisposition to experience these other kinds of text-objects as epitomizing multimodality will render the modal character of alphabetic print texts imperceptible, in the same way that Western chamber music performances are misidentified as experiences of absolute music purified of theatrics, which are associated with only such genres as, say, operas and stadium rock concerts. Further, it might risk encouraging the fundamental error in the conception of modality as countable. While we might allow for abstracting distinct modes as a means of analysis—separating out, for example, in the case of music, pitch from rhythm and duration and timbre and all these from, say, performer gestures, or sound from sight and smell—there is always the danger of mistaking the terms of analysis for the reality, and thereby slipping from the model of reality resulting from that analysis—e.g., multimodality—to belief in the reality of the model (see Bourdieu 29). We neglect, in such instances, the effect of our process of abstraction on our conception of that which we have analyzed, and then confuse that effect with the actual phenomenon under consideration.

In other words, just as it would be wrong to justify attention to what we have learned to recognize as "multimodal" texts by arguing that they, too, are "writing" (the point Alexander and Rhodes make [17]), we should not attempt to redeem alphabetic print texts by insisting that they, too, are "multimodal." The former strategy, as Alexander and Rhodes observe, reinforces the privileging of (a particular notion of alphabetic print) writing even in the terms used to elevate other kinds of compositions; the latter strategy merely reverses this by subscribing to an ideology of multimodality whereby more of what is assumed to be countable is always better. And, more significantly, both strategies reinforce the attribution of effects to features of the text-objects in question. But as Williams reminds us, we need to "break from the common procedure of isolating the object and then discovering its components" and instead "discover the nature of a practice and then its conditions" (*Problems* 47).

Attention to the reading practices that render specific features of a text-object remarkable and others not, and what they render those features remarkable for, and with what consequences for readers, is, as I've already suggested, one strategy by which to get at what Williams argues for. But these reading practices would then have to be explored in terms, too, of the conditions of such practices, as part of those practices. That is to say, practices themselves must be understood as contingent and (therefore) material and social rather than individual choices or habits or universals. So, for example, in addition to exploring the various practices by which students (and other readers) mark (or decline from marking) or take notes on academic alphabetic print texts, and the conditions encouraging such practices and the effects on meaning, learning, and pleasure that these may have, we can also explore—in the sense of experimenting with (and reflecting on)—alternative practices in such reading. And, of course, we can investigate the features attended to, and taken for granted, by following default formatting for word-processing software, in composing and circulating texts. For example, we can explore the differences that might result from opting (or not) for default font style and size, line spacing, margin size, not to mention paper versus digital "files" and use of images, graphs, sound clips (and not), and the conditions of such practices (time, labor, equipment, training, as well as intent and submission requirements). Thus, in addition to considering, as Wysocki advises, the spaces of pages, we can have students question the spaces in which they encounter those pages—being read or written—and what might account for those experiences, what alternative spaces might be claimed for those encounters, and what conditions shape the spaces available and their availability.

One outcome of such explorations might well be, of course, that students will opt for conventional forms of alphabetic print text—but with a deeper appreciation for the deployment of such forms. From the perspective of those advocating what are more typically recognized as "multimodal" compositions, this might be seen as evidence of pedagogical failure, given the promised ostensibly enriching effects of composing using more of the modes understood as discrete and countable. But from the perspective I've been advancing here—what Cynthia Selfe, Timothy Lockridge, and I have termed a *transmodal* perspective (Horner et al.)—such an outcome would be entirely legitimate, since modality is understood as practice rather than text-object element, and since the aim is not the production of particular kinds of text-objects (as in, this week one alphabetic print essay due; next week one multimodal composition due, with more points for more modes) but rather composers' and readers' increasingly conscious concern with modality as social practice.[6] My students, asked to experiment in their compositions with modality, showed various degrees of versatility with playing with images, font style, color, size, layout, and videoclips (versatility testifying to their different levels of access to and experience with these practices). But when told to revise one of their earlier essays, using modality in whatever way they thought best, most opted for the conventional. After being assured, in response to their questions, that they didn't have to add video clips or other features to their writing if they didn't want to, they attested that they found it not simply easier but more appropriate for their purposes to opt for conventional modality. While they appreciated some of the unconventional modal features of some of their colleagues' writing (as creative or as giving new perspectives on the general issues the course was addressing), they also saw most (though not all) of these features as interfering with their pursuit of knowledge. (The exception was that their attempts to find images and the like to include in their experiments inevitably, if unintentionally, expanded the range of their research.) While "not hating on" the unconventional, as one student put it, they saw it as largely irrelevant. But from a transmodal perspective, such decisions were evidence of pedagogical accomplishment insofar as even the default was critically considered and chosen rather than unwittingly followed. They were opting not for fewer features but, instead, those that a dominant ideology of multimodality has blinded us from recognizing as modal features. Thus, from a transmodal perspective, students can come to see the modal practices that currently constitute conventional writing which that ideology has kept hidden. And, from a transmodal perspective, modality is neither an unquestioned given (the default) nor even an array of choices but, instead, the always emerging outcome of their practices, and of those engaging with their compositions.

From a transmodal perspective, in other words, students' decision to iterate conventional practices with modality is itself agentive. Indeed, just as, from a translingual perspective, a writer's iteration of conventional locutions is agentive in reinforcing, and thereby introducing difference into, that practice, from a transmodal perspective, my students' decision to perpetuate (what they took to be) conventional alphabetic print textual practices in their writing was agentive in reinforcing, and thereby introducing difference into, those practices: renewing them. That difference becomes apparent once we locate their compositions spatiotemporally as material social practices. Any sense of their being merely "the same" arises from neglect of the spatiotemporal character of those practices.[7]

Carey Jewitt, Jeff Bezemer, and Kay O'Halloran note that the "social semiotic idea . . . that there are inherent social affordances in resources" does not mean "you cannot attempt to use modes in ways that have not been used but rather to acknowledge that the ease with which modes can be used for a task differs, as do the modal means, and therefore meaning will be shaped differently" (82). Jewitt, Bezemer, and O'Halloran account for this difference in ease in terms of history: affordances, they say,

> are the outcome of long periods of social action with physical-material resources . . . through which resources are shaped by how they have been taken up by different societies as a means of shaping meaning. It is the traces of this social "work" that adhere to modes and become a part of its affordances. (82)[8]

While this account refreshingly breaks from the prevailing tendency to attribute inherent properties to abstracted modes, it mistakes historical dominance for totality, ignoring the ways in which alternative and oppositional social practices of modality, and even traditions of such practices, have all along posed quite different uses and meanings for modality. And, of course, history is neither a fait accompli nor a story of uniform outcomes. Nor is the seemingly "same" meaning produced through following the easy path of what a particular resource "affords" ever entirely the same, given the inherent difference produced by every reiteration of a given practice.[9]

Thus we can ask of any modal practice, including the seemingly most conventional, what it might achieve, under what conditions (see Wysocki 59). Inevitably, some modal practices will reinforce conventional practices of modality. But in so doing, they will thereby change these practices both by reinforcing them (thereby rendering them more reinforced) and by virtue of who is now taking them up. For example, the decision of many of my students to go with Times 12-point font, double-spaced black ink on white background texts in conventional student essay manuscript layout reinforced this set of practices and thereby changed those practices by rendering them more reinforced and practices which they themselves engaged.

Trimbur and Press have noted that while "multimodality is not new, nor is it a break from the past," multimodality *is* new "as a *term*, as a *conceptual terrain*" (21). Just as the "new literacy studies" has to do not with new forms of literacy but, rather, with new ways of conceptualizing literacy (as Street has insisted ["New Literacy Studies" 28]), so multimodality has to do, or should have to do, not with new forms of composition but with a new way of conceptualizing composition. Such studies can do so by posing modality not as a new element or set of elements for composers to deploy but, rather, as a new set of questions to ask about composition.

In place of neoliberalism's pursuit of the new, innovative, and effective, identified with commodifications of communicative practices, we can question the concrete labor practices responsible for any effects those practices accomplish, the conditions of those practices, and the different effects in the seemingly same, and the same in the seemingly different. To ask these questions would rematerialize modality as social practice, recognizing modality as the outcome of those practices, and recognizing those practices as shaped by while shaping material social conditions. Those questions are pertinent not to specific kinds of compositions but to all compositions, alphabetic print text included. And, given the inherent difference that any practice with modality produces through the concrete labor of composers (including those practices of reading/listening/

viewing/feeling compositions), the answers to those questions will inevitably be contingent, depending as they do on the practices of those taking up that labor—which, as practice, is where modality appears. Modality is the site, means, and outcome of our composing practices—what we work with, and on, and rewrite. It is what we compose, and transform, through our practices.

Notes

1. As Claire Lauer notes in her study of use of the terms *multimedia* and *multimodality*, composition scholarship uses the two terms interchangeably, with use of one or the other "contingent upon the context and the audience to whom a particular discussion is being directed" (226).

2. On the problems of prevalent invocations of affordances, see Paudel (ch. 4), Prior (26–28), Wysocki (59–60n1).

3. See, for example, the concrete labor of the translators, and all those engaged with the various versions of documents worked on, which Laura Gonzales describes in her essay for this collection.

4. The definition is attributed to nineteenth-century Polish philosopher and mathematician Hoene-Wroński, and was cited as influential by twentieth-century French composer Edgard Varèse ("INART 55").

5. For a comparable analysis of schooling in seeing practices, see Grasseni.

6. For a different but complementary conceptualization of transmodality, see Murphy. For a discussion of mediation in the production of modality, see Paudel.

7. On the difference arising from the temporal location of an utterance, see Pennycook; Lu and Horner.

8. See also Wysocki, who, like Jewitt et al., acknowledges that "constraints of communication materials are often social and historical." But Wysocki then suggests that we "ask after the constraints as we teach or compose [to] help us understand how material choices in producing communications articulate to social practices we may not otherwise wish to reproduce" (56).

9. On the difference produced through reiteration, see Pennycook (43).

Works Cited

Alexander, Jonathan, and Jacqueline Rhodes. *On Multimodality: New Media in Composition Studies*. Conference on College Composition and Communication / National Council of Teachers of English, 2014.

Bernhardt, Stephen A. "Seeing the Text." *College Composition and Communication*, vol. 37, no. 1, Feb. 1986, pp. 66–78.

Botstein, Leon. "Listening through Reading: Musical Literacy and the Concert Audience." *Nineteenth-Century Music*, vol. 16, no. 2, Autumn 1992, pp. 129–45.

Bourdieu, Pierre. *Outline of a Theory of Practice*. Translated by Richard Nice, Cambridge UP, 1977.

Calvet, Louis-Jean. *Towards an Ecology of World Languages*. Translated by Andrew Brown, Polity, 2006.

Canagarajah, A. Suresh. "'Nondiscursive' Requirements in Academic Publishing, Material Resources of Periphery Scholars, and the Politics of Knowledge Production." *Written Communication*, vol. 13, no. 4, Oct. 1996, pp. 435–72.

Carr, Nicholas. *The Shallows: What the Internet Is Doing to Our Brains*. W. W. Norton, 2011.

Dor, Daniel. "From Englishization to Imposed Multilingualism: Globalization, the Internet, and the Political Economy of the Linguistic Code." *Public Culture*, vol. 16, no. 1, Winter 2004, pp. 97–118.

Flores, Nelson. "The Unexamined Relationship between Neoliberalism and Plurilingualism: A Cautionary Tale." *Plurilingualism in TESOL*, special issue of *TESOL Quarterly*, vol. 47, no. 3, Sept. 2013, pp. 500–20.

Ganahl, Rainer. "Free Markets: Language, Commodification, and Art." *Public Culture*, vol. 13, no. 1, Winter 2001, pp. 23–38.

Grasseni, Cristina. "Video and Ethnographic Knowledge: Skilled Vision in the Practice of Breeding." *Working Images: Visual Research and Representation in Ethnography*, edited by Sarah Pink et al., Routledge, 2004, pp. 15–29.

Horner, Bruce. "Rewriting the Difference of Multimodality: Composing Modality and Language as Practice." *Bridging the Multimodal Gap: From Theory to Practice*, edited by Santosh Khadka and J. C. Lee, Utah State UP, 2019, pp. 263–84.

Horner, Bruce, et al. *Translinguality, Transmodality, and Difference: Exploring Dispositions and Change in Language and Learning*. Enculturation/ Intermezzo, 2015, intermezzo.enculturation.net/01.htm.

Hull, Glynda A., and Mark Evan Nelson. "Locating the Semiotic Power of Multimodality." *Written Communication*, vol. 22, no. 2, Apr. 2005, pp. 224–61.

"INART 55 History of Electroacoustic Music: Edgard Varèse (1883–1964)." *Pennsylvania State University*, www.personal.psu.edu/faculty/m/e/meb26/ INART55/varese.html. Accessed 17 June 2019.

Jewitt, Carey, et al. *Introducing Multimodality*. Routledge, 2016.

Kress, Gunther. "Gains and Losses: New Forms of Texts, Knowledge, and Learning." *The Influence of Gunther Kress' Work*, special issue of *Computers and Composition*, vol. 22, no. 1, Dec. 2005, pp. 5–22.

———. "Multimodality." *Multiliteracies: Literacy Learning and the Design of Social Futures*, edited by Bill Cope and Mary Kalantzis, Routledge, 2000, pp. 179–200.

Kubota, Ryuko. "The Multi/Plural Turn, Postcolonial Theory, and Neoliberal Multiculturalism: Complicities and Implications for Applied Linguistics." *Applied Linguistics*, vol. 37, no. 4, Aug. 2016, pp. 474–94.

Lauer, Claire. "Contending with Terms: 'Multimodal' and 'Multimedia' in the Academic and Public Spheres." *Computers and Composition*, vol. 26, no. 4, Dec. 2009, pp. 225–39.

Lea, Mary R. "Reclaiming Literacies: Competing Textual Practices in a Digital Higher Education." *Teaching in Higher Education*, vol. 18, no. 1, 2013, pp. 106–18.

Leppert, Richard. *The Sight of Sound: Music, Representation, and the History of the Body*. U of California P, 1993.

Lu, Min-Zhan, and Bruce Horner. "Translingual Literacy, Language Difference, and Matters of Agency." *College English*, vol. 75, no. 6, July 2013, pp. 582–607.

Mills, Kathy Ann. "A Review of the 'Digital Turn' in the New Literacy Studies." *Review of Educational Research*, vol. 80, no. 2, June 2010, pp. 246–71.

Murphy, Keith M. "Transmodality and Temporality in Design Interactions." *Journal of Pragmatics*, vol. 44, no. 14, Nov. 2012, pp. 1966–81.

Paudel, Hem Sharma. *Mediation in Literacy: Language, Technology, and Modality*. 2015. U of Louisville, PhD dissertation.

Pennycook, Alastair. *Language as a Local Practice*. Routledge, 2010.

Prior, Paul. "Moving Multimodality beyond the Binaries: A Response to Gunther Kress' 'Gains and Losses.'" *The Influence of Gunther Kress' Work*, special issue of *Computers and Composition*, vol. 22, no. 1, Dec. 2005, pp. 23–30.

Selfe, Cynthia L. "The Movement of Air, the Breath of Meaning: Aurality and Multimodal Composing." *College Composition and Communication*, vol. 60, no. 4, June 2009, pp. 616–63.

———. "Response to Doug Hesse." *College Composition and Communication*, vol. 61, no. 3, Feb. 2010, pp. 606–10.

Small, Christopher. *Musicking: The Meanings of Performing and Listening*. Wesleyan UP, 1998.

Stein, Pippa. "Representation, Rights, and Resources: Multimodal Pedagogies in the Language and Literacy Classroom." *Critical Pedagogies and Language Learning*, edited by Bonny Norton and Kelleen Toohey, Cambridge UP, 2004, pp. 95–115.

Street, Brian. "The Future of 'Social Literacies.'" *The Future of Literacy Studies*, edited by Mike Baynham and Mastin Prinsloo, Palgrave Macmillan, 2009, pp. 21–37.

———. *Literacy in Theory and Practice*. Cambridge UP, 1984.

———. "New Literacy Studies." *Language, Ethnography, and Education: Bridging New Literacy Studies and Bourdieu*, edited by Michael Grenfell et al., Routledge, 2012, pp. 27–49.

Trimbur, John. "Essayist Literacy and the Rhetoric of Deproduction." *Rhetoric Review*, vol. 9, no. 1, Autumn 1990, pp. 72–86.

Trimbur, John, and Karen Press. "When Was Multimodality? Modality and the Rhetoric of Transparency." *Multimodality in Writing: The State of the Art in Theory, Methodology and Pedagogy*, edited by Arlene Archer and Esther Breuer, Brill, 2015, pp. 19–42.

Williams, Raymond. *Marxism and Literature*. Oxford UP, 1977.

———. *Problems in Materialism and Culture: Selected Essays*. Verso, 1980.

Wysocki, Anne Frances. "awaywithwords: On the Possibilities in Unavailable Designs." *The Influence of Gunther Kress' Work*, special issue of *Computers and Composition*, vol. 22, no. 1, Dec. 2005, pp. 55–62.

Yancey, Kathleen Blake. "Made Not Only in Words: Composition in a New Key." *College Composition and Communication*, vol. 56, no. 2, Dec. 2004, pp. 297–328.

Something Borrowed, Something New: Multimodal Composition through the Reclamation of Vernacular Literacies

Sara Cooper

> A composition is an expression of relationships—between parts and parts, between parts and whole, between the visual and the verbal, between text and context, between reader and composer, between what is intended and what is unpacked, between hope and realization. And, ultimately, between human beings.
>
> —Kathleen Blake Yancey

One of two scrapbooks Harriet Riley inherited from her great-grandmother, "Ma Dink," by way of her mother, is a repurposed ledger book, its pages "stiff with glue" and corners worn round (Riley, *Memory's Urn* 01:12). The words "Ledger 1912 to 1916" are hand-printed in uneven block letters on its cover (fig. 1). Indeed, what appears within—a collage of images cut from women's magazines, newspaper clippings, handwritten notes, greeting cards, poems, and hymns—is a kind of accounting, the registering of life.

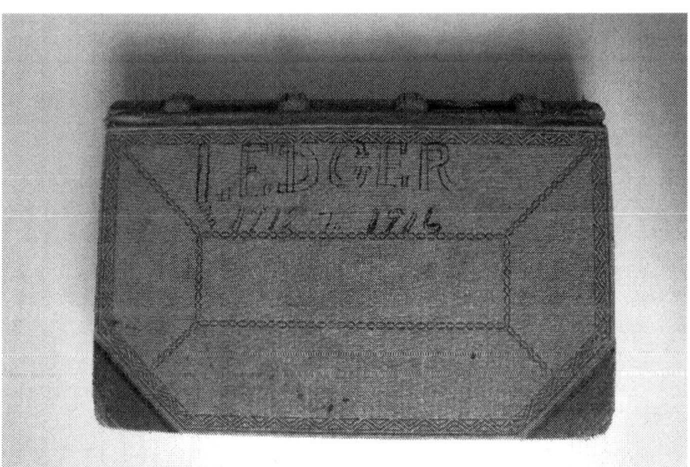

Figure 1. Ma Dink's first scrapbook, a repurposed ledger book

Harriet brought the book to the first session of a six-week digital storytelling workshop I conducted in Houston, Texas, in which participants, mostly women, composed in response to vernacular written artifacts—letters, postcards, recipes, diaries—of the sort kept in an attic or a shoebox under the bed.[1] The book's object-ness is startling. Everything about it, from the cursive notes that fill the gaps between images to the stained pages, call to mind the hands that made and have handled it over the years. When you see the book, you want to touch it. The evidence of use by multiple generations, the images of towns, country, home, and family, recall the body and the public and private spaces the body occupies.

The text is multimodal in its meshing of image and text, and incorporation of multiple genres that are multimodal themselves, but also in the way Jody Shipka and other scholars of multimodality (Ball and Charlton; Kress; Prior, "Writing"; Selfe; Wysocki; Yancey) remind us that all writing, not just digital composing, is: not "static artifact" (Shipka 13), but always "situated, mediated, . . . dispersed" and "layered with multiple histories" (Prior, "Writing" 189–90). Ma Dink's ledger book also foregrounds, makes tangible, the embodied multimodal nature of all linguistic meaning-making that Hannah Rule describes in her essay in this volume. Here, words are "objectified," to borrow from Rule's reading of Gunther Kress: they are textured, spatially charged, visceral, and, like children's lettered building blocks, handled in playfully kinesthetic ways.

Harriet's digital story (Riley, *Memory's Urn*), itself a multimodal revision of her great-grandmother's scrapbooks, recounts the relationship the women in her family have maintained with reading, writing, the South, and preserving personal and public history. If Harriet's story represents a kind of multimodal revision of Ma Dink's scrapbooks, the books are also a product of Ma Dink's own revisionary practice—of her domestic circumstances, of the tension she felt between private and public space, of the material makeup of her life. The two writers, Harriet and Ma Dink, by way of their shared history, are collectively engaged in a process of "re-purposing" (Bakhtin qtd. in Prior, "Writing" 189) wherein alphabetic texts are made new—and new meanings are made—through their interactions with and through multiple mediums, genres, and modes, each of which carries its own sociocultural associations and relations to power.

In his essay in this collection, Bruce Horner defines modality as a social practice and draws on Louis-Jean Calvet to remind us that modalities are "reinvented, renewed and transformed in every interaction." In so doing, Horner builds on Brian Street's "ideological model of multimodality," which Horner describes as "attend[ing] to the interplay of practices with and ideological beliefs about modality/ies." For the women I describe here, this process of radical repurposing, especially of vernacular artifacts like letters, journals, and scrapbooks associated with domestic space and devalued in literary contexts, presents opportunity for a kind of feminist revision of not only alphabetic texts but also the composers' relations to practice, to modal ideologies, and to their own agency as makers and mergers of domestic and public, vernacular and literary space.

This essay draws on frameworks of feminist geography, semiotics, and multimodal composition to pinpoint how alphabetic text—itself material and always socially situated (see Horner's essay in this volume; Prior, "Writing")—changes when translated from one genre and medium to another, from one set of modes to another, and from one context to another by women actively (re)reading and repurposing their complex and historically situated relations to the conventions of physical and textual, public and private spaces. Attending to such specific and situated processes of translation is a particularly generative practice for moving beyond oversimplified assertions about the multimodal nature of all texts toward understanding how the "complex practices inherent in communication" (Reichert Powell, this volume) are lived and negotiated, especially by those who have historically been disenfranchised by the rules of our semiotic tools.

Genre, Medium, Mode—and Remediation

To best reflect how alphabetic text exists and transforms in the composing practices, texts, and contexts I describe here, it is worth pausing to define terms, especially as they relate to one another; this is particularly important given that the language we use in our disciplinary conversations to describe semiotic acts can be slippery. Definitions of words like *genre*, *medium*, and *mode*—used to describe meaning-making—can be unstable, shifting, and cross-pollinating, even tending toward the hybrid.[2] This is in part because the communicative phenomena such words describe are themselves social and situated, and in part because of the vastness of the endeavor: defining how language (in its multitude of forms) works. As Pegeen Reichert Powell notes in her introduction to this volume, the word *multimodality* "by definition, is all communication across all time."

Cheryl Ball and Colin Charlton define mode as a "way of meaning making, or communicating" (43). Modes refer particularly to sensory experience, and include linguistic, visual, aural, gestural, spatial, and the combination of these (New London Group); Rule, in her essay in this collection, also emphasizes another, the kinesthetic mode, as of particular significance when considering the embodied nature of all composing. The kinesthetic is especially relevant to the descriptions that follow of the physicality, or made-ness, of Harriet's and Ma Dink's compositions.

While definitions of multimodality abound, I find Tracey Bowen and Carl Whithaus's most productive: "the conscious manipulation of the interaction among various sensory experiences . . . used in the processes of producing and reading texts" (7). Here the emphasis is on making—especially the maker's agency in managing an *interaction*—and on text as both made and received. Multimodality occurs in the interplay between maker, making, made, and received.

Following Prior and Anne Wysocki, Bowen and Whithaus further emphasize the importance of understanding multimodality in relation to genre. The two concepts, they argue, are "cross-fertilizing influences that shape the development of written documents" (2). Discussing mode but not genre, or vice versa, ignores the layers of semiotic activity and sociocultural context at play when composing with or reading alphabetic text.

The makers I describe here are orchestrating interaction between sensory experiences (modes), medium[3] (writing, voice, screen), layers of genre (a postcard, a scrapbook, a digital story), and the social and textual conventions associated with each. The New London Group defines genres as "forms of text or textual organization that arise out of particular social configurations or the particular relationships of the participants in an interaction" (75). As with Bowen and Whithaus's definition of multimodality, the focus is on interaction, here between text and social context. The ways in which genres are read and understood are rhetorical—that is, they shift depending on reader, composer, and context. Prior, also viewing genre as socially constructed, insists we "conceptualize genres as involving production, reception, distribution, and representation," stages he views not as "separate . . . but as co-present dimensions of discourse with multiple and changing configurations over time" ("Speech Genres"

22). By reconfiguring and re-presenting, or remediating, genres (Prior, "Speech Genres"; Shipka), Ma Dink and Harriet remediate (and reassign value to) modes, including alphabetic text. By remediating modes—combining the aural and the alphabetic in a digital story, for example, or separating a magazine image from its text—they remediate genre, acting within and upon the stages Prior names.

This process has the potential to become a strategy by which makers claim agency. As Michel de Certeau asserts, subjugated groups often respond to imposed values through a process of "expectation, negotiation and improvisation" (xvi). The resulting texts reflect "interests and desires that are neither determined nor captured by the systems in which they develop" (xvii). In such cases there is a negotiation between social-textual rules and conventions—belonging to predefined genres, mediums, modes, and their interaction—and the creative acts that insist on their subversion and, ultimately, redefinition.

In their discussion of mode, medium, and genre, Ball, Tia Scoffield Bowen, and Tyrell Brent Fenn ask whether the "meaning of . . . contained text changes when the interface changes" (34). Assuming a sociocultural approach to texts (Prior, "Writing"), the answer is yes. Harriet's and Ma Dink's texts certainly bear this out. Altering mode, genre, or medium changes how a text interacts with sociocultural practices belonging to particular histories. Glynda A. Hull and Mira-Lisa Katz relate this phenomenon to identity and social status: every sign system has a "different potential for enacting a self" (Urciuoli qtd. in Hull and Katz 46), and "some [have] more status in certain societies, communities, and historical moments than others" (Hull and Katz 46). It is worth considering, then, what happens when multiple sign systems—literary and vernacular genres, alphabetic text and image—literally interact, overlap, are placed in conversation through multimodal, multigenre texts.

Bowen and Whithaus suggest multimodalities have the potential to become "liberating vehicles," allowing users to "break . . . with convention in both pedagogy and production." They are careful not to suggest that modes are inherently liberatory, however, citing writers in their edited collection who identify ways in which "new modes of composing create their own set of conventions that shape or even limit students' composing processes" (6). It is not a question of whether or not, or even which, multimodal composing processes are liberatory but instead a question of how the relations between composer, text, and context are realized. This view corroborates the social and situated definition of multimodality forwarded here (Horner, this volume; Prior, "Writing"; Wysocki). By defamiliarizing "available designs" (New London Group), composers (like Harriet and Ma Dink) have the opportunity to cocreate conventions and their relation to the sociocultural values embedded in those conventions to better suit what they are communicating about themselves and the literal and figurative spaces they inhabit.

Page as Landscape, Landscape as Page

The texts I am analyzing here manage and make fluid the interaction between multiple modes and genres as means of negotiating boundaries between public and private geographic and textual spheres. The page here (be it analog or digital) is not only the container for content related to domestic and civic spaces but also a kind of geography itself—a landscape the reader or writer experiences in space and time, where space and time, through a subversive relation to genre conventions and artifacts signifying private and public spaces, are alterable. The page, in this case, becomes a space where the user, not unlike de Certeau's user of a city, claims agency through a practice of making (a path, a text) that subverts or circumnavigates established structures or forms and their sociocultural contexts. What Kathleen Yancey says of poets and composers of other alternative text forms applies here: makers "use the page as partner to create meaning" (92).

This is where, when considering written artifacts traditionally produced by women, cultural geography, and especially feminist geography, becomes pertinent. The feminist geographers Mona Domosh and Joni Seager describe home, for women, as a "geographical anchor" with which their "identities are bound up . . . in complex ways" (31). Within these spaces, they argue, women experience a "shifting and blurring" of the "distinction between the private and the public" (34). Women may experience home, Domosh and Seager argue, as a place that embodies their "'integrative selves' . . . as mothers, wives, and workers," or as "a trap that isolate[s] them from the rest of the world" (33). Texts like Ma Dink's scrapbook and Harriet's digital story engage with this tension while also challenging traditional divides identified by feminist geographers between culturally gendered spheres: public and private, highbrow and lowbrow, literary-imaginative and utilitarian (Domosh and Seager).

The scrapbook, itself a genre typically associated with women, and the digital story (which I will argue is one modern iteration) become containers for other feminized and feminist genres (letters, postcards, greeting cards) deemed lesser because of their use by women and tendency toward personal subjects (Huff 6–10). To apply Cynthia Huff's discussion of journaling to this broader range of genres, such "marginal discourse[s]" are "excluded from the artistic hierarchy . . . [and] at the edge of our communication field" (8). Ma Dink, Harriet, and others marginalized by a patriarchal literary aesthetic use this positioning—at the edge of publicly legitimized composing space—as a creatively productive vantage point. As outsiders unbeholden to established norms or pressure to maintain and revere a "static" text (Shipka 13), these women revise (a word that literally translates as *see again*) and recontextualize material, including alphabetic text, to better reflect their own experience and better suit the narrative they are composing about their own lives as citizens of civic and domestic spaces. They resituate "woman's work," to borrow from Maureen Goggin's discussion of needlepoint, as a "rhetorical tool" (312).

This kind of recontextualizing is especially significant given the sociocultural baggage associated with what is traditionally considered women's writing, especially works that combine multiple textual and tangible artifacts. As Suzanne L. Bunkers writes:

> For many years, scholars presumed that women's diaries, journals, letters and memoirs were highly secretive, carefully guarded texts, written only by one author and not intended to be read by anyone else. Such texts came to be labeled "private" writings, that designation not only signaling their classification as texts but also relegating them to what was judged "woman's sphere"—the private rather than the public realm. (17)

What careful study of women's personal writing reveals is that diaries, and I would argue scrapbooks, digital stories, and other forms that blend and allude to a woman's material experience, are both public and private at once. Composers of such texts enact a "tactical" (de Certeau) relation to genre and mode, challenging the public-private binary and associated sociocultural expectations by existing simultaneously within and outside of geographic spaces and the literary ones that mirror them.

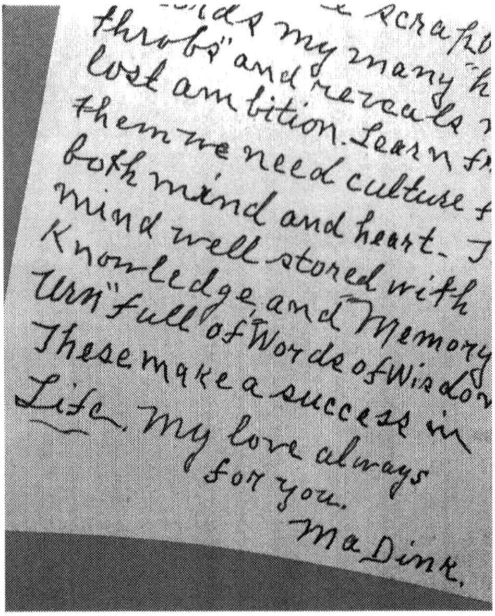

throbs" and reveals my
lost ambition. Learn fr
them we need culture f
both mind and heart. T
mind well stored with
Knowledge and Memory
Urn" full of Words of Wisdom
These make a success in
Life. My love always
for you.
Ma Dink.

Figure 2. Inscription in Ma Dink's second scrapbook

Ma Dink's Ledgering

As Harriet recounts in her digital story, her mother, Lib, received the first of Ma Dink's scrapbooks at age seven. This was shortly after Lib's mother passed away from tuberculosis and four years after her father died in a car accident (Riley, *Memory's Urn* 02:11). Harriet surmises that Ma Dink, then seventy-eight and likely unable to take in her newly orphaned granddaughter herself, created the two scrapbooks to "[help] her granddaughter . . . in the only way she knew how, by giving her the[se] poems, stories, and letters" (04:47–55). She gave Lib the second book on her sixteenth birthday (03:37–44). These are, in a sense, how-to manuals for surviving in the world, or more precisely surviving as a young woman in it. Ma Dink's purpose and audience are evidenced throughout both texts, but most directly in the inscription of the second book (fig. 2):

> This little scrapbook records my many "heart-throbs" and reveals my lost ambition. Learn from them we need culture for both mind and heart. The mind well stored with Knowledge and "Memory's Urn" full of "Words of Wisdom." These make a success in <u>Life</u>. My love always for you. Ma Dink. (03:37–04:00)

Ma Dink's preface diminishes divides between mind and heart, wisdom and memory, concepts that are themselves gendered. It also reflects what Bunkers identifies as a common practice among diarists, and one that challenges the perception that journals are purely private spaces: including upfront one's purpose for writing (17).

Figure 3. Collages in Ma Dink's scrapbook depicting the glorification of domestic duty

Harriet reads Ma Dink's statement about her "lost ambition" as reference to her identity as a writer and to her unsuccessful attempts at publishing (Riley, *Memory's Urn* 04:05–18). A number of the hymns and verses included in the books are her own. Also included is a rejection letter, addressed to her, from the *Christian Times*. The above dedication, in its acknowledgement of an outside audience and allusion to her desire to make her compositions public, suggests Ma Dink sees the book as having a place in the public sphere, if not the more prestigious sort of sphere after which she occasionally sought. In this way the books, and Ma Dink's admission, exist as a circumnavigation, as de Certeau describes, of more official and elitist literary spaces. The texts themselves, and alphabetic text and genres they contain—a hymn, a personal note, a rejection letter—assume new meaning through their interaction with one another and their medium.

Many of the collages included in the ledger book simultaneously refer to, and challenge, the glorification of domestic duty through the texts Ma Dink has selected, their arrangement on the page, and especially their relation to one another. A two-page spread includes multiple images (presumably cut from women's magazines) of flowers and one of a woman, hair in a pleasant bob, holding a bouquet and looking flirtatiously at the camera (fig. 3). The caption reads: "Oh, won't you come over to my house?" A line of text on the same page, affixed alongside an image of ivy, reads, "Guests won't need a second invitation to the home that is beautified with—." The text cuts off, is interrupted by a picture of Chinese wisteria. The spaces between images are filled with Ma Dink's handwritten notes about the symbolic significance of the pictured flowers: white lilies are "sweetness and purity." Under "white rose" she's written "I am worthy." Her cursive notes interpret the official texts on the page, her handwriting synecdoche for the body that is always involved in responding to a text, and, as Rule argues, in any meaning-making act. The cursive-filled spaces combined with the fragmented text complicates the suggestion, by other elements of the spread, that a woman's worth is bound up in her ability to care for a home.

Domestic imagery is further complicated by the inclusion, throughout the books, of images and text related to public space: hymns about the American flag, a picture of Lincoln and Mary Todd. A page featuring postcards from Meridian, Mississippi, and Mississippi State Teachers College in Hattiesburg also includes an image of a Madonna with child, referencing not only spirituality or religion but also the traditionally female sphere of childrearing (fig. 4). This image repeats elsewhere in the book. One page includes a postcard Ma Dink likely received from her son while he was stationed at Camp Beauregard in Louisiana. It depicts a soldier atop a war plane embracing a woman's ghostly figure (fig. 5). Again, handwritten notes contextualize, and personalize, these texts. Representations of public space, of what Domosh and Seager designate a male realm, are in conversation with feminized genres (postcards and women's magazines) and imagery, evidence of the composer's hand (choosing, arranging, annotating), and renegotiated audience.

Figure 4. Scrapbook collage including postcards from Meridian, Mississippi

Figure 5. Postcard likely from Ma Dink's son from Camp Beauregard, Louisiana

Perhaps most surprising is the ubiquity, in the scrapbooks' pages, of pioneering women, their photographs accompanied by biographical notes—both printed and handwritten—listing their accomplishments: Evangeline Booth, first woman to hold the post of general; Jane Addams, the second woman to win a Nobel Peace Prize; Martha Berry, founder of schools for the poor and, as Ma Dink notes, "repeatedly voted one of America's greatest women"; and First Lady Ruth Cleveland. These are women who have made a place for themselves in male-dominated public spaces and, here, become a part of a choir of voices Ma Dink is conducting to educate her granddaughter and, perhaps indirectly by way of the text's geographic movement, future generations of women in her family about how a woman might challenge geographic (including domestic) limitations.

These books, then, are multigenre in another way—part memoir, part history, part instruction manual. They are also a chronicle of a literacy practice and, as Harriet notes, likely "kindled [her] mother's love for books" (Riley, *Memory's Urn* 03:07–08). This in turn, she notes, led to Harriet's own love of language, which she has passed down to her daughters (Riley, Personal interview). The scrapbooks provide instruction not only on how to live but on how to read and write in, toward, and through life. "For many women," Bunkers writes, "diaries and journals have been the only autobiographical records left behind" (23). That Ma Dink's books are overtly multimodal attests to the kind of work she was doing—making tangible the circumstances of her life through her manipulation of text as material; she ultimately revises her relation to geographic and textual space by blurring boundaries between image, text, and genres connotative of the private (child rearing, beautifying the home) and public (historical figures, patriotic symbols, a teacher's college).

Ma Dink's books blend original poetry and hymns, considered elite literary genres, with less elite "literate activities" (Prior, "Writing" 189) belonging to the domestic sphere, like images of gardening and child rearing (expressed through content) or greeting cards and pages torn from women's magazines (expressed through genre). The books are literal expressions of the porous borders between spheres, since the composer is physically removing artifacts from one genre, value set, and historical context into another. Collage of the sort Ma Dink is composing is read spatially, the eye moving in some cases haphazardly from image to image, as well as chronologically through the turning of pages.

Citing Paul Saenger, Wysocki describes the page as a "space" that "both shapes and grows out of how we understand what words, texts, and readings are. . . ." She notes Susan Howe's reading of Emily Dickinson's unconventional dashes, for example, as a response to "an American desire to tame space by shaping wilderness . . . whether wilderness be the dark forest at one's door or the imagined darkness of women's internal lives" (304). In this description geographic space, textual space, and gendered space are enmeshed. The page, and even the "visuality of alphabetic text" has the potential to enact a physical and internal landscape and even, as Wysocki argues, inspire change in "practices and beliefs" (306).

Bakhtin argues that in literature, time "thickens, takes on flesh, becomes artistically visible" while space becomes "charged and responsive to the movements of the plot, and history" (84). Time is made tangible and visceral in Ma Dink's books through the material wear of the objects being arranged, the experience of flipping through these thick and rippled pages, and the inclusion of artifacts representative of particular moments in a private and public history. Space, characterized here by the friction created when disparate elements rub up against one another, is particularly charged.

Digital Story as Feminist Revision

Digital storytelling provides opportunity for further feminist revision of alphabetic text, and I would argue many kinds of texts, in equally if differently subversive ways. While digital technology is often considered a male sphere (evidenced by the lack of women in technology-related fields), and a public one (democratizing publishing), digital storytelling has the potential to become the site for a kind of feminist counterpublic that engages technology in an alternative way. This type of storytelling's reliance on multimodal collaging (of image and sound), tendency toward personal stories (if often contextualized in public or historical ones), and emphasis on the material embodiment of its subject (photographs of objects, the human voice as overlay) is akin to traditionally female-dominated arts like scrapbooking, quilting, and weaving. Harriet's translation of Ma Dink's scrapbooks into a digital story exemplifies this possibility.

Harriet's digital story opens with the following text, read as voiceover in her soft Mississippi accent:

> I have two handmade books that my mother kept in the bottom drawer of her bedroom desk. She had very little from her childhood. And I don't ever remember her talking about these books or who made them. But as a child I often went into her room when she wasn't there, sat down on the carpeted floor, carefully and quietly opened that drawer, and thumbed through the larger book with its colorful pictures. (Riley, *Memory's Urn* 00:04–27)

As the viewer listens to this narrative, images of the two books—their covers, leather spines, warped pages (fig. 6)—flip past, then fade into an old photograph of her mother as a girl (fig. 7). We pause on the girl's face long enough to notice the cracks in the paper, lines veining her skin and cutting across her eyes, as Harriet says of her mother: "I don't remember her talking about these books or who made them" (00:11–15).

Harriet goes on to tell the story of these books—why they were made, and how they have become, for her, a point of entry into understanding multiple generations of women in her family and their relation to literacy and the practice of preserving history. Photographs Harriet has taken of these scrapbooks, and especially the intricately composed pages, make up

Figure 6. Warped pages of Ma Dink's scrapbook

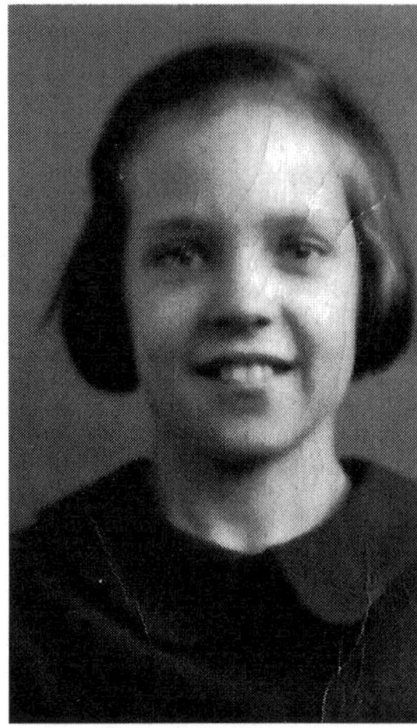

Figure 7. A photograph of Harriet's mother from Ma Dink's scrapbook

the bulk of the visual material for the film, followed by old family photographs, newspaper clippings, and maps. In the digital story, the visual material is collaged with aural elements—voiceover, music, and sound effects.

The layers here are multiple and intricate, reflecting what Shipka calls the "complex and highly distributed processes associated with the production of texts (and lives and people)" (13). They overlap like colored filters over a stage light, or a stack of transparencies on an old-school projector, each containing a different piece of information that contributes to and changes the overall picture. There is the texture of Harriet's voice, itself a text written with the sounds of her and her family's geographic migrations, the idioms she's inherited, her gender, age, and demeanor; there is the original written text of the voiceover, not pictured but present as Harriet reads from a document she wrote and rewrote, first as prewriting in response to prompts about objects, then as a written draft she would have to pare down and rearrange to fit the images she would eventually use; there are stories, and stories about stories, as Harriet contextualizes Ma Dink's work in a future lineage to which she wouldn't have been privy; there are the photographs Harriet took of the objects themselves, deliberately positioned and framed; there are the backdrops for these photos—a wood floor or open drawer, domestic images referencing Harriet's home, but also by association her mother's, grandmother's, and great-grandmother's homes, and more generally the domestic spaces in which women do their work; and there are the objects themselves—photographs, maps, scrapbooks—that, as fragments of lived lives, suggest infinite and unknowable pasts; finally, in each of these layers are the multiple contexts and histories that, as Shipka reminds us, make all texts multimodal—undetectable lines of connection moving off the page and into the world these objects and bodies and texts have occupied or come to represent at various times, for various audiences, and in various physical spaces.

Each of these elements, interacting with one another, the medium (screen), and genre (digital story), indeed informed by medium and genre, changes when brought into this particular multimodal context. The photograph of Harriet's mother as a child, paired with Harriet's voiceover noting the silence in a family, becomes a silent marker of a life. Its cracks make the passing of time Harriet describes literal and material. Harriet's voiceover text, similarly, transforms in the presence of this photograph. We become viscerally aware of the multiple and complex histories to which she refers, to the evidence of these lives as held by the objects they've left behind. The texts within Ma Dink's books also change as Harriet curates image and alphabetic text, revising their relations to one another and the world. As all stories are, Harriet's is the product of a series of decisions: what to keep and what to leave out. In this story, Harriet has prioritized evidence of Ma Dink's embodied craft(ing)—her handwriting, original hymns, collaged pages, rejection letter. Ma Dink's handwriting appears in thirty-four frames, her signature in eight. To draw again from Rule's work in this collection on embodied meaning, "linguistic processes are bodily processes, physical actions involving sensation, sensorimotor engagement, three-dimensional objects, spatial relations, and the creative construction of meaning." In Ma Dink's and Harriet's work, these processes are foregrounded and laid bare on the page.

At one point in the digital story, Harriet says of her mother, Lib: "She was in a new town and a home where she felt unwanted" (03:09–12). On the screen is a poem by J. Danson Smith, clipped from a newspaper and included in Ma Dink's scrapbook. It opens, "Take Heart, ye saints! Refuse to be discouraged!" Harriet, through this combination of words and image, has curated an exchange between Lib's struggle and Ma Dink as personal and religious mentor. The context here is complex. This is a poem written by a man and featured in a public, masculine medium (the newspaper), mediated through a feminine genre (the scrapbook), and then mediated again by Harriet's digital story, itself a kind of feminist revision. Medium, genre, mode, and sociocultural histories are embedded like Russian dolls. In a similar move, Harriet describes the solace she imagines her mother found in these books and how this ultimately inspired her love of reading. The text on the screen reads: "the strong go on" (03:17).

Not unlike its mentor text, Harriet's digital story merges geographic spaces with domestic ones. While animated lines move across a map connecting a series of cities and towns where Harriet's mother lived, Harriet's voiceover focuses on her mother's personal experience within these locations: a dorm room, a city where she taught school, the town in which she lived after marrying, a desk drawer in Meridian (00:30–46). While the map suggests representation and communication of public space, Harriet's words inscribe private, personal, and domestic geographies onto that space.

This kind of layering, where image is not a literal representation of the voiceover text but an agent that nuances meaning, is a common practice in digital storytelling. In Harriet's story it is used to demonstrate a mentoring relationship between granddaughter and grandmother focused on literacy. If Ma Dink's books are, in part, a chronicling and passing down of her own literacy practices, Harriet's story brings this process to the forefront, merging it with her own and her mother's literacy practices. The physical artifacts of Harriet's story combine with the audible ones to create a text in which the voice and process of these two composers are layered upon one another. And whereas Ma Dink's text blurs boundaries between image and text through juxtaposition and overlap on the page (a postcard next to a handwritten note), Harriet's text allows for multiple texts (voice-over and filmed objects) to exist simultaneously. We hear and see (at least) two texts at once. The result is a literacy narrative that spans generations and individual texts, a multigenerational text representative of a new kind of women's work. Texts are no longer static artifacts stuck in a patriarchal history and geographical space; they are part of a process of recording, preserving, and revaluing history centered on the materiality of text and women's lives. Ma Dink's story, through this process, is both further fragmented and made more whole.

Knitting toward Revision

Huff suggests textile arts traditionally practiced by women reflect the "networking" role women often play in families and communities, bringing together disparate elements to form a whole (12). To extend this metaphor to the composing of texts, scrapbooks and digital stories might be seen as doing similar work. They introduce the potential to revise meanings of alphabetic text not by altering language but through a revision process centered on fragmenting, recombining, and recontextualizing. By engaging with textual artifacts, especially those that are gendered or classed, composers stand to gain a more liberatory relation to literacy. The composers actively redefine their relation to meaning-making, potentially transitioning from passive receiver to active creator of convention. They also call attention, through the process, to the materiality of writing as linked to the materiality of living.

As Huff suggests, diaries that include "physical memorabilia: a picture postcard, a newspaper account, a pressed flower . . . testif[y] to women's joining of the inner and the outer, the mental and the physical, as they witness connections between body and mind, between the actual and the symbolic" (11). Much of what is told in Harriet's digital story is carried in the artifacts themselves. No longer relegated to women's spaces, the domestic, or kept between locked book covers, the artifacts are made public, given literal voice. If women, as purveyors of the domestic realm, have traditionally been sequestered to private spaces, this work emphasizes both dissonance *and* connection—with one another, with multiple histories, with the outside world. To again return to Domosh and Seager, the composers I discuss here make this process of "shifting and blurring" the literal through the manipulation of texts and textual conventions (34).

Harriet, in an interview, says Ma Dink's scrapbooks inspired in her mother, and eventually in her, a desire to preserve history by "saving things that were meaningful to her." There is, in these scrapbooks and Harriet's story, an attention to the material nature of childrearing, housekeeping, moving about the world: "My mother kept family scrapbooks the whole time we were growing up with things like the program from our kindergarten graduations, newspaper clippings pertaining to our family, glass from the window of the Hotel Roosevelt where she and my sister were staying in New Orleans when Hurricane Betsy hit in 1965." Harriet, similarly, has a collection of scrapbooks that include family photos, poems, images, and travel mementos. This desire to archive, to press a lock of hair into a baby book or affix a photograph to an album page, to take note of one's surroundings, feels similar to what motivates the writing of more established literary genres. As Harriet says, the personal essays she also writes are as much for her daughters as any outside audience: "I want them to have a written record of my life." Her audience is at once public and private. She draws a parallel between this work and the letters her mother wrote to her three children after they moved away, full of "ordinary daily activities" and "thoughts." "I treasure the ones I still have," she says. "I think we all (all three generations) had our children in mind when we wrote" (Riley, Personal interview).

As Harriet's and Ma Dink's work demonstrates, multimodal texts, whether analog or digital, emphasize the material nature and sociocultural contexts of all texts, including alphabetic ones. When engaging traditionally gendered vernacular artifacts and a process of pastiche, they also offer a revised understanding of texts, alphabetic and visual, as a kind of geography experienced in time. This is achieved, especially, by adapting texts and genre conventions that make room for, make tangible, and place in conversation the textual and material evidence of a lived life.

Enacting Vernacular Literacies in the Classroom

The kind of life writing Harriet and Ma Dink practice in their digital storytelling and scrapbooks is not foreign to the composition classroom. Instructors of first-year writing often assign personal narratives early in a semester as a way to begin where the students are and honor (their) lived experience as applicable to a substantive writing practice. The literacy narrative, a common iteration of such assignments, invites students to reflect on and chronicle their personal histories with texts. It would be a natural and productive extension of such assignments to ask students to consider histories beyond their own experiences, examining literacy artifacts from prior generations of their families.[4] What might come of a student's attending to a grandparents' love letters, or an old photo album, as objects of scholarly research? Such practices have the potential to incite metaconversations about literacy itself, especially as manifested in less conventional or extracurricular forms (Gere). These practices invite questions about why certain kinds of meaning-making are valued over others in academic contexts and how this valuing impacts the ways we perceive and construct identity. Such conversations challenge public-private binaries and are particularly relevant in college classrooms where students may feel pressure to leave home literacy practices at the door.

Asking students to translate such artifacts into digital stories could encourage their own reevaluation and reframing of personal and public histories. Again, this process invites metareflection on composing practices themselves, and how medium, mode, genre, and their interaction affect which stories are told. I would argue this is especially important given recent trends toward formulaic writing as valued in high-stakes testing contexts. Many first-year students are coming from four years in high school where they learned to write to test genres, with little opportunity to experience the complex and meaningful relation between a text's form and content.[5]

Rather than seeing semiotic practices as static, this kind of work invites students to consider how "knowledge can be embodied in different kinds of representations and [that] some kinds of knowledge lend themselves better to certain representations than to others" (McCorduck qtd. in Shipka 7). This acknowledgement of the relation between genre, mode, medium, and power, and of the situated and social nature of all meaning-making, seems a feminist endeavor, if not as explicitly so as in the works I discuss here. Through such projects, students might trouble, as this volume asks us to do, a conception of alphabetic text as static monolith, viewing it instead as rhetorical and always in relation to the modes, mediums, genres, and social contexts through which it is read.

Notes

1. During one of our first workshops, I asked participants to respond to the following writing prompts focused on the artifacts they'd brought with them: Describe the object. What are its uses? Where has it lived? Describe its homes. Who or what do you associate with this object and why? What was the object's significance to this person or these people? What time does it bring to mind? Do you associate it with a season? A year? A time of day? Describe one to three specific moments when this object was in the hands of one of its users.

2. The title of Wysocki's influential article "awaywithwords" and Rule's homage to it in this volume with a description of composition as "seeinglanguagingfeelingmoving" point to shortcomings of the language we use to describe meaning-making; such hybrid words enact the role of the spatial in the linguistic while troubling boundaries between seemingly static concepts.

3. Ball et al. describe *media* as the means by which "modes of communication are produced and distributed for public consumption," though they note, too, Kress's assertion in a 2011 keynote address that "trying to create distinctions between 'mode' and 'medium' has become useless" (33).

4. One cannot assume, of course, that all students have a stash of vernacular literacy artifacts in their parents' attic. Alternative assignments might include asking students to analyze literacy artifacts from their own lives or those available in online archives like *College Women* (collegewomen.org), a collection of scrapbooks, letters, diaries, and photographs from women attending the earliest women's colleges.

5. It could be interesting to ask students what story a particular test essay genre tells about writing, literacy, history, and identity.

Works Cited

Bakhtin, Mikhail. *The Dialogic Imagination: Four Essays.* Translated by Caryl Emerson and Michael Holquist, U of Texas P, 1983.

Ball, Cheryl E., and Colin Charlton. "All Writing is Multimodal." *Naming What We Know: Threshold Concepts in Writing Studies*, edited by Linda Adler-Kassner and Elizabeth Wardle, Utah State UP, 2015, pp. 42–43.

Ball, Cheryl E., et al. "Genre and Transfer in a Multimodal Composition Class." Bowen and Whithaus, pp. 15–36.

Bowen, Tracey, and Carl Whithaus, editors. *Multimodal Literacies and Emerging Genres.* U of Pittsburgh P, 2013.

Bunkers, Suzanne L. "Diaries: Public *and* Private Records of Women's Lives." *Legacy*, vol. 7, no. 2, 1990, pp. 17–26.

de Certeau, Michel. *The Practice of Everyday Life.* Translated by Steven Rendall, U of California P, 1984.

Domosh, Mona, and Joni Seager. *Putting Women in Place: Feminist Geographers Make Sense of the World.* The Guilford Press, 2001.

Gere, Anne Ruggles. "Kitchen Tables and Rented Rooms: The Extracurriculum of Composition." *Writing and Community Engagement: A Critical Sourcebook*, edited by Thomas Deans et. al., Bedford/St. Martin's, 2010, pp. 34–49.

Goggin, Maureen Daly. "An 'Essamplaire Essai' on the Rhetoricity of Needlework Sampler-Making: A Contribution to Theorizing and Historicizing Rhetorical Praxis." *Rhetoric Review*, vol. 21, no.4, 2002, pp. 309–38.

Huff, Cynthia. "'That Profoundly Female, and Feminist Genre': The Diary and Feminist Practice." *Women's Studies Quarterly*, vol. 17, no. 3–4, Fall–Winter 1989, pp. 6–14.

Hull, Glynda A., and Mira-Lisa Katz. "Crafting an Agentive Self: Case Studies of Digital Storytelling." *Research in the Teaching of English*, vol. 41, no. 1, Aug. 2006, pp. 43–81.

Kress, Gunther. *A Social Semiotic Approach to Contemporary Communication*. Routledge, 2010.

The New London Group. "A Pedagogy of Multiliteracies: Designing Social Futures." *Harvard Educational Review*, vol. 66, no. 1, Spring 1996, pp. 60–92.

Prior, Paul. "From Speech Genres to Mediated Multimodal Genre Systems: Bakhtin, Voloshinov, and the Question of Writing." *Genre in a Changing World*, edited by Charles Bazerman et. al., The WAC Clearinghouse / Parlor Press, 2009, pp. 17–34, wac.colostate.edu/books/perspectives/genre/.

———. "Writing, Literate Activity, Semiotic Remediation: A Sociocultural Approach." *Writing(s) at the Crossroads: The Process-Product Interface*, edited by Georgeta Cislaru, John Benjamins Publishing Company, 2015, pp. 185–202.

Riley, Harriet. *Memory's Urn*. *YouTube*, 29 Apr. 2014, www.youtube.com/watch?v=KcPFgFSG5ws.

———. Personal interview. 26 Oct. 2015.

Selfe, Cynthia L. "The Movement of Air, the Breath of Meaning: Aurality and Multimodal Composing." *College Composition and Communication*, vol. 60, no. 4, June 2009, pp. 616–63.

Shipka, Jody. *Toward a Composition Made Whole*. U of Pittsburgh P, 2011.

Wysocki, Anne Frances. "awaywithwords: On the Possibilities in Available Designs." *Multimodal Composition: A Critical Sourcebook*, edited by Claire Lutkewitte, Bedford/St. Martin's, 2013, pp. 302–08.

Yancey, Kathleen Blake. "Looking for Sources of Coherence in a Fragmented World: Notes toward a New Assessment Design." *Computers and Composition*, vol. 21, no. 1, Mar. 2004, pp. 89–102.

Beyond Page Design: Writing as Multimodal Embodied Meaning

Hannah J. Rule

In their contribution to *Naming What We Know: Threshold Concepts in Writing Studies,* Cheryl E. Ball and Colin Charlton describe an oft-repeated claim: "all writing is multimodal." Support for this idea comes mainly through the impossibility of its other, namely that "there is no such thing as a monomodal text" (43). To illustrate, Ball and Charlton point to a standard-issue academic research essay—composition's ur-genre—as a text perhaps presumed to be monomodal. But, the authors emphasize, "such a text is recognized from its linguistic mode *and* its visual and spatial arrangement on the page (title, name block, double spacing, margins, default font size, formulaic structure, etc.)" (43; emphasis added). That is, an alphabetic essay reveals its multimodality only when its design or visual features—the nonlinguistic elements that border and order the linguistic ones—are recognized.

As their encyclopedic genre directs, Ball and Charlton are echoing a familiar refrain in composition, one they attribute especially to the New London Group (42). Jody Shipka links the same claim to others, including Judith Wooten and Anne Wysocki, who reiterate that no text is really monomodal because "even print-linear alphabetic texts are provided meaning potentials based on the visual design of the page" (Shipka 12). Seeing writing and multimodality in this way—with multimodality as always already a condition, if on the literal periphery, of traditional alphabetic texts—is certainly familiar. And doing so could be, too, a kind of strategy. Claiming that writing is already multimodal urges us to accept that multimodality isn't something additional to teach, but just another dimension of what we already do. Such a move may make the enormity of our instructional edict today feel more possible. In our age of perpetual digital revolutions, pulling multimodality closer to our center has become even more imperative. As a part of this effort, compositionists have conceptualized students more as designers than writers (see, for example, George) and have conceptualized our discipline more in terms of, in Derek Owens and Tara Roeder's terms (in this volume) "composition and design" rather than strictly "writing." This collection too intervenes in this challenge, asking how we can interrupt tendencies toward fashioning writing-versus-multimodality binaries (see Reichert Powell, in this volume) and asking after the status of writing in light of a broad acceptance that composition must help its students acquire ranging multiliteracies attuned to the changing demands of a translingual and digitally connected world.

I do not disagree with the claim that all writing is multimodal. But, along with Pegeen Reichert Powell (in this volume), I too wonder about the assumptions that tend to get us to this claim. One assumption worth questioning is that multimodality is primarily a characteristic of texts themselves, a notion reflected in the appeal to the visual and spatial components of an academic essay, like margins or headings. Shipka has countered this assumption, arguing that multimodality is rather a routine condition of all communicative processes (12–13). No matter the nature of any resulting products, Shipka observes, composing processes always involve myriad cross-modal activities, like listening, inscribing, reading, speaking, sketching, gesturing, and so on. I align with Shipka, and with Bruce Horner (in this volume), in believing that a product-focused conception of multimodality is limited and limiting. And the way I will argue here for intermingling the multimodal and the linguistic relies on constructing modalities in relation to meaning-making processes, not on the characteristics of products.

In so doing, it is a second assumption embedded in the claim that all writing is multimodal that I wish to focus upon: that the linguistic mode is principally distinct from multimodality. We may grant writing multimodality; we repeat that multimodal features will share the page or screen with the linguistic—but, I note, only on the edges or only where words aren't. Our view tends to be that it's words, and then everything else. And it is not just the familiar claim I began with that can propagate this linguistic isolation: familiar schemes that continue to influence how we think and talk about multimodality like multiliteracies or multiple intelligences have done so, too (Dunn; Gardner, *Frames*). While these frameworks open our instruction to access and learning difference, they at the same time perpetuate the notion that the linguistic is a special mode fundamentally isolated from visual, spatial, kinesthetic, and other modalities.

This collection aims to think expressly about writing in profound relation with multimodality, not as something put aside or on pause while we continue to welcome in, and add on, composing in multiple modes. Following this purpose, I too will claim that all writing is multimodal, but in a manner that disrupts the tacit instinct to separate words from other modalities. Instead, I construct linguistic meaning as itself multimodal and multisensory, as visual-linguistic-kinetic-spatial processes without absolute demarcations. To support this adjustment, I first establish how foundational texts have shaped (and reflect) our tendency to isolate the linguistic. I then complicate that instinct by exploring scholarship on embodied meaning, a perspective that sees language processes as bodily ones involving sensation, sensorimotor engagement, three-dimensional objects, and spatial relations. Dissolving strong distinctions between word- and multimodal-meaning processes continues to be critically important. Doing so is key, for one, to dismantling the stubborn notion that word-dominant meaning-making is rigorous while multimodal making is easy and categorically nonlinguistic.

Words, and Everything Else: The Linguistic as Isolated from Multimodality

Since even before the field's modern inception, compositionists have in different ways worked to stretch our domain beyond alphabetic writing (e.g., Palmeri). Patricia A. Dunn, for instance, has worked to deconstruct composition's "primacy of language" ideology (18), which both presumes writing as the chief mode of knowledge and intellect and devalues the varied means that individuals also use to make meaning and communicate understanding. Inviting in a range of communicative modes, including "visual, aural, spatial, emotional, kinesthetic, or social ways" (1), helps make the "linguisto-centric" (50) domains of schooling and society more accessible and inclusive. Dunn names this move beyond words alone variously: alternative formats, multiple literacies, diverse intellectual pathways, Friere's multiple channels, and multiple intelligences (3).

The latter is, of course, the central term of Howard Gardner, a psychologist whose theory of multiple intelligences gained prominence among literacy educators in the 1990s. Gardner's goal in *Frames of Mind: The Theory of Multiple Intelligences* is to "expand and reformulate our view of what counts as human intellect" (4) beyond its narrow equivalence with the Western cultural dominance of "*rationality, intelligence,* or the deployment of *mind*" (5). While schooling and testing procedures implicitly measure intellect through "logical or linguistic problem solving" (24), Gardner uncovers how intelligences are better understood to move across a broader range of "musical, bodily, spatial, and even personal symbol systems" (26). Like Dunn, Gardner explodes our tacitly narrow and exclusionary measures by exposing intelligences, instead, as capacious and multidimensional.

Gardner and Dunn each expose the modes through which we might newly recognize knowing. Their terms—multiple intelligences and multiliteracies—are not, I recognize, equivalent to multimodality. Compositionists tend to see multimodality most in terms of communication, often as a condition of texts themselves or sometimes more expansively in terms of communicative processes. However, I want to here link multiliteracies, multiple intelligences, and multimodality (and risk collapsing their differences) because of the similar ways in which the *multi* in these terms becomes characteristically nonlinguistic. That is, in our general discourse around multimodality, compositionists seem to set aside the linguistic as a domain fully separable from multimodality. This habit can be exemplified in the pedagogical uptake of Gardner's theory in a 1995 issue of *English Journal*, discussed below. The habit echoes too in the discourse of Gunther Kress and the New London Group, two figures tightly associated with our working conceptions of multimodality. One consequence of routinely isolating word meaning from other modalities is that we leave the nature of the linguistic uninterrogated and unaffected by other modes.

In *Frames of Mind*, Gardner establishes some ground reflected in compositionists' tacit views of multimodality. For one, at the outset, Gardner describes the intelligences—linguistic, musical, spatial, and so on—as "*relatively autonomous*" (8). And it is not just that Gardner encourages us to see categorical differences, it is also that the linguistic feels even more autonomous in that logical-mathematical and "linguistic competence" have long been the premium measures in education (337). That is, the other intelligences in Gardner's scheme feel even more like they are in contradistinction because language is already familiarly installed in testing, educational, and cultural discourses. In other words, even as educators might welcome multiple modes, our immersion in the "primacy of language" ideology (Dunn 18) pushes us to leave the linguistic distinct and at our center still.

In his own contribution to the *English Journal* issue on multiple intelligences in 1995, Gardner reflects on how his psychological theory had been forwarded by educators and on the relation of this theory to English education specifically ("Multiple Intelligences"). He allows for the (ideologically) common sense claim that English could be conventionally considered "a subject that traffics only in linguistic intelligence." But instead he advises that multiple intelligences should help English practitioners "make use of and stimulate the full gamut of human intellectual strengths and proclivities" (17). Gardner sees multiple intelligences as a "catalyst" for shifting baseline assumptions and practices in English classrooms. Under the direction of multiple intelligences theory, students are understood as individuals with a range of capacities and interests across symbol systems. Multiple pathways for understanding through those systems, including performance, movement, drawing, and so on, can be made available to students as varying means to express understanding and knowledge.

Opening up varying pathways is one way to describe the method advocated by English pedagogue Peter Smagorinsky in his contribution to the multiple intelligences issue. Smagorinsky begins by describing how he had begun soliciting literary interpretations through "unconventional types of compositions" (19). Rather than just writing, Smagorinsky's students were invited to take advantage of ranging symbol systems to "act, dance, draw, soundtrack, and otherwise express their conception of the English curriculum" (20). One advantage of these "non-linguistic activities" (19) is engagement. Smagorinsky claims that those who rarely turn in homework (which can be presumed is some form of writing) will spend "all weekend producing elaborate video productions dramatizing their interpretations of literary relationships" (19). That is, students who stage videos are provided a chance to demonstrate their "understanding of literature in ways not accessible through their writing" (19). As directed by Gardner's views, Smagorinsky describes video, drawing, or dancing interpretations as engaging many of the "same developmental processes" as writing as well as those "*not* available through writing" (22). As such, Smagorinsky sees Gardner's "powerful, comprehensive theory" (21) as a means to pitch nonlinguistic activities to skeptical colleagues, swaying them to believe that students who were not writing were not merely "playing games" (20).

The activities that Smagorinsky describes remain familiar, effective, and important. But I'm interested in the subtleties of how those practices are described, as I see embedded in his commentary enduring assumptions about multimodality and the linguistic. First, established in Smagorinsky's discussion is the idea that making a video or a skit is somehow not serious or intellectual but may instead be seen as "playing games." Again, this is not how Smagorinsky himself sees these types of compositions but how other, skeptical educators might. Questioning the rigor of composing across modalities, though, still echoes today—it rings loudly, for example, in Shipka's anecdote about a professor's dismissive response to her student's research essay on ballet shoes (2). This dismissiveness can linger in compositionists' views today, too—perhaps more so than we think. A second major assumption is that activities like those Smagorinsky describes are nonlinguistic. This terminology suggests that language, word meaning, comprehension, and other expressly language-associated processes somehow fully evacuate from processes of multimodal meaning-making. In naming his video example a "nonlinguistic activity," Smagorinsky covers over the linguistic dimensions of a video product—words as scripts, spoken lines, captions, and so on. But also, as Shipka and as Horner (in this volume) help us see, the term *nonlinguistic* covers over, too, the ranging processes involved in the making of the video, not the least of which would entail more word-driven practices of reading, analyzing, quoting, and narrating of whatever literary text prompts the video's production. Smagorinsky's language in his discussion, if unwittingly, reinforces the isolation of linguistic meaning-making by suggesting that communicative acts like performance, video, or drawing are wholly separate (and at risk of being less intellectual) from writing or word work. But somehow, multimodal compositions, like videos, get at understandings and meanings "not accessible through . . . writing" and that are "other than the logical and linguistic realms" (19, 25). In this manner, the kinesthetic or spatial or musical (or a blend of all these modalities) is resolutely not the linguistic; those who "won't write" will make a video; Smagorinsky's friend is a "good writer" but "cannot wrap a birthday present to save her life" (21). In short, we get the message that multimodal making is, essentially, not words. So, in our familiar thinking, we reserve intellectual and rigorous words on one hand and push everything else onto the other, possibly as games and certainly wholly nonlinguistic.

The nuances in Smagorinsky's discussion helps me expose the ways in which the advancement of multiple intelligences as antidote to the "primacy of language" has in part had the effect of still isolating the linguistic from other modes. As our unquestioned domain, the linguistic recedes from our consideration. Said another way, in our move to be open to other modes, the linguistic is counterintuitively reified in our thinking through its presumed difference and isolation from the visual, spatial, performative, musical, and so on.

These assumptions arise similarly across formative scholarship on multimodality. In their seminal "A Pedagogy of Multiliteracies," the New London Group (NLG), like Gardner and Dunn, puts language or "mere literacy" at the center of traditional instruction and offers "by contrast" a focus on multiliteracies, or "on modes of representation much broader than language alone" (New London Group 64). Note the subtle isolating gesture of the phrase "language alone." The focus of multiliteracies is upon modes that are instead "much broader" (64), leaving unclear the status and relation of language to multimodality. The NLG's modal categories are also familiar and align generally with Gardner and Dunn's schemes: visual, audio, gestural, spatial, linguistic, and multimodal (the latter to connote "interconnection among the other modes" [78]). And while the NLG includes the "linguistic" right alongside other modes, there is still the sense that words are of a particular and different sort. For instance, the NLG categorizes "various semiotic systems" into language, and everything else: "the grammars of languages, and the grammars of other semiotic systems such as film, photography, or gesture" (74). The wording here makes available the idea not only that linguistic grammar is entirely separate from other modalities' but also that other modalities' grammars, in spite of being quite different, can be nonetheless grouped together. In their gesture of broadening, the NLG reinforces our tendency to separate the linguistic and multiple modes.

Kress too can set aside the linguistic mode in his exploration of multimodal meaning. For instance, in his 1996 book *Before Writing: Rethinking the Paths to Literacy*, Kress familiarly posits the rise of multimodality by observing the seismic shifts in communicative modes hastened by the digitized world (Reichert Powell, in this volume, cites a similar impetus).

He perceives these shifts in terms of changing times, musing that "my generation's valuation of language as primary may no longer be shared by younger generations" (143). In other words, the world is no longer as writing-dominant as it (supposedly) once was (5). Kress symbolizes the disappearance of words from the multimodal-visual-digital world more than once through the figure of the front page of a "tabloid newspaper." For Kress, this symbolic page serves as prime evidence that "[p]rint is, literally, being pushed off the page" (2). Here again is the tacit presumption that meaning in multiple modes means meaning only through the non-linguistic. Perhaps, if prompted, we can readily counter Kress's figure. For one, we know today that words and writing persist; indeed, as many have noted, digital and information revolutions have meant that more people are writing much more now than in any time in history (e.g., Brandt). And yet and still, we largely presume that when we're thinking about multimodality we are not thinking about language. Words are "pushed off the page." We move "beyond" words, beyond "mere literacy." We invite in "non-linguistic activities" by adding on multimodal composing.

In focusing so intently on the nuance of these scholars' descriptions, it may seem I am just mincing words. What does it matter if these innovative scholar-practitioners tend to separate words from other dimensions entailed in making meaning and knowledge? Does it matter much if they fail to expressly comingle the linguistic with other modes? It makes sense, after all, that if we aim to multiply the modal practices of composition, then we would need to focus least on the mode most familiar. But still the assumptions that surface through these close readings are important, as they reflect our collective habits of differentiating. This habit of subtle separation may actually more perpetuate than disrupt the "primacy of language" ideology, as many still remain skeptical of multimodal making because of its supposed core differences from alphabetic writing.

This risk can be exemplified as it erupts in a skeptical response to the *English Journal*'s issue on multiple intelligences. In his response letter, Alan Pierpoint offers his own practice scenario in which he describes a quiz he gave that allowed students to choose their modes of response: a "traditional" essay topic, a creative dialogue between characters, or a drawing of a battle map (12). None of his students, he reports, chose the essay and only two crafted a dialogue. The rest were maps. He wonders in a rather sarcastic rhetorical question why so many chose the drawing, expressing absurdity at the notion that he could have "23 spatial-kinesthetic learners, and no verbal-logical ones" (12). His questioning reveals a host of assumptions. For one, Pierpoint hyper-focuses on the modal features of his students' products rather than on the modes entailed in producing one of these answers. He does not seem to consider much how the kind of intellectual problems established in his prompts might most steer his students' choices. For some reason, too, he fails to see his dialogue prompt as entailing the linguistic. And he certainly doesn't imagine how his supposedly purely visual-spatial "map" option must at least to some extent involve linguistic meaning. Pierpoint doesn't reflect on these points likely because he already has his answer: "The picture is easier than the essay" (12). And here, a pulse that runs deep still in everyday as well as composition's imaginary: the picture, song, podcast, oil painting, dance performance, skit is always easier than the rigor of word work. But I wonder: On what basis do Pierpoint and many of us make the blanket claim that the picture is easier? And that the picture is finally and fully separable from language? What do we think we're doing when we have students use alphabetic writing to communicate their thinking and understanding? What do we believe about the nature of the writing itself as a mode, outside of our general insistence that it is always already somehow distinct from other symbol systems?

Today, as instructors and as a field, we know more fully the value of, and the urgent need to teach through, multiple pathways, a shift owed in large part to the scholar-practitioners I've just discussed. We may no longer much embody the heights of Pierpoint's skepticism. But we do still habitually separate words from everything else.

Gardner warned about how neat categorization can be seductive in our thinking. In his move to multiply the range of symbol systems through which intelligences may be perceived by discussing them as "*relatively autonomous*" (*Frames* 8), he understands that we risk accidentally believing that *strictly separated* describes also how intelligences operate in the world. But those operations are simply not so tidy. Gardner emphasizes that separating intelligences is only strategic; his categories "are fictions—at most, useful fictions—for discussing processes and abilities that (like all of life) are continuous with one another" (70). Similarly, though our discourse habits may suggest otherwise, multimodality is not isolated from writing in acts of composing and communication unfolding in the world. Said another way, we no longer benefit from the rhetoric of moving beyond words. Rather, we need ways now to dispense with the unuseful fiction that words are of a fundamentally different sort than other modalities. We need a different operating assumption: that all modalities are much less separable than our previous schemes have sorted them. As I argue next, work on embodied meaning, which sees linguistic meaning-making as embodied, dimensional, and multimodal, can help give shape to this kind of alternative imaginary.

The Linguistic as Multimodal: The Philosophy of Embodied Meaning

In *Before Writing*, the same book where he pictures words being pushed off the page, Kress provides an alternative route for conceptualizing the development of meaning-making processes. Kress focuses on how, before they start school and face the impositions of the print literacy regime, children compose spontaneously, dynamically, and "in an absolute plethora of ways, with an absolute plethora of means, in two, three, and four dimensions" (xvii).[1] Children enact the worlds and activities of pirates or superheroes or teachers through any modalities available to them: "toys and constructions of various kinds; Lego blocks; cardboard boxes; blankets; chairs; corners of rooms; pens and paper; scissors, paste and paper; and so on" (8–9). But, Kress emphasizes, these spontaneous practices are discounted in school.

One way Kress builds print acquisition upon these multimodal meaning instincts is by suggesting that children may approach alphabetic text as aesthetic object. He observes that children's multimodal instincts enable them

> to treat print, which is too often seen as a unidimensional medium, as multimodal, as a complex semiotic system; and it is this disposition, which makes it possible for them to make inroads into the great complexity of alphabetic writing. For children, alphabetic writing is clearly multimodal: it is blocks of print, letter-shapes; media—such as newspapers, birthday cards, books; genres; it is an aesthetic object which can be used in design; a medium of meaning; a drawing of sound; and so on. (97)

Kress's compelling conceptual strategy here to connect print to multimodal meaning practices in a sense objectifies words. Because children associate composing with three-dimensional stuff, as they attack print literacy they will tend to see and want to manipulate print as additional objects—print as shapes, blocks, or texts-objects like a card or book. In this way, Kress puts language right on the same plane as Lego sets, couch cushions, pens, or a cardboard box—words too are things that can be designed, pasted, or hammered into meaning. By exploring the multimodality of our meaning-making instincts, Kress reverses the common (modern, Western) assumption that alphabetic-print literacies are primary and first. He comingles linguistic and multiple modes, imagining the linguistic as the kind of acquired add-on to already established multimodal and dimensional instincts toward meaning. Kress thus works against linguistic isolation by seeing multimodality at the center of meaning (or, as in his title, before writing). In this final section, I build from Kress's reversal that puts multimodality, not isolated alphabetic writing, at the center of meaning-making. But instead of building this bridge by imagining alphabetic text as designable object, I focus on the philosophy of embodied meaning as a means to disrupt the ways we tacitly separate words from everything else.

As we have embraced multimodal composing, compositionists have not much examined or reconsidered our presumptions about linguistic meaning, outside of our entrenched belief that writing is knowing. Writing is presumed as the chief mode of knowing (Dunn); and knowing—that "intellectual competence," "rationality," or "deployment of mind" (Gardner, *Frames* 5)—is delivered through writing. But what sustains this primary association? That rigor, I suspect, is in part anchored by the abstraction we associate with language. We assume that words are filed in our minds and systematically accessed as a matter of transcendent mind. As the psycholinguistics and cognitive science scholar Raymond W. Gibbs puts it, conventional views hold that "meaning is best understood as abstract and disembodied symbols," or a "hypothetical construct . . . that must be studied from a formal objectivist perspective" ("Embodied Experience" 1, 13). Arthur M. Glenberg and Michael P. Kaschak add to this characterization, stating that language is often seen "as a symbol manipulation system: Language conveys meaning by using abstract, amodal, and arbitrary symbols (i.e., words) combined by syntactic rules" (558). This view supports the association between writing and intellect, but also may fuel the ways the linguistic is so readily isolated from other modes. The New London Group, for example, describes "mere literacy" as the focus on "language only . . . conceived as a stable system based on rules such as mastering sound-letter correspondence" (64). Gardner, too, reproduces the language-as-abstraction view in his discussion of school modes: "[I]n the standard classroom," Gardner writes, "teachers talk, often presenting material in abstract symbolic form and relying on inanimate media such as books and diagrams in order to convey information" (*Frames* 357). We think of alphabetic writing as abstract, computational, cognitive, systemic, a complex code to master, a means of information processing. And so, we conclude, the essay must be more abstract, more rational, and thus more difficult than (and distinct from) the picture. But, just as Dunn suggests that the "primacy of language" is an ideology that can be budged out of its totalizing position, so too can (and should) we search for other ways to understand linguistic meaning-making.

One such way is through embodied meaning, a part of a broader network of research and philosophy "in the new sciences of the embodied mind" (Johnson xi). Bridging philosophy, linguistics, psychology, and cognitive science and taking modern shape beginning in the 1970s, embodied meaning suggests that linguistic meaning is not a matter of symbolic computation but rather one of visual, motor, and perceptual action.[2] Gibbs provides a helpful introductory summary of this perspective, writing:

> [P]rocessing linguistic meaning is not a matter of understanding what words mean, but includes the perception of physical objects, physical events, the body, and other people in interaction. The meaningful representation of language includes both a depiction of what has happened and potential perceptions and embodied actions that may take place in the future. Linguistic meaning, therefore, is inherently embodied . . . ("Embodied Experience" 13)

From this perspective, linguistic processes are bodily processes, physical actions involving sensation, sensorimotor engagement, three-dimensional objects, spatial relations, and the creative construction of meaning. As I will continue to unpack, this hypothesis is suggestive in the question of writing's relation to multimodality as it invites us to take on a tangled and nested rather than separate and categorical relation among modalities. That is, taking on an embodied meaning perspective urges us to mix up modal categories, to see the linguistic no longer as a rarified and abstract modality but as one continuous with and always already entailed in the visual, gestural, spatial, and so on.

I push us toward this connection with caveat and caution. Work on embodied meaning is expansive, interdisciplinary, emerging, and, in many areas, still tentative, speculative, and critiqued.[3] Especially as an outsider—a compositionist rather than a linguist or cognitive scientist—I will surely by some marks fail to capture the nuances of this research. Nevertheless, I see two core ideas from embodied meaning research as particularly illuminating for conceptualizing dynamic multimodality within the linguistic: embodied simulation and meaning as embodied action.

The concept of embodied simulation suggests that linguistic meaning is not received or transacted nor a matter of translation into the language of thought. Rather, meaning is a matter of bodily enaction. The simulation hypothesis is summarized by the cognitive science scholar Benjamin Bergen as such: "we understand language by simulating in our minds what it would be like to experience the things that the language describes" (*Louder* 13). That is, when we hear, read, or write words, we "soft-assemble" (Gibbs, *Embodiment* 201) meaning by performing the possibilities of that language through spatial, perspectival, textural, and other three-dimensional details. Evidence for simulation processes in part comes from "introspection" (Bergen, "Embodiment" 144): individuals report that they consciously experience simulated imagery in their mind's eye while engaging language. Bergen describes this idea with a simple example:

> Processing the words *pink elephant* leads many people to have conscious visual-like experiences in which they can inspect a non-present visual form with a color that looks qualitatively like it's pink and has a shape that looks qualitatively like that of an elephant, from some particular perspective. (144)

Evidence for simulation processes, though, comes not just from anecdotes of experience like Bergen describes but largely from quantitative measures like reaction time and eye-tracking.[4] This kind of research demonstrates a connection between individuals' understanding of language and their bodily movements or interactions implied by the language. For example, if an individual reads the sentence *Sam turned the key in the ignition*, as Ernest Davis puts it, that individual would find it "easier to turn their hand clockwise than counterclockwise" (1). This is because, according to simulation theory, that individual was just consciously and subconsciously simulating the embodied action implied in that sentence.

One dimension of simulation phenomena related to our conscious introspective experiences and that illustrates the mixed modal dimensions of meaning-making is perspective-taking: "This view proposes that . . . speakers and listeners create construals of the different perspectives, and shifts of perspective, of the objects and actions described by language" (Gibbs, "Embodied Experience" 3). Gibbs exemplifies this concept with a close exploration of how we might simulate a complex sentence, like "*As far as the eye could see, stalks of corn were bending as waves under the battering force of a surging curtain of rain*" ("Embodied Experience" 3).[5] We may assume that we get meaning from this sentence through just a simple mental schema of rain on a field (3). But it is not simply the gist of meaning, not a simple symbolic representation or abstraction, that individuals seem to simulate. Rather, Gibbs emphasizes the "embodied richness" of simulation (3), which involves taking complex and roving perspectives within a detailed imagined scene. He describes several possible perspectives that may be required to understand this sentence: for example, we first may take the perspective of the eye as it scans across the horizon; then a broader spatial perspective would be necessary to enact the shape, orientation, and expanse of the corn stalks; then a relational and action-oriented perspective might be taken to account for the force of the rain bending the stalks. Perspective-taking reveals how simulation is not a simple, static, or flat visual process. Simulation is better understood as an active, three-dimensional, even transmodal[6] experience that unfolds with visual, relational, spatial, linguistic, and kinetic contours.

The language-image connection established in simulation is not new, nor is it exclusive to embodied meaning perspectives. Indeed, imagery evokes a history as long as the discipline of rhetoric itself (Sadoski and Paivio ix). But this relation has been understood most commonly as a long-standing tension, one "between an abstract, verbal emphasis and a concrete, imaginal emphasis in cognition and learning" (27). This tension is familiar in our everyday thinking—it's abstract language on one hand and visuality or multimodality on the other; it's a left-brained person as language and logic-oriented versus a right-brained person as creative and image-oriented. Simulation helps collapse this binary, establishing instead a melded connection of words and dynamic, embodied imagery.

Simulation emphasizes imagery as action, making the connection between word and image better conceived as *languaging as visioning* in an active, contextualized, experiential, and socially and culturally constrained way. But simulation should not be understood as simply involving the isolated domain of seeing with the eyes or in the "mind's eye," as Bergen often puts it (e.g., *Louder* 16). As evidenced in examples I've provided, imagery entails not only visuality but also spatial relations, orientations, affect, and movement. Kristie Fleckenstein's work on what she calls "imageword" underlines this point. While Bergen can tend to tacitly reinforce a dominating link between simulation and seeing, Fleckenstein forwards a more complex view, namely that imagery

> comes in an unending stream and a range of individual modalities. Rarely do these modalities remain neatly demarcated. Images tend to nest a range of senses, resulting in meanings that are collaborative products of sound, sight, and touch, providing full and resonant . . . significance to meaning. "Seeing" doesn't occur alone or in isolation but is accompanied by feeling. After all, the physiological system of visualization includes the apparatus to detect texture. (19–20)

Fleckenstein exposes how modalities nest in imagery, and by extension, simulation. Plainly, simulating language is imaging, is moving, is feeling. Making meaning with language is itself a profoundly multimodal process or, as Bergen puts it simply: "Understanding language, in multimodal ways, is a lot like being there" (*Louder* 92).

Simulation demonstrates not only connections among words and dimensional imagery but also between the linguistic and the kinesthetic. Embodied meaning philosophy asserts that "real bodily action is at the root of meaning conveyed by language" (Glenberg and Kaschak 563). Demonstrated largely by fMRI imaging studies, this connection suggests that as far as the brain is concerned, understanding language about actions, from the concrete to the abstract, is similar to doing those actions in the world. As Bergen describes this relation:

> When people are processing language about motor actions, there's an increased signal in motor areas, as compared with language not about motor actions. . . . [L]anguage that describes visual scenes leads to an increased signal coming from the brain's vision system.

> For instance, language about motion leads to increased activity in the medial temporal lobe, which houses a region implicated in the visual processing of motion. ("Embodiment" 147)

While these conclusions have been variously challenged (Bergen, "Embodiment" 147), the point here is nevertheless suggestive for conceptualizing meaning-making processes multimodally as, here, language is a kinesthetic endeavor.

One specific angle that helps establish the meaning-action link is the indexical hypothesis, a concept most attributed to Glenberg. This idea suggests that sense-making is akin to a rapidly unfolding, trial-and-error process of attempting to coordinate objects, actions, and relations implied by language. After words and phrases are indexed, or related to imagistic, associative, and culturally shaped memories of those objects and in ad hoc fashion, an individual will imagine the possibilities of embodied action with, or the "affordances" of (Glenberg and Kaschak 558), those objects. Meaning emerges once those actions and things "mesh," or coherently fit together, "according to the constraints on embodied possibilities in the real-world" (Gibbs "Embodied Experience" 3, 4). The indexical hypothesis emphasizes that we try out linguistic meaning through our embodiments, or again, that we "soft-assemble" it. Languaging, in this way, is an active doing. And "meaning is action-based" (Glenberg and Kaschak 559). These insights help conceptualize language and motor action coterminously. Our bodily movement and our language understanding share much of the same real estate in the brain and our object-oriented kinesthetic experiences ineluctably shape the meanings we make with words.

These few implications from embodied meaning research can help reshape our assumptions about multimodality. For just one example, in the *English Journal* issue referenced above, Bruce Pirie describes his approach to what he calls "kinesthetic English." In his "walk this way" activity, students are asked to move as a character would in a given scene. Under the influence of multiple intelligences, this movement would likely be seen as a kind of translation, a way to make meaning that is not accessible through alphabetic writing. However, under the direction of embodied meaning, those kinesthetic actions are not an alternative pathway that stands fully outside the linguistic. Instead movement is perhaps the essential avenue through which rich linguistic meaning can be made in the first place. Indeed, the kinesthetic choices students make as they move, their gestures and sounds and spatial sequencing, do not and could not emerge in isolation; those choices are necessarily steered by and inseparable from word-oriented reading, comprehension, analysis, and selection processes. Pirie too suggests a dynamic interplay of modalities, emphasizing that "we are hardly ever working only in a kinesthetic mode" (50). For Pirie, in the "walk this way" exercise, students "move (kinesthetically), see others move (visually), talk about it (verbally and interpersonally), and reflect on it (intrapersonally)" (50). The implications of embodied meaning push this interplay even further: modes are not just sequentially and separately engaged, as Pirie has it here, but simultaneously enacted. The linguistic never separates from the kinesthetic movement of a character but intertwines, as students might quote a character while gesturing and imagining the scene or character three-dimensionally in their mind's eye. Languaging is doing is feeling is seeing is moving.

I've only here introduced a small bit of embodied meaning research. But I hope that this introduction helps undermine how we relate writing and multimodality. Embodied meaning suggests that linguistic meaning unfolds in the same dimensions as do multimodalities. Meaning-making with words—writing and reading and speaking and listening—is not rarefied or distinct or more rigorous (though, I suppose, language could be more economical or directive). All writing is indeed multimodal, but not just in the design features of a page or in the multimodal nature of all composing processes. Rather, all composing is multimodal in the inherent modal overlaps of meaning-making. The linguistic is never only the linguistic, the visual never just the visual, the kinesthetic never just the kinesthetic. As meaning moves and is made and remade, the linguistic flows among modal streams and entanglements. The multimodal capacities and differences of our bodies and the three dimensions of our lifeworld experiences are the foundations of all our capacities to understand and to communicate. All composing is multimodal in that all meaning-making itself is profoundly multimodal.

Finding ways to see linguistic meaning as multimodal embodied meaning diffuses our sense of needing it to be words and everything else. And mixing up modalities is especially important given how we tend to worry perpetually about perceived losses in literacies. As I was writing this essay, I came upon an article expressing just such a worry: that kids just aren't writing anymore. Citing the rise of *Snapchat*, *Instagram*, increasing video and image content on *Facebook*, and other statistics around digital media habits, the authors proclaim resolutely that "picting is the new literacy" (Norris and Soloway). Along the way to this claim, the authors do share some useful detail about current media practices. But like Kress's figure of the image crowding words off the page, their central claim is entrenched in the fundamental distinction between words and everything else. The authors wonder at the article's close, "When will the U.S. Congress express laws in images? When will venture capitalists express business plans in pictures?" I hear in these questions a cynicism, that familiar picture-is-easier position, a call to see an abject absurdity in the idea that pictures, alone and isolated, could ever deliver something so complex and serious as law or technical documents. This prognostication about picting, though, is overwrought: it separates images from language; it ignores how other modal dimensions, like the aural, sonic, gestural, musical, and more, are no doubt all mixed up with words and pictures in the meaning and media environments the authors describe.

As we careen deeper into imagined futures that are thought to be continuously somehow more imagistic, I can feel the word wardens among us (self not discluded) entrenching themselves further, lamenting the seeming loss of difficulty or critical skills and the fundamental not-imageness of alphabetic writing. It thus remains ever more imperative to soften the isolation of writing from multimodalities. Instead, we might proceed believing that all meaning-making processes are ones that invoke and provoke multisensory, embodied, and multimodal relations. We can relinquish page design as the bedrock argument with which writing becomes multimodal. We can dispense with unuseful fictions that, if unwittingly, isolate, categorize, and strictly demarcate modalities. Instead we can move toward imagining the linguistic with everything else, toward composition as seeinglanguagingfeelingmoving, perhaps.

Notes

1. NCTE's "Position Statement on Multimodal Literacies" echoes this point: "Young children practice multimodal literacies naturally and spontaneously. They easily combine and move between drama, art, text, music, speech, sound, physical movement, animation/gaming, etc."

2. My understanding of embodied mind philosophy in relation to language and meaning has been shaped most by Gibbs, Bergen, Glenberg, Lakoff and Johnson, Johnson, and Shapiro. A central book in this area is one likely familiar in composition: *Metaphors We Live By*. In it, Lakoff and Johnson establish metaphor as the basis of routine language use. This metaphoric conceptual

system for our understanding is grounded by embodied experience, in spatial, kinesthetic, visual, and sensory orientations of bodies. And the embodied grounding of metaphor is the way scholars extend the implications of simulation to abstract language and concepts (e.g., Bergen, *Louder* 198–203).

3. Like any disciplinary ground shift, work in embodied meaning garners critique related to its novelty, methods, and lack of determined comprehensiveness—for example, that embodied meaning processes have not yet been shown to be necessary or sufficient mechanisms for language understanding (Bergen, "Embodiment" 144). Lakoff and Johnson's work in particular has also been rightly critiqued for its problematic assumptive appeals to universal embodiments (e.g., Vidali; Altman; Hayles) for perpetuating "objectivist presuppositions in positing a universal body unmarked by gender, ethnicity, physical disability, or culture" (Hayles 164).

4. An example of these kinds of studies may illuminate. In one such study, participants were first asked to learn a set of actions prompted by a symbol: if they saw a *, they would make a grasping motion with their fist; seeing a # prompted them to swallow. Participants were shown a symbol, performed the matching action, and then were presented with a metaphorical phrase that would either match or mismatch the action just performed (e.g., the sentence *Swallow your pride* appears after the prompt to swallow). They were asked to press a button when they felt they understood that phrase. Results showed that participants were "about half a second faster" in pressing the button when the actions matched than when they didn't (Bergen, *Louder* 200). This difference in time is in part explained by the involvement of the motor cortex: "understanding a metaphorical action phrase, like *grasp a concept*, activates the motor apparatus responsible for performing the same action; in other words, mentally simulating the metaphorical action" (Bergen, *Louder* 200).

5. Simulation processes have been demonstrated not just with the kind of concrete language demonstrated in this example but also in the case of abstract concepts and metaphor (Gallese and Lakoff; Santana and de Vega).

6. Horner et al. advanced the term *transmodal* recently as a way to move away from "understanding modality and linguality in terms of fixed ('defined') categories and practices" and to emphasize the dynamism of modal and communicative experience.

Works Cited

Altman, Meryl. "How Not to Do Things with Metaphors We Live By." *College English*, vol. 52, no. 5, Sept. 1990, pp. 495–506.

Ball, Cheryl E., and Colin Charlton. "All Writing is Multimodal." *Naming What We Know: Threshold Concepts in Writing Studies*, edited by Linda Adler-Kassner and Elizabeth Wardle, Utah State UP, 2015, pp. 42–43.

Bergen, Benjamin K. "Embodiment, Simulation, and Meaning." *The Routledge Handbook of Semantics*, edited by Nick Riemer, Routledge, 2015, pp. 142–57, www.cogsci.ucsd.edu/~bkbergen/papers/ESM.pdf.

———. *Louder Than Words: The New Science of How the Mind Makes Meaning*. Basic Books, 2012.

Brandt, Deborah. *The Rise of Writing: Redefining Mass Literacy*. Cambridge UP, 2015.

Davis, Ernest. "Embodied Simulation as a Theory of Language." *Computer Science Department at New York University*, cs.nyu.edu/davise/papers/bergen.pdf. Accessed 20 June 2019.

Dunn, Patricia A. *Talking, Sketching, Moving: Multiple Literacies in the Teaching of Writing*. Boynton/Cook, 2001.

Fleckenstein, Kristie S. *Embodied Literacies: Imageword and a Poetics of Teaching*. Southern Illinois UP, 2003.

Gallese, Vittorio, and George Lakoff. "The Brain's Concepts: The Role of the Sensory-Motor System in Conceptual Knowledge." *Cognitive Neuropsychology*, vol. 22, no. 3, May 2005, pp. 455–79.

Gardner, Howard. *Frames of Mind: The Theory of Multiple Intelligences*. Basic Books, 1983.

———. "Multiple Intelligences as a Catalyst." *English Journal*, vol. 84, no. 8, Dec. 1995, pp. 16–18.

George, Diana. "From Analysis to Design: Visual Communication in the Teaching of Writing." *College Composition and Communication*, vol. 54, no. 1, Sept. 2002, pp. 11–39.

Gibbs, Raymond W., Jr. "Embodied Experience and Linguistic Meaning." *Brain and Language*, vol. 84, no. 1, Jan. 2003, pp. 1–15.

———. *Embodiment and Cognitive Science*. Cambridge UP, 2006.

Glenberg, Arthur M. "How Reading Comprehension Is Embodied and Why That Matters." *International Electronic Journal of Elementary Education*, vol. 4, no. 1, 2011, pp. 5–18.

Glenberg, Arthur M., and Michael P. Kaschak. "Grounding Language in Action." *Psychonomic Bulletin and Review*, vol. 9, no. 3, pp. 558–65.

Hayles, N. Katherine. "The Materiality of Informatics." *Configurations*, vol. 1, no. 1, Winter 1993, pp. 147–70.

Horner, Bruce, et al. "Thinking about Multi (or Trans-) Modality, and Trans (or Multi-) Linguality: Power, Ideology, and Emerging Questions." *Digital Rhetoric Collaborative*, 6 Oct. 2014. www.digitalrhetoric collaborative.org/2014/10/06/thinking-about-multi-or-trans-modality-and-trans-or-multi-linguality-power-ideology-and-emerging-questions/.

Johnson, Mark. *The Meaning of the Body: Aesthetics of Human Understanding.* U of Chicago P, 2007.

Kress, Gunther. *Before Writing: Rethinking the Paths to Literacy.* Routledge, 1997.

Lakoff, George, and Mark Johnson. *Metaphors We Live By.* U of Chicago P, 1980.

The New London Group. "A Pedagogy of Multiliteracies: Designing Social Futures." *Harvard Educational Review*, vol. 66, no. 1, Spring 1996, pp. 60–92.

Norris, Cathie, and Elliot Soloway. "Picting, Not Writing, Is the Literacy of Today's Youth." *THE Journal*, 8 May 2017, thejournal.com/articles/2017/05/08/picting-not-writing.aspx.

Palmeri, Jason. *Remixing Composition: A History of Multimodal Writing Pedagogy.* Southern Illinois UP / NCTE, 2012.

Pierpoint, Alan. Response to "Letters: Winners, Losers, and Multiple Intelligences." *English Journal*, vol. 85, no. 2, Feb. 1996, pp. 11–12.

Pirie, Bruce. "Meaning through Motion: Kinesthetic English." *English Journal*, vol. 84, no. 8, Dec. 1995, pp. 46–51.

"Position Statement on Multimodal Literacies." *NCTE*, 17 Nov. 2005, www.ncte.org/positions/statements/multimodalliteracies.

Sadoski, Mark, and Allan Paivio. *Imagery and Text: A Dual Coding Theory of Reading and Writing.* Lawrence Erlbaum, 2001.

Santana, Eduardo, and Manuel de Vega. "Metaphors Are Embodied, and So Are Their Literal Counterparts." *Frontiers in Psychology*, vol. 2, article 90, May 2011, pp. 1–12.

Shapiro, Lawrence. *Embodied Cognition.* Routledge, 2011.

Shipka, Jody. *Toward a Composition Made Whole.* U of Pittsburg P, 2011.

Smagorinsky, Peter. "Multiple Intelligences in the English Class: An Overview." *English Journal*, vol. 84, no. 8, Dec. 1995, pp. 19–26.

Vidali, Amy. "Seeing What We Know: Disability and Theories of Metaphor." *Journal of Literary and Cultural Disability Studies*, vol. 4, no. 1, 2010, pp. 33–54.

Translating Modalities: Interactions between Digital and Alphabetic Modes in Professional Translation Work

Laura Gonzales

Over the last two decades, there have been numerous ongoing conversations, both in the field of rhetoric and composition and in related fields, regarding what counts as or what is considered multimodality and multimodal communication (New London Group; Shipka, "Including" and *Toward a Composition*). On the one hand, multimodality as a disciplinary term has direct ties to digital technologies and digital media, encompassing the use and manipulation of "still and moving images, animations, color, words, music and sound" in digital contexts (Takayoshi and Selfe 1). Early conceptions of multimodality, specifically within rhetoric and composition and the subfield of computers and composition, tied the concept to writing, and more specifically to writing in digital spaces. For example, the New London Group's position statement, published in 1996, directly states that "literacy pedagogy must now account for the burgeoning variety of text forms associated with information and multimedia technologies" (61). In its early development, multimodality emerged in academia partly as a consequence of the need to reconceptualize writing beyond alphabetic texts.

Yet, on the other hand, as definitions of multimodality continue to shift and emerge, scholars like Jody Shipka, Cynthia Selfe, and Janine Butler (among many others) remind us that multimodality is always embedded in our communicative practices, including (but not limited to) writing and using (but not always bound to) digital tools (Shipka, "Including"). As Gabriela Raquel Ríos clarifies, multimodality has been practiced in non-Western communities for decades, as "Indigenous peoples have historically used music, dance, theater, and other types of non-textual practices to make meaning, and we still do" (89). Indeed, scholars researching multimodality through culturally situated frameworks continue to argue that although the disciplinary concept of multimodal communication may be new, multimodal practices that encompass and extend beyond alphabetic writing have always been in place, particularly in non-Western cultures (Banks; Butler; Haas).

The essays in this collection collectively argue that there is in fact "no discrepancy" between alphabetic and multimodal texts, since alphabetic and multimodal elements are not "competing propositions" (Reichert Powell, this volume). Rather than treating modes as discreet entities, recent work in multimodality has pushed rhetoric and composition to further consider—and to teach students to consider—the ways that modalities (including but not limited to alphabets) interact in specific rhetorical situations where the context, purpose, and audience guide the exigence and effectiveness of a communicative event (Horner et al., *Translinguality*). As Bruce Horner argues in his essay within this collection, specific elements of communicative practice (e.g., languages, modalities) are often "abstracted" from "the concrete labor of practitioners—composers, listeners, viewers, readers." This type of abstraction can lead to the erasure, as I will further demonstrate in this essay, of the labor, lived experiences, and particular communicative strengths of communicators who rhetorically navigate communication for both themselves and for their communities.

In this essay, I introduce the activities of translation and the labor of translators as potential sites for studying the interactions between alphabetic and digitally mediated modalities in situated cultural-rhetorical contexts. Having both worked as a translator and studied translation processes across institutions for a number of years (see Gonzales), I have had the opportunity to witness how the transformation of information across named languages (e.g., Spanish, English) elicits intricate and rhetorically situated interactions between languages and modalities. Further understanding translation practices in context, I argue, can help rhetoric and composition scholars to continue theorizing and teaching multimodality beyond the limitations of any single modality, language, or genre. By grounding my analysis of multimodal communication in the work of professionals who adapt content across languages (Spanishes and Englishes) for their specific communities, I contribute to this collection's goal of illustrating the intricate and ongoing relations among modalities in both alphabetic and digitally mediated communication, while also honoring the labor of the professional communicators who complete this work. As I will further demonstrate, analyzing the work of translators and the activities of translation can help the field of rhetoric and composition move away from limiting conceptions of multimodality to teaching and learning digital technologies, orienting toward a closer examination of how modalities interact in specific cultural-rhetorical situations.

Why Study Translation as Multimodality?

Recently, scholars in rhetoric and composition extended discussions of multimodality to further consider the multimodal elements embedded in what is sometimes described as multilingual communication, emphasizing the various ways through which movements across languages encompass the "multiple, dynamic, and malleable" practices typically associated with multimodal composition ("NCTE Definition"). For example, in "Composition 2.0: Toward a Multilingual and Multimodal Framework," Steven Fraiberg traces the relations between languages and modalities in Israel, providing a framework for studying the "complex blending of multimodal and multilingual texts and literacy practices in our teaching and research" (what he calls "code mashing"; 102). This call for interrogating the relations between languages and modalities in situated contexts has since been taken up by several scholars in and beyond rhetoric and composition (Butler).

Most recently, proposing the *trans* prefix as an alternative to the *multi* in multimodality, Horner, Selfe, and Tim Lockridge argue for a "focus on work across boundaries of language and modality rather than seeing our task as one of selecting from a menu of languages and modalities" (*Translinguality*). Thus, some proponents of multimodality and transmodality emphasize the need to further consider how modalities are not static, bound entities but are instead fluid practices deployed and mitigated in specific contexts and situations, within and beyond the boundaries of standardized written English.

Although there are numerous frameworks for researching language fluidity from a wide range of disciplines and fields (e.g., translanguaging [García and Li Wei], translingualism [Horner et al., "Language Difference"], code meshing and code mashing [Young and Martinez; Fraiberg]),

I focus specifically on translation due to the practical nature and the history of this practice and profession. When translators adapt information across named languages (e.g., Spanish, English), they make rhetorical decisions as they present information to audiences from various linguistic and cultural backgrounds. In making these decisions, translators have to consider the specific histories and backgrounds of their intended audiences, understanding regional and historical variations of specific languages (e.g., Spanishes, Englishes) that might influence how information is perceived in a particular instance or utterance.

For example, translators have to use different Spanishes to reach Mexican American audiences from particular socioeconomic backgrounds than they do when translating for Spanish-speaking communities from Spain (see Torrez 291–92), whose version of Spanish derives from Catalan, a European language used in parts of Spain and France. Throughout their translation processes, translators have to consider orientations to language and culture embraced by their intended audiences, making rhetorical decisions about which words in their linguistic repertoires would be most appropriate to use in specific translation scenarios. Thus, translators move through and shift the various modalities encompassed in their communicative repertoires, making deliberate rhetorical decisions about which practices to represent in their final translations and which alphabets to draw from to represent ideas to a specific community.

In addition to issues of linguistic variations, contemporary translators also have to consider issues of visual design and media when completing translations. When translating a birth certificate or medical record, for instance, translators have to translate both alphabetic information and visual data to render a translation that will be understood by an individual who does not speak the source language of the original document. As translators adapt information for their communities, they fluidly work through modalities, thus transforming both the content and form of a mode based on a specific rhetorical situation and situated exigence.

Method

As part of a larger project (see Gonzales) to understand the multimodal practices enacted during translation activities, I worked with two communities of translators over a period of three years. I specifically chose to work with Latinx translators who work across Spanishes and Englishes rather than working with participants who speak languages in which I am not fluent. While I acknowledge the colonial histories embedded in both Spanish and English, by working with immigrant, Latinx individuals who identify Spanishes as their first language, and with whom I identify, I can present a more nuanced, ethical, and thorough analysis that accounts for multimodal processes, products, and lived experiences.

The two organizations that I discuss in this essay are Knightly Latino, a bilingual, college-student-run news broadcasting organization located in Orlando, Florida, and the Language Services Department, a small translation and interpretation business located within the Hispanic Center of Western Michigan, a nonprofit organization serving Latinx communities in Grand Rapids, Michigan. During my work with both organizations, I traced how participants adapted information from Spanish to English (and vice versa) for various purposes, including translating news stories into Spanish for communities in Orlando and translating technical documents such as birth certificates, medical records, and education transcripts for Spanish-speaking immigrants who aimed to use these documents in English-dominant spaces within the United States.

Following emerging calls for embracing multimodal methods in rhetoric and composition (Butler; McKee and DeVoss), I incorporated visual data collection and analysis methods to help me understand data in various dimensions, including those best understood through alphabetic and digitally mediated practices. By employing a multimodal research practice, I aimed to decentralize the distinction between alphabetic and digital modalities in both writing and research, highlighting the ways through which alphabetic and digitally mediated technologies provide helpful avenues for understanding and practicing communication. For example, in tracing translation activities, I used visual methods to not only account for what my participants were doing during my data collection periods but to also understand and acknowledge the environments, locations, and positionality of this work within its broader rhetorical and cultural contexts (Pigg).

The methods I employed in this project included video and screen cast recordings of translation processes, in addition to artifact-based interviews and field notes collected during my conversations with translators at two research sites over the course of three years. These methods yielded 449 hours of video data, not including the three years of physical observation and the relationship-building encompassed in the various stages of this project. Although the specific coding mechanisms I employed stem beyond the scope of this essay, in the data narratives below, I highlight examples of how alphabetic and digital modalities were enacted during my collaborations with translators at both research sites.[1] Through these examples, I showcase how translators blur commonly accepted distinctions and boundaries between alphabetic and digital modalities, focusing less on discreet tools, alphabets, and platforms and more on the collective rhetorical impact of language transformation. In this way, the data narratives presented in the following sections illustrate the ways in which alphabetic and digital modalities are collaborative, rather than "competing," entities (Reichert Powell, this volume).

Data Narrative 1: Mirror Translations in the Language Services Department

The Language Services Department is a small business situated within a bigger nonprofit organization intended to provide services for Latinx communities in and beyond Grand Rapids, Michigan (Gonzales and Turner). Although the Language Services Department charges a small fee for written translation services (e.g., translating Web sites, technical documents, transcripts), all of the department's profits are reinvested in the social programs provided by the nonprofit organization, the Hispanic Center of Western Michigan. Thus, while the Language Services Department operates as a professional, stand-alone organization, some of the structural elements and resource limitations commonly found in nonprofit organizations also play a role in the Language Services Department. For example, although the Language Services Department employs more than fifteen translators who have extensive training and experience, the department itself does not have access to many of the technological tools and software available in a for-profit business. Thus, through their work in the Language Services Department, translators adapt and make do with the technologies that are available. This often entails completing extensive design activities using general word processing software like *Google Docs* and *Microsoft Word*.

The most common type of project to enter the Language Services Department is the translation of technical documents such as birth certificates, legal documents (e.g., court reports), and education records. After moving to the United States from South and Central American countries, Latinx community members often have to translate these documents to gain residency, enroll in school, and qualify for health insurance (among other purposes). For this reason, the Language Services Department provides low-cost document translation to community members. Further, translators within the organization must be trained in technical translation and must have at least a working knowledge of government requirements for translated documents eligible to be used in legal transactions. In 2015, the Language Services Department translated approximately 5,600 legal, medical, and education documents for members of the community.

Although the language on these technical documents is often limited (the documents range from one to two pages, or one hundred to three hundred words), much of the work in these types of translations requires that translators design and redesign logos, seals, and other visuals across languages. To ease language accessibility in technical translations, and to ensure that government agencies will accept translated technical documents, the Language Services Department provides clients with mirror translations, which consist of translated documents that identically match the design, layout, and formatting of the original text. Because the Language Services Department does mirror translations, graphics like the seals must all be translated and designed before the translated document is considered complete.

Due to the frequency of translations requiring seals (birth certificates, medical records), the Language Services Department's greatest source of intellectual property has become its extensive, editable document library of translated seals and stamps, built over the course of twenty-seven years. Seals and stamps are categorized into birth, death, and marriage certificates, educational and medical records, and other technical document templates organized by the country of origin of each original text. Although designers (e.g., Web designers, user experience researchers, graphic designers) don't necessarily use the term *translation* to describe their work, as I have argued in other places (see Gonzales and Turner) there are ongoing and expanding connections between design and translation professions. These connections continue to grow as the lines between visual, alphabetic, and digital modalities blur with the

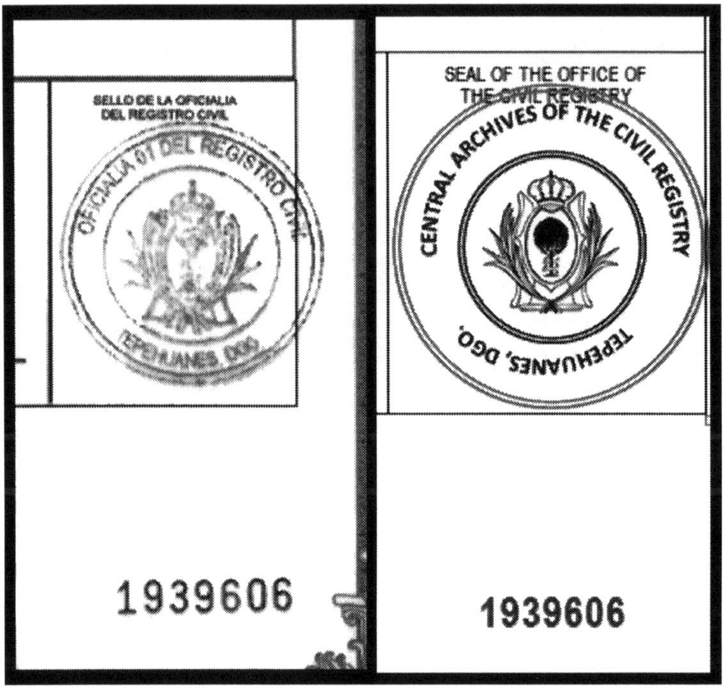

Figure 1. Birth certificate seal from Tepehuanes, Durango, Mexico

increased use of digital technologies across the world. Although translators may have historically been trained to focus solely on alphabetic language transformation, as figures 1–3 illustrate, translation work now entails alphabetic, visual, and digital manipulations, where translators have to recreate (using word processing and sometimes visual design software) intricate designs that incorporate their translated alphabetic texts. Figures 1–3 portray various seals and figures that were designed by translators during my data-collection period.

In figure 1, the image on the left is a picture from the original birth certificate seal submitted for translation at the Language Services Department; the image on the right is a screenshot from the translated design. As evidenced in these two images, employees in the Language Services Department must translate the information contained in the seal (e.g., Central Archives of the Civil Registry) and must also include the images and logos in the translated document for reference. In this way, translators also act as designers in the translation of birth certificates, ensuring the usability of translated documents by providing mir-

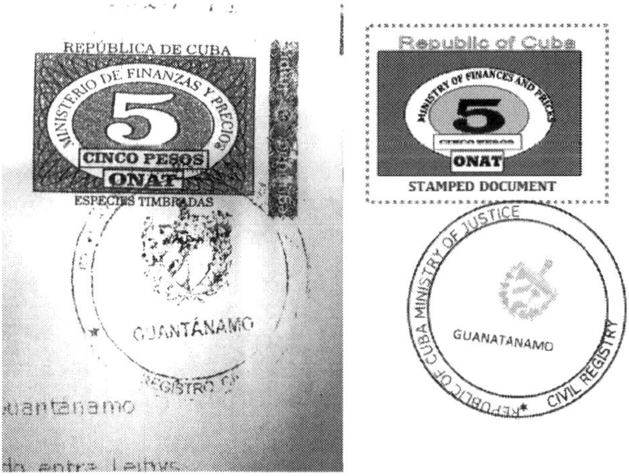

Figure 2. Educational record stamps from Cuba

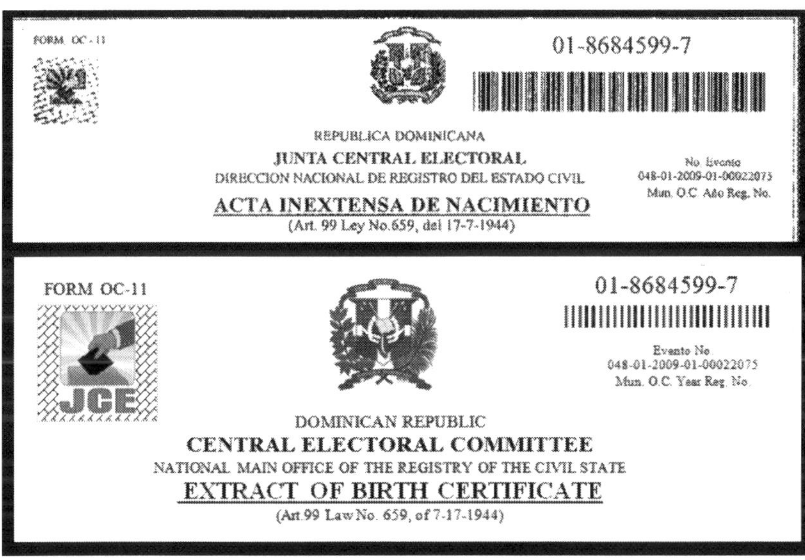

Figure 3. Birth certificate barcodes and seals from the Dominican Republic

ror translations that can be clearly understood in both the original and the target language. The image on the left in figure 2 is a picture from the original education certificate submitted by the client. On the right is the image designed and translated by an employee from the Language Services Department. The translated phrase "stamped document" signals that the client paid the due taxes on her original document. This in turn provides added credibility to the translated document, indicating to the English reader that the educational record was submitted to and accepted by the Cuban embassy.

In recent years, government agencies have been providing ways for individuals to digitally verify the authenticity of technical documents such as birth certificates. Although translators cannot recreate digital barcodes on such documents (as depicted in figure 3), it's important for translators to still place barcodes and their corresponding verification numbers in the right position on finalized documents. In this way, government agencies can verify the validity of these technical documents via a verification number (such as the "event number" ["Evento. No."] pictured in figure 3). As evidenced in figures 1–3, the translation of technical documents, at least for participants in the Language Services Department, requires culturally situated, multimodal, multilingual design. To complete these mirror translations, translators have to manipulate the language of each document (translating complex legal language from Spanish to English) while also recreating intricate government seals and logos in a way that will make the visual content accessible to readers in English.

As translators complete mirror translations, the focus of their composing process rests on effectively communicating technical information in both Spanish and English for the various stakeholders who will engage with a particular document. While translators certainly use multimodal elements in their combination of alphabetic and visual modalities, the focus of the translation activity itself remains on the specific rhetorical context in which these genres will be used. To complete mirror translations, translators have to understand the specific technical genre they are working with, the nationalities of the stakeholders who will be using this document, and the technical elements required on both the source and target texts engaged in this interaction. In these specific activities, translators use but also manipulate and adapt modalities to make their work accessible, searching *Google* for seals and logos, recreating visual elements in *Microsoft Word* and *Google Slides*, and repositioning information so that it can be read on both alphabetic and visual levels. In this way, mirror translations encompass complex interactions between modalities, interactions that are grounded in material exigencies like enrolling children in school, finding a new medical doctor, or facilitating legal proceedings.

Data Narrative 2: Multimodal Interactions in Localizing Machine Translation

At my second research site, I got the opportunity to study translation with bilingual news-broadcasting students at Knightly Latino, a university campus news network that focuses on writing and translating news stories to meet the needs of the Latinx community in Florida (see "Nicholson News"). I worked closely with two student translators at this organization, recording their computer screens during translation projects and holding post-translation interviews to better understand my participants' translation practices. During these interviews, the translators and I watched portions of their screen recordings together and then talked about what was taking place during these recordings. I asked translators questions like, Why did you decide to use this particular definition or digital translation tool? Why did you go to that specific Web site while you translated? In this way, the post-translation interviews helped me further understand how participants made decisions and coordinated resources as they translated information.

During one of her translation screencast recordings, one of my participants, Natalie, was translating a news story originally published in English, titled "Development Plans Threaten Orlando Park." The story described a new housing development set to be built on the grounds of a popular park in Orlando. As she translated this story during a thirty-minute writing session, Natalie used *Google Translate* thirty-two times to find possible translation options or to double-check the translations she came up with on her own. Despite her thirty-two visits to *Google Translate*, Natalie only used fourteen of the Spanish words the site suggested for her final article. The rest of the times, according to Natalie, *Google Translate* suggestions served as inspiration for her translation process. For example, Natalie began translating her news story from English to Spanish by looking up the word *threaten* using *Google Translate*. She wanted to translate this word as it was used in the article's title, "Development Plans Threaten Orlando Park." *Google Translate* identified four options: *amenazar*, *proferir amenazas contra*, *acechar*, and *amagar*. Rather than using any of the initial options, however, Natalie searched for Spanish translations of the word *harm*. *Google Translate* provided nine options for this translation and Natalie decided to use the first option, the word *daño*, in her final article.

During her artifact-based interview, Natalie explained that she didn't use any of the initial suggestions provided by *Google Translate* because "the word threaten seemed to be translated into something more related to physical harm. If I *amenazar* someone, for example, I'm threatening them physically. Threatening a park is completely different, so I decided to look up options for the word harm because I thought that might give me results that are more like harming a physical object instead of a person." In this example, Natalie brought in her own understanding of the word *amenazar* as it would be understood by her audience; and to get a more accurate translation of the word *threaten* in Spanish, Natalie brought in her understanding of the English language by looking up the synonym *harm* and using those results instead. In this way, Natalie explained, the translations provided by *Google Translate* "are just inspiration sometimes. I wouldn't have thought of the word *dañar* on my own necessarily, but seeing that *amenazar* was an option helped me think of similar words to look up in Spanish and English. The *Google* translations gave me options." For Natalie, *Google Translate* served as a tool to help or inspire her own abilities to move between languages, rather than as a tool to find specific translation answers.

Although Natalie's translation event can be considered multimodal on several levels, including the word processing she was using to compose her translation on a computer and the various digital tools she used to make translation decisions, it is the activity, rather than the discreet mode or tool of translation, involved in this process that perhaps required the most rhetorical manipulation in this example. While Natalie navigated several Web sites and platforms throughout her translation process, many of these multimodal elements would remain invisible to someone who only witnessed the product of Natalie's translation (without taking into account her process). As Paul Prior explains in "From Speech Genres to Mediated Multimodal Genre Systems," "multimodality is a routine dimension of language in use, as utterances can only happen in embodied, material, multisensory, multi-semiotic worlds" (27). By navigating the machine-translation algorithms of *Google Translate* through her specific cultural-rhetorical lens, Natalie managed to make information both accessible and localized to her specific audience, thus leveraging the rhetorical elements of multimodality in both process and product. As Natalie's example illustrates, while the product of a writing event may appear to be strictly alphabetic (specifically, here, in a finished written translation), the process of translation work itself frequently entails multimodal activities that can be further recognized in rhetoric and composition scholarship and pedagogy (Shipka, *Toward a Composition*).

Data Narrative 3: Embodied Multimodality in Translation

Although the visible elements of translators' work encompass several multimodal elements in both process and product, through my work with translators at the two organizations depicted in this essay, I was also able to account for several embodied modalities that are frequently at play during the language adaptation process. These modalities include embodied gestures like pointing and signing as well as internalized, non-visual modalities that translators experience as they draw on their cultural knowledge to make linguistic decisions. For example, in figure 4, Sara, a translator and the director of the Language Services Department, sits in front of her computer as she translates a flyer for an upcoming community event titled People Helping People. While Sara completed her flyer translation, she had two computer monitors with many screens

Figure 4. Sara, director of the Language Services Department, points to her computer screen as she translates a flyer.

open. Although it is unclear in the figure itself, Sara consulted several digital tools to complete this translation, including *Word Reference* (www.wordreference.com/), to find word-translation options. Figure 4 also shows Sara pointing her finger at the screen: as Sara moved her fingers back and forth across the screens, she envisioned and decided between various sentence structures that would facilitate understanding for, and appeal to, Spanish-speaking users interacting with this flyer, using the motion to cover and combine phrases as she translated.

During her artifact-based interview, Sara explained that although she coordinates several digital resources while she translates, translators must frequently "feel their way" into their translation. "Feeling" translations involves not only seeing words digitally on a screen but also testing out how users will engage with information in their material contexts—with a printed flyer, a multi-layered Web site, or other materials that extend outside of digital spaces. To feel translations, translators may engage in conversations while standing and gesturing, sit in various rooms with different types of lighting to look at a document, or print digital materials in a large font to see how words fit on a printed page. Often, this type of work requires translators to think back to their previous experiences hearing, reading, or writing in various languages in different situations, reencountering the interactions that make up translators' constantly expanding index of cultural knowledge. As Hannah Rule explains in her essay within this collection, "linguistic meaning is not received or transacted nor a matter of translation into the language of thought. Rather, meaning is a matter of bodily enaction." As translators transform a word, they recall their previous experiences with that word and with the other people, tools, and technologies involved in previous interactions, enacting multimodality not only in material spaces but also through their embodied experiences. Thus, when studying translation, accounting for modality requires an accountability to context, mode, physical space, and culture.

Implications

By analyzing how translators adapt information across languages, I was able to see and experience the rhetorical coordination of modes that takes place as translators transform ideas from one language to another. Because language is constantly in motion, the words we use to describe specific concepts or ideas shift and transform with our cultural norms and practices. Translators, to maintain expertise in language transformation, also have to echo this flexibility and fluidity, constantly changing their practices as languages and linguistic patterns evolve. Translation is a multimodal practice in that it requires

- the decentering of alphabetic language—and of alphabetic, written language in English (what some scholars describe as *standard written English*)—as the single or most important element of communicative practice (Horner et al., *Translinguality*);
- the rhetorical awareness of how modes and genres function in different contexts and for various audiences (Butler);
- the purposeful and rhetorical layering of modes and media, with critical attention to how modes like visuals, sounds, and words work together in creating meaning for various stakeholders (Takayoshi and Selfe); and
- the critical understanding of how communicative practice is always rhetorically and culturally situated (Guerra; Shipka, *Toward a Composition*).

For translators like Sara, Natalie, and others, working across semiotic resources and layering communicative practices is not a stylistic choice or preference. Instead, translation practices are situated both in a specific rhetorical situation (e.g., as a birth certificate is being transformed from Spanish to English) and in the cultural history and experience of the individual translator(s) completing this task. For example, if Sara in the Language Services Department is translating a birth certificate, the strategies she uses to navigate translation moments in that project will depend on the situation that prompted the exigence for the translation (e.g., a mother needs to enroll her child in school) and on her skills, training, and experience as a translator (e.g., Sara's cultural background, her training and knowledge of translation dictionaries, and how she may be feeling when the translation project arrives). Thus, orienting to multimodality through translation work can help researchers and teachers in rhetoric and composition understand the cultural influences and the rhetorical context fueling the interactions between modalities in situated communicative moments. In translation work, the distinction between alphabetic and digital modalities is decentralized, as modality is enacted based on rhetorical exigence and navigation on the part of the translator.

In "Cultivating a Rhetorical Sensibility in the Translingual Writing Classroom," Juan Guerra illustrates the importance of connecting communicative practices to culture and experience, explaining:

> [W]e falter in our efforts to help our students understand what a translingual approach is because we have been leading them to think that we expect them to produce a particular kind of writing that mimics what we call code-meshing rather than getting them to understand that what we want instead is for them to call on the rhetorical sensibilities many of them already possess but put aside because of what they see as a jarring shift in context. (231–32)

As Guerra argues, some recent efforts to embed linguistic difference in the composition classroom have been unsuccessful, but not because writing teachers are not welcoming or encouraging students to use their entire linguistic and composing resources. Rather, these pedagogical challenges arise when teachers fail to understand how students' linguistic resources (including but not limited to alphabetic and digital modalities) are always tied to broader cultural-rhetorical contexts. In other words, we experience challenges in teaching language diversity (and, I would argue, multimodality) when we tell students to translanguage or to work across languages and modalities in the classroom without setting up the cultural-rhetorical environment that will facilitate these interactions.

Rather than merely pushing students to incorporate modes and languages in our classroom projects, translation teaches us the importance of recognizing how these languages and modalities are tied to various histories and lived experiences, and how the specific layering of these communicative resources and practices may have real consequences in the lives of our students and their communities. Just like Sara in the Language Services Department relives her experiences with language when translating a document, students in our classrooms and professionals in our workplaces may be reliving and sharing their lived experiences as they blend languages and semiotic resources through their work. Translating or translanguaging together, then, requires us as teachers and researchers of rhetoric and writing to support the language work that students and professionals engage in, appreciating the practices that students deploy not as adherences to or deviations from our own expectations but rather as evidence of communicators' own rhetorical and cultural labor.

Note

1. For a more thorough discussion of the method and methodology used to analyze translation data in this project, see Gonzales.

Works Cited

Banks, Adam J. *Digital Griots: African American Rhetoric in a Multimedia Age*. Southern Illinois UP, 2011.

Butler, Janine. "Where Access Meets Multimodality: The Case of ASL Music Videos." *Kairos*, vol. 21, no. 1, Fall 2016, kairos.technorhetoric.net/21.1/topoi/butler/index.html.

Fraiberg, Steven. "Composition 2.0: Toward a Multilingual and Multimodal Framework." *College Composition and Communication*, vol. 62, no. 1, Sept. 2010, pp. 100–26.

García, Ofelia, and Li Wei. *Translanguaging: Language, Bilingualism and Education*. Palgrave Macmillan, 2014.

Gonzales, Laura. *Sites of Translation: What Multilinguals Can Teach Us about Writing, Rhetoric, and Technology*. 2016. Michigan State University, PhD dissertation.

Gonzales, Laura, and Heather Noel Turner. "Converging Fields, Expanding Outcomes: Technical Communication, Translation, and Design at a Non-profit Organization." *Technical Communication*, vol. 64, no. 2, 2017, pp. 126–40.

Guerra, Juan C. "Cultivating a Rhetorical Sensibility in the Translingual Writing Classroom." *College English*, vol. 78, no. 3, Jan. 2016, pp. 228–33.

Haas, Angela M. "Race, Rhetoric, and Technology: A Case Study of Decolonial Technical Communication Theory, Methodology, and Pedagogy." *Journal of Business and Technical Communication*, vol. 26, no. 3, 2012, pp. 277–310.

Horner, Bruce, et al. "Language Difference in Writing: Toward a Translingual Approach." *College English*, vol. 73, no. 3, Jan. 2011, pp. 303–21.

Horner, Bruce, et al. *Translinguality, Transmodality, and Difference: Exploring Dispositions and Change in Language and Learning*. Enculturation/Intermezzo, 2015, intermezzo.enculturation.net/01.htm.

McKee, Heidi A., and Dànielle Nicole DeVoss, editors. *Digital Writing Research: Technologies, Methodologies, and Ethical Issues*. Hampton Press, 2007.

"The NCTE Definition of 21st Century Literacies." *NCTE*, 28 Feb. 2013, www.ncte.org/positions/statements/21stcentdefinition.

The New London Group. "A Pedagogy of Multiliteracies: Designing Social Futures." *Harvard Educational Review*, vol. 66, no. 1, Spring 1996, pp. 60–92.

"Nicholson News: Knightly Latino." *Nicholson School of Communication / University of Central Florida*, sciences.ucf.edu/communication/knightly-latino/. Accessed 21 June 2019.

Pigg, Stacey. "Emplacing Mobile Composing Habits: A Study of Academic Writing in Networked Social Spaces." *College Composition and Communication*, vol. 66, no. 2, Dec. 2014, pp. 250–75.

Prior, Paul. "From Speech Genres to Mediated Multimodal Genre Systems: Bakhtin, Voloshinov, and the Question of Writing." *Genre in a Changing World*, edited by Charles Bazerman et al., WAC Clearinghouse / Parlor Press, 2009, pp. 17–34, wac.colostate.edu/books/perspectives/genre/.

Ríos, Gabriela Raquel. "Performing Nahua Rhetorics for Civic Engagement." *Survivance, Sovereignty, and Story: Teaching American Indian Rhetorics*, edited by Lisa King et al., Utah State UP, 2015, pp. 79–95.

Shipka, Jody. "Including, but Not Limited to, the Digital: Composing Multimodal Texts." *Multimodal Literacies and Emerging Genres*, edited by Tracey Bowen and Carl Whithaus, U of Pittsburgh P, 2013, pp. 73–90.

———. *Toward a Composition Made Whole*. U of Pittsburgh P, 2011.

Takayoshi, Pamela, and Cynthia L. Selfe. "Thinking about Multimodality." *Multimodal Composition: Resources for Teachers*, edited by Selfe, Hampton Press, 2007, pp. 1–12.

Torrez, J. Estrella. "Somos Mexicanos y Hablamos Mexicano Aquí: Rural Farmworker Families Struggle to Maintain Cultural and Linguistic Identity in Michigan." *Journal of Language, Identity and Education*, vol. 12, no. 4, 2013, pp. 277–94.

Young, Vershawn Ashanti, and Aja Y. Martinez. *Code-Meshing as World English: Pedagogy, Policy, Performance*. NCTE, 2011.

Part Two

Modality in Texts and in the Classroom

The Places of Writing on the Multimodal Page

Matthew Davis and Alex Mueller

The page has always been multimodal, accommodating varying verbal and nonverbal elements from illustration to punctuation, but the mass reproduction and conventionalization of its layout, its accepted fonts, and its thin margins have given writing its pride of place on the printed page. In Sigrid Norris's terms, writing carries a high "modal intensity" on the printed page: it serves as the primary mode of meaning-making, carries the majority of the semiotic weight, commands attention, and structures interaction with other modes (83). We can recognize the varying levels of intensity of many other nonverbal modes across printed pages in books or student essays but the vast majority of printed pages we encounter are dominated by writing. In fact, as contributors to this volume hasten to point out, the extreme degree of the modal intensity of alphabetic text has led to the mistaken characterization of print culture as monomodal, as if nonalphabetic ways of making meaning on the page have disappeared from view.

To punctuate the error, John Trimbur and Karen Press argue that "print culture is as thoroughly multimodal in its practices of text production as the present digital age, though in different ways, with different effects, accomplished by different means" (22). While Trimbur and Press helpfully recognize the limits of using the term *multimodal* to characterize conceptual differences of communication over time, their argument does not account for what Norris would call the "modal complexity," or the level of intricacy of the relations between multiple modes (79). As Bruce Horner argues forcefully in his essay in this volume, the usefulness of multimodality for analysis is extremely limited when it is reduced to counting modes within a given text. By calling a page multimodal, then, we are not referring to the fact that on any given page we can count more than one mode. Instead, we follow Gunther Kress's sense of modes as those socially constructed and materially available resources for making meaning through space and time (79–81). Modes are neither fully isolatable from one another nor fully reducible to one another. In analysis, then, we prefer not to count modes—as if that were possible—but instead to think about the waxing and waning complexity of the interrelations among ways of representing meaning. In this essay, we focus on those interrelations as they appear on the page—a culturally available space for representing meaning and shaping human textual attention. Within read-write digital platforms, for example, this modal complexity is often extremely high, offering multiple modes of interaction through sound files, video illustration, and even space for readerly annotation. And while some printed contexts exhibit such high levels of modal intensity, we want to suggest that the page has not been as multimodally complex since the Middle Ages, before the age of the mass-produced, printed book.

Prior to the advent of the printing press, the page—the medieval manuscript page—was often complexly multimodal, containing elaborate scripts, rubrications, and illuminations; the medieval page was a multimedia experience for its community of readers, viewers, and listeners (Carruthers; Mak). Both writing and the page are, and always were, visual: rendered in multicolored acrostics, historiated initials, and varying sizes of script (Mitchell; Drucker, *Graphesis*). In this essay, we argue that the knowledge of this history compels us to orient our reading and writing pedagogy newly to the page, particularly its design elements: not just images and text but the entire mise-en-page, the layout, the arrangement, and the spaces for annotation and interaction. Digital texts—particularly within development of Web 2.0 text technologies—have reinvigorated our attention to the page as a site of multimodality (Shipka; Wysocki; Yancey). In terms of modal complexity, the digital page is multimodal in ways the printed page cannot be: in its speed and scale of activity and its coordination of audio, moving image, and responsive design. But what comparing these historical moments shows even more clearly is that the page is now a place that enables forms of textual activity both new and old: clicking, scrolling, reading, embedding, interacting, commenting, annotating.

For Johanna Drucker, this recognition of digital page design as a visual and dynamic form of knowledge production means that "we face the challenge of reading interface as an object and of understanding it as a space that constitutes reading as an activity" ("Reading Interface" 213). Just as medieval scribes, rubricators, and illuminators designed the page with future glossators and commentators in mind, digital composers must consider page designs as interfaces that both facilitate the elegant reading of their alphabetic text and invite the interactions of future readers. The teaching of composition, then, must prepare students to consider carefully the visual, spatial, and aural dimensions of the page as a multimodal interface. To some extent, this pedagogical orientation requires the "design thinking" advocated by Derek Owens and Tara Roeder (in this volume), but rather than challenge the modal or institutional supremacy of writing, we call for a renewed focus on the design of writing, both in the consumption and production of pages. While such a pedagogy culminates in the student creation and design of multimodal interfaces, this essay argues for increased attention to the reading and analysis of the places of writing on the page, tracing its history as both a visual image and a space for readerly activity from medieval classroom manuscripts to first-generation Web sites to annotation platforms.

The Places of Writing on the Preprinted Page

As Alberto Manguel cleverly puts it, "Like a skeleton supporting the skin of the text, the page disappears in its very function, and in that unprepossessing nature lies its strength" (120). In the midst of flipping through the average printed book, magazine, or student essay, it is often easy to forget about the page, which has become so naturalized as an interface for reading that we rarely stop to notice its features. It is only when we encounter an awkward or unconventional page layout that we awaken to what Manguel calls "the page's tyranny" (123): the visual limitations of textual display, which dictate presentational features from the size of the font to the spaces for margins. By allowing for bottomless pages, expandable text, and hypertext navigation, digital environments promise to free us from this oppression, but it only takes a few clicks to arrive at a Web site that is nearly unnavigable in its labyrinthine architecture. To resolve this problem of eye scatter, graphical user interface designers create text columns that are approximately thirty characters in width, thereby maximizing readability and minimizing scrolling (Vandendorpe 136–42). The effect of this practice is not only a remediation of the printed newspaper, which has always used columns for efficiency and space, but also a return to the *pagina*.

The *pagina* was not a page but rather an eight-to-twelve-centimeter-wide block of writing on a papyrus scroll, designed to be read aloud from top to bottom as it was unrolled. Once the codex book arrived in the first century CE, the *pagina* became a feature of the page, retaining its lanky shape but often in duplicate form, as two columns side by side (Mak 4). Because the codex additionally freed one hand, which had been previously required to hold the scroll to turn the discrete leaves of the book, these folios eventually absorbed the *paginae* they hosted, becoming what we now definitively call *pages* (Vandendorpe 135–36). The emancipated hand also had the luxury to assume a new occupation, glossing: inscribing annotations between lines or into the margins of the page. In the twelfth century, this phenomenon led to a further innovation of the placement and size of columns, which varied according to space reserved for readerly commentary. As Malcolm Parkes has suggested, this development introduced a design challenge that compelled medieval authors and commentators to create an organization of subject matter (*ordinatio*) on the page that would make the texts easier to consult, read, and annotate. *Ordinatio* was often accomplished through the precise placement of rubrics, red-lettered or underlined words or phrases that would offer guidance to the reader seeking chapter titles, source citations, or even particular parts of an argument (36–58). For Ivan Illich, this development means that "[t]he visual page is no longer the record of speech but the visual representation of a thought-through argument" (99). Through this transformation, the page becomes more than a script for oral performance: it becomes a visual object that absorbs the text as merely one aspect of its pictorial repertoire.

In addition to enhancing the visuality of writing, medieval manuscripts were often produced with the anticipation of readerly interventions and additions. This orientation to the future of the book resulted in page layouts that either included wide margins for the insertion of annotations or large sections of the page left vacant for extensive commentary. These pages then became spaces for potential accretion, designed for the use of additional text creators who could mark and recirculate the page to yet other readers to continue the cycle. This attention to the delivery of the page is what Jim Ridolfo and Dànielle Nicole DeVoss call "rhetorical velocity," or "the strategic theorizing for how a text might be recomposed (and *why* it might be recomposed) by third parties, and how this recomposing may be useful or not to the short- or long-term rhetorical objectives of the rhetorician." While Ridolfo and DeVoss are primarily describing the digital forms of delivery that consider the future appropriation, remix, and redistribution of material online, this design consideration was also central to preprinted environments such as the manuscript page.

While the salience of this point could be made with the commentary traditions of a number of theological texts, such as the *Glossa Ordinaria*, or legal books, such as the *Decretum*, we have selected one canon of pedagogical texts, Aesop's fables, as a representative example for analysis. These tales of animals are known for their moral lessons, but they were primarily used in medieval classrooms for reading and writing instruction. Students and teachers would insert interlineal glosses, usually Latin synonyms, to challenge their expanding vocabulary and then rewrite these fables, both in abbreviated and elaborated forms. Most crucially, though, students and teachers appended extensive commentaries to fables in their manuscripts, which regularly occupied more space on the page than the fables themselves. While such an emphasis on textual amplification encouraged readerly additions, many manuscripts reached a saturation point at which the accommodation of commentary caused the page to become flooded with textual annotation.

The transition to print in the fifteenth and sixteenth centuries reflects how writers and printers developed new page formats and organizational features that dispelled much of the confusion caused by such an emphasis on rhetorical velocity. In the case of Aesop's fables, the widely various and dynamic commentary tradition became reduced to a single commentary, the *Aesopus moralizatus*, which eventually transformed fable reading into an exercise in abbreviation, not amplification. The *Aesopus moralizatus* contains academic commentaries that provide both moral and allegorical interpretations between, and sometimes in the margin of, each fable (fig. 1). The *Aesopus moralizatus*'s accommodation of interpretation within the text itself reflects the long-standing medieval practice of allocating adequate space in the margins of the manuscript page for glosses and commentary by teachers or students. The printed versions of the *Aesopus moralizatus*, however, reproduce one canonical commentary, which is in great contrast to the variety of commentaries that exist in the manuscripts of their medieval predecessors (Wright xxiii). The prospect of printing unruly and lengthy commentaries, which often appeared in the margins, between lines, and even between selections of text, was surely formidable and it is no surprise that printers chose more manageable and standardized layouts for their editions (Wheatley, *Mastering Aesop* 82). Just as the accumulation,

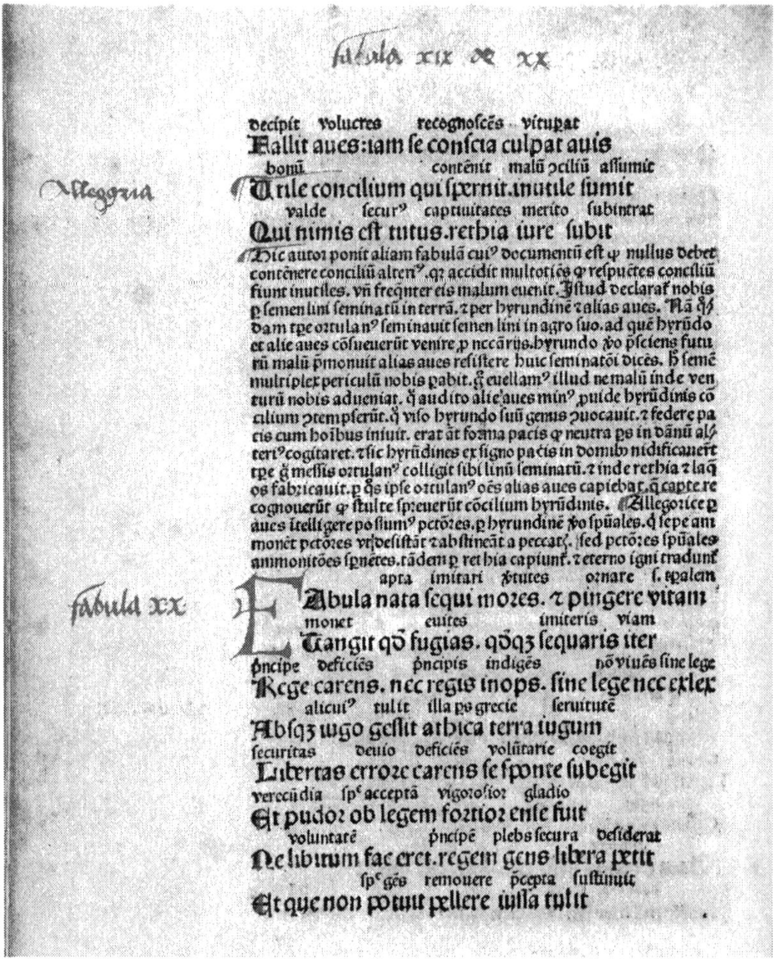

Figure 1. *Esopus moralizatus*, printed by Heinrich Quentell in Cologne in 1489. From the Huntington Library, San Marino, California, MS 99974.

circulation, and replication of fables had been more volatile, so too had been the fables' interpretations. In fact, the commentary of the earlier medieval classroom often displaced the fables themselves. For example, in one mid-fifteenth-century manuscript, *Codex Claustroneoburgensis 1093*, the commentary that accompanies the *elegiac Romulus* is so lengthy that it overwhelms the fables inscribed in the middle of the pages (fig. 2). Even the prologue to the fables had to be divided into two parts to accommodate the effusive exegeses (fol. 350v–352r). This excessive emphasis on commentary is so widespread in the existing manuscripts

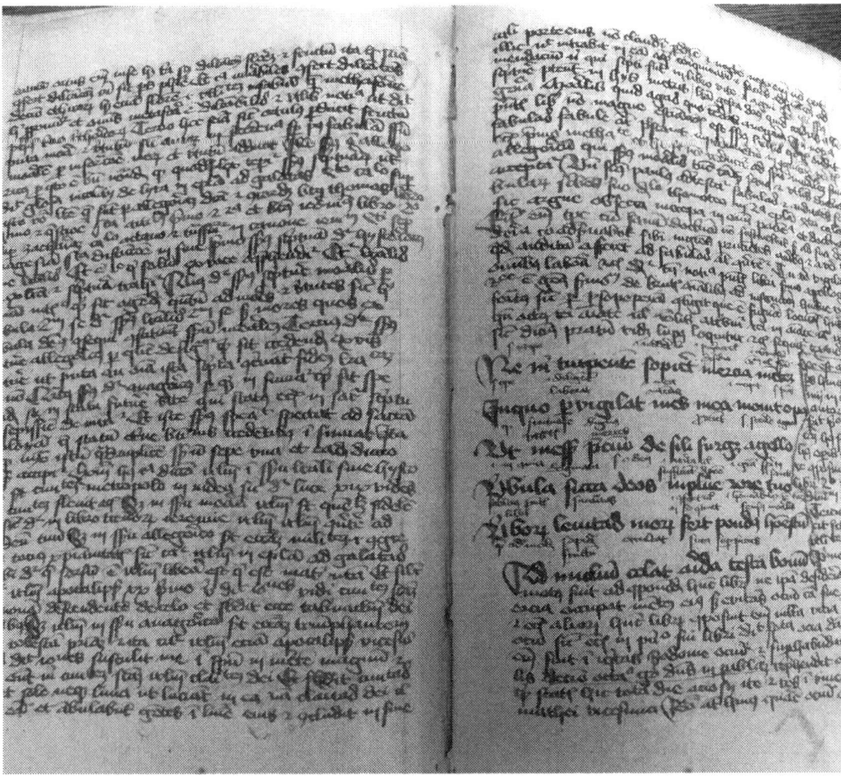

Figure 2. The prologue to the mid-fifteenth-century elegiac *Romulus*, in larger script, surrounded by overwhelming commentary, in smaller script. From *Codex Claustroneoburgensis 1093*, Stiftsbibliothek Klosterneuburg, fol. 350v–351r.

that it is reasonable to conclude that the *elegiac Romulus* was composed specifically for the pedagogical production of classroom commentaries (Wheatley, "*Fabulae*"; Wright xvii–xviii). If this is the case, the text serves the commentary, overturning the standard assumption that interpretation is extraneous to its object. In the case of the medieval fable, the commentary completes the text.

While early printers worked valiantly to accommodate such Aesopic amplification, the demand to create editions that were mass-produced, readable, reproducible, and cost-effective led to the attenuation of the social function and annotative authority of the fabular reader. The pages of printed books reduced the spaces previously open for future commentary and the eventual inheritors of medieval manuscripts regularly cut off the margins of books altogether when they were rebound. This compromise has resulted in a textually dominant and uniform design of the page that is almost completely determined by authors, editors, publishing companies, and software designers, which has in turn meant that the features of the page have become increasingly shaped by the pages' value as commodified objects for individuals to consume, not produce. By eliminating future readers as amplifiers of the page, printed text has come to pervade the page, so much so that such writing spaces are now considered to be monomodal. As Trimbur and Press suggest, such characterizations of print as monomodal are ideological claims that occlude the inherent multimodality of alphabetic text (21). We recall this prehistory of the printed page, however, to emphasize that the ideology of monomodality emerges from specific material conditions, which often make unavailable a rich array of composing modes previously available in the shared culture of medieval books—from visual markers, such as manicules that refer future readers to key passages and invite commentary, to marginal apparatuses, such as rubricated citations and key terms that facilitate hypertextual connections within and across texts. And while multimodality may represent its own neoliberal ideologies of innovation and countable objects of design (see Horner's essay in this volume), the material conditions of digital pages make available social modes of readerly interaction, like amplification and annotation, which are high-speed and large-scale extensions of practices that predate the age of print. This historical context is crucial to consider because digital pages face the same dilemma as printed pages: How can the page accommodate readerly additions and also maintain readability? Put another way, How might we encourage designs of the page in which the page's elements remain objects of critical inquiry and visual forms of knowledge production?

The Places of Writing on the Digital Page

As we have outlined, Drucker's charge to read the printed page as an interface—as both an object and a space ("Reading Interface")—illuminates how the page constitutes, invites, and limits readerly writing as activity. Reading the page as an interface can also illustrate how it constitutes and invites a writerly reading experience: a place for the remediation of writing and of the printed page. Such a transformation of the page also remaps readerly attention according to the modal affordances of old and new media (Bolter and Grusin).

This remediation and transformation is evident in *Welcome to Pine Point*, a 2011 webtext by The Goggles (Michael Simons and Paul Shoebridge), which was sponsored by the National Film Board of Canada. The webtext has been variously described as an "interactive web documentary" ("Welcome"), a "cross-platform project . . . and an interactive documentary" (Simons and Shoebridge), and a "liquid book" (Pitzer). It tells the story of Pine Point, an abandoned Canadian mining town in the Northwest Territories, which was built ex nihilo for mining purposes in the 1950s, flourished as a small mining town in the 1970s, and—after the mine was depleted—was closed and abandoned in 1988. The story of Pine Point is moving and emotional, staging in turns the joys of small-town life, the hardships that boom-and-bust extraction capitalism wreaks on human life, and the nostalgia that townspeople have for their shared pasts. *Welcome to Pine Point* is built from materials found on *Pine Point Revisited*, a Web site by a former resident of the town, Richard Cloutier.[1] The original Web site archives the history of Pine Point in Web 1.0 fashion (fig. 3).

The interactive documentary, *Welcome to Pine Point*, on the other hand, is a text of remarkable multimodal intensity and complexity: fluid,

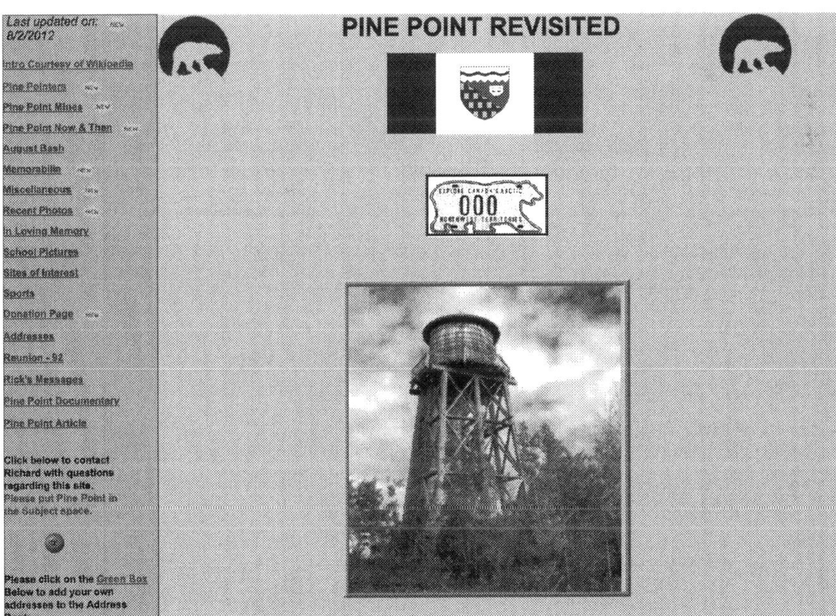

Figure 3. The home page of *Pine Point Revisited*

interactive, and responsive design that incorporates amateur video and old news footage, music and music videos, found and recorded audio, voiceovers, interviews, audio and textual overlays, animated text and images, linear and nonlinear navigation, government documents, and old photos, among other materials. Both the original Web site and the interactive documentary are assemblages—in most cases, assemblages of many of the same materials. But given the different experiences of the webtexts (that is, if our reactions and our students' reactions to them are indicative of differences), we argue that the two texts function both similarly and differently as objects and as spaces that constitute writing and reading as an activity; this similarity and difference is built through the use of multimodality to construct the page as a phenomenon for directing and addressing attention. Here, we attend to the modal complexity and intensity in both works—to the construction, reconstruction, and remediation of the page—to understand how these pages constitute different objects that create different kinds of reading experiences, and also function as spaces that invite different kinds of textual activity.

There are two versions of the home page of *Pine Point Revisited*, and both transport users to an earlier era of Web page design (pinepoint revisited.homestead.com; pinepointrevisited.homestead.com/Pine_Point .html). Upon loading, a left-side navigation bar links to multiple pages that house picture galleries, donation and memorial pages, and an address book that in both form and function resembles a database. On one version (updated 2 Aug. 2012) some pages are marked with yellow and red GIFs highlighting them as "new"; on the other (updated 27 Aug. 2015) the colors are muted and the GIFs are gone. The site visit counters differ on each page as well. Both versions mix image borders, image types, and fonts in configurations almost totally absent from the current moment of standardized design. In other words, the layout is not generic in our current sense, its modal complexity much different than the templates that currently guide most amateur (and much professional) page design. And neither is its design responsive to device or scaling. On the home page and elsewhere on the site, one navigates with substantial scrolling; in terms of structure, all pages are centrally linked on the home page—one must always navigate back through that hub. The site has no sound, and the only moving images are the flashing yellow and red GIFs on the older version (fig. 3). Compare that to the page from *Welcome to Pine Point* shown in figure 4 (though the interactivity of the page is impossible to capture in a still image). In it appears a book—a remediation of

Figure 4. A screen capture from *Welcome to Pine Point*

a book—representing a Web site composed of digitized print materials. There is a redesign of the navigation bar (lower left), which is itself a remediation of a printed table of contents. This navigational aid hides itself from the experience of the page but pops up when the viewer hovers over it—making all sections equally accessible during each moment of reading and viewing (ironically, much the same way that sections are always equally accessible in a print book). As one reads and navigates the page, slow, soft music (the theme song of the documentary) plays on repeat in the background. The page evidences not only heightened multimodal complexity—including modes unavailable in print—but also increased modal intensity. Through interactivity, the page here becomes less a place for a staging of specific multimodal interactions and more a space for a constrained set of multimodal possibilities. One's navigation of the webtext determines which of those possibilities actualizes on the page.

Just as the content of the home page of *Pine Point Revisited* remediated and transformed into more intense and complex multimodal relations in *Welcome to Pine Point*, the visual representations of the people of the town are similarly transformed. *Pine Point Revisited* contains a number of gallery pages, where each image is clickable and reveals another gallery. On the page shown in figure 5, the first fifteen images of the "people of Pine Point" link to galleries with additional sets of captioned images—the full set including hundreds of digitized photos. The final three images—numbered 16, 17, and 18—are identical to each other and

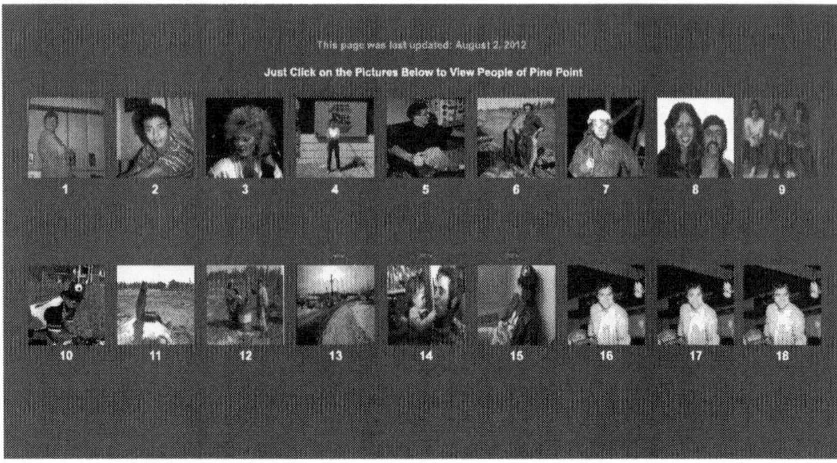

Figure 5. Gallery of people from Pine Point in *Pine Point Revisited*

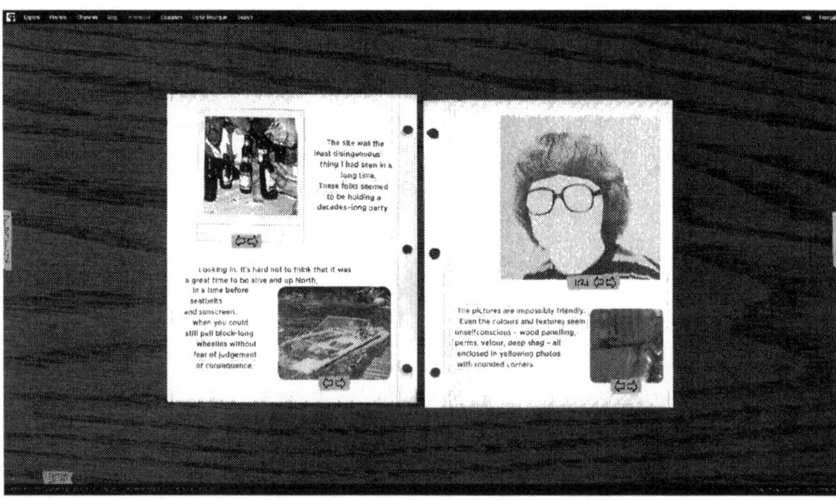

Figure 6. An interactive photo album page from *Welcome to Pine Point*

do not link to additional galleries. There is neither sound nor moving images, though a few flashing GIFs do proclaim some images or galleries are "new." The overall effect of the page, then, is of a set of materials meticulously curated and annotated, but without much attention to accessible design.

Contrast this with the remediated and interactive photo album pages from *Welcome to Pine Point* (fig. 6). Embedded within the page design are images from the *Pine Point Revisited* galleries, recontextualized among each other depending on what the reader-viewer clicks and in what order. The experience of the (remediated) pages depends on reader interactivity. When the reader-viewer clicks back and forth across the photo album page, the click is accompanied by the exaggerated sound of a printed page turning; the theme song continues to play on repeat and the noises of people having a party—sounds of people mingling, voices hooting, bottles clinking together—play for the first twenty seconds or so.

The point in comparing these two texts is not to laud one while denigrating the other. Nor is it to make the case that more multimodality is better. Instead, the point is to illustrate the ways that digital pages construct readerly and writerly attention through multimodal intensity and complexity. There's a hint to this link on the About This Project page of *Welcome to Pine Point*: "This was supposed to be a book." It is, of course, not a book. But what it is remains somewhat up in the air. When asked in an interview, "What is this thing?," Shoebridge replies: "Because we were book guys, we kept a lot of the old handmade book-like things, in keeping with that medium-is-the-message concept. We tried to emphasize what each medium does well. Keeping the words as writing rather than voiceover narrative was something we wrestled with at the start, but I think we're happy we kept it as words" (Pitzer). Here Shoebridge is using "medium" in the way that we use mode—hence his indicating writing and voiceover as separate media. Differences of vocabulary aside, his remarks point up the ways the creators purposefully constructed the modal intensities and complexities offered in new media environments, particularly as operationalized through the remediation and transformation of the book. In addition, for them, this work is done by looking to historical precedent—the book, the page—to construct their webtext.

So what—or where—is the *pagina* here? *Welcome to Pine Point* is certainly not the wide block of writing on a papyrus scroll, nor particularly the printed page, though it incorporates elements of both. Is it fitting to say that the screen has absorbed the page, the way folios eventually absorbed the *paginae* they hosted? And, if so, how do we use the history of the page to learn to read new interface objects and accept new invitations for textual activity?

Pedagogies of the Page

We argue that the knowledge of the history of the page—difficult, partial, and in flux though it may be—compels us to orient our writing pedagogy newly to textual design elements: not just to individual modes but to purposeful engagement with modal intensity and complexity. With our students, we must attend to the entire mise-en-page, layout, the arrangement, and the spaces for readerly and writerly interaction that our texts might construct. Just as medieval scribes, rubricators, and illuminators designed the page with future glossators and commentators in mind, digital composers must consider designs that facilitate both the elegant reading of their alphabetic text and rhetorical velocity. Here, we illustrate how digital annotation—one kind of engagement with the page, inflected through the material and social affordances of Web 2.0 technology—involves students in the history of and possible futures for the multimodal page.

The affordances of Web 2.0 technology that enable users to annotate—that is, append writing, image, or video to existing texts, images, or videos—webtexts are now so ubiquitous throughout the Internet as to disappear in their very function. Almost every Web site invites user response through a variety of graphical features of the page, ranging from a Contact Us window, to a sidebar chat, to a commentary feed. While the data acquired from such annotations is often used to enhance user experience, it is also often used for product development or to create metrics for market analysis. This consumerist approach to Web page design leads to visually attractive and comfortable interfaces, but rarely do such pages accommodate divergent interests of their viewers, causing a slowing, if not a complete stoppage, of their rhetorical velocity, particularly if such recomposing is not oriented toward producing capital for the Web site's stakeholders.

As we encourage our students to attend to the page as a unit of attention, then, we want also to prepare them to consider the interpretive, cultural, economic, and political implications of graphical user interface design, particularly when incorporating space for viewer response or content creation. To accomplish this, we believe it is important to provide opportunities for students to engage critically with a wide variety of annotation platforms in an effort to identify the underlying assumptions that determine the place of readerly writing on the page (Schacht; Nair). We ask students to respond to course readings using different varieties of digital annotation and then to reflect on their user experience, answering questions such as, How does the design of each page invite or resist certain types of annotation? How do the annotations contribute to the visual representation or production of meaning on the page? For the purpose of this essay, we will describe this pedagogical approach to one such platform: the commercially successful site *Genius* (genius.com).

Among the many annotation sites available, such as MIT's *Annotation Studio* (www.annotationstudio.org) and the University of Virginia's *Prism* (prism.scholarslab.org), perhaps the most visually stimulating is *Genius*, which began as the hip-hop commentary platform *Rap Genius* in 2009 and has recently expanded beyond rap and song lyrics to include a variety of annotatable objects, ranging from poetry to *Netflix* series' scripts to album cover art. Students are particularly attracted to this site because of its seemingly endless interactivity, including its manicules for upvoting or downvoting suggested annotations; its competitive and multifaceted system of gaining annotative and editorial authority through the accumulation of "IQ"; and its audio and visual options, including music videos, sound files of poems, and color-coded text highlighting. Meera Nair has developed one pedagogical approach to the site, called "Annotation Exercises for Fiction Boot Camp," which helps students create high-quality annotations focused on tracking literary elements, particularly characterization and theme (Schacht, pars. 36–38). Consider, for example, the *Genius* page devoted to Sylvia Plath's regularly anthologized poem "Metaphors," which contains the text of the poem in a column on the left side of the page, as well as a slightly thinner column on the right dedicated to annotations for each line (fig. 7). Underneath the text of the poem is a row of social media icons, which allow the annotators to readily share the page to *Twitter* and *Facebook* or embed the page in their own Web sites. Annotations only appear when highlighted lines are clicked, which transforms the commentary into a digital palimpsest that can be peeled back to reveal annotations relevant to particular lines. Once a highlighted line is clicked, an annotation appears in the right-hand column, followed below by a list of "improvements" to the annotation, which are suggestions for revision to the existing annotation.

While students often emphasize how provocative and motivating *Genius* is, they also express frustration about its usability and its resistance to interpretive speculation. At first glance, creating annotations is simple: commentators highlight a word or passage and then type a comment in a text box. However, annotations that haven't been verified by designated "editors" (users who have a high *Genius* IQ) are flagged in red, appear visually suspect, and may be eventually eliminated altogether. And in the case of short texts, such as "Metaphors," and those that have been extensively annotated, it is impossible to add a new annotation.

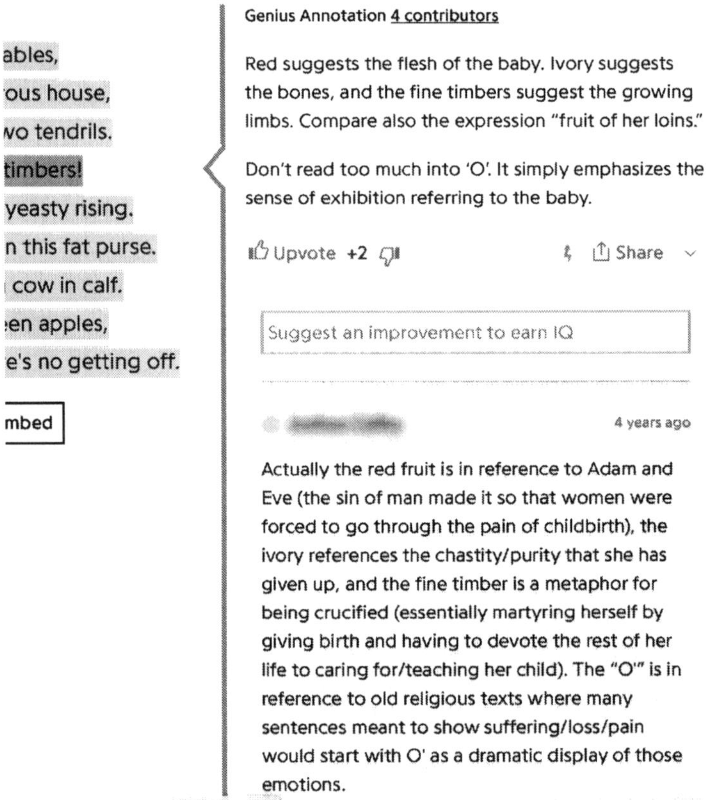

Figure 7. The *Genius* page devoted to Sylvia Plath's "Metaphors," captured 27 Mar. 2019

Instead, users can merely suggest improvements to existing annotations, which require additional approval by other users before they can be incorporated into the annotation itself. Students notice that riskier interpretations often get coded as a "stretch" and are rarely added to existing annotations because the authorized comments are mostly descriptive or contextual in nature. The multivalence of a particular phrase, such as Plath's "red fruit," is not valued because the purpose of *Genius* annotation is not to accommodate multiple interpretations of particular lines but rather to create an authoritative commentary, much in the style of the *Aesopus moralizatus*, in which one moral per fable sufficed. This annotative authority is also visually represented on *Genius* pages in the placement of the suggested improvements below the approved annotation. If we examine the comments on "red fruit," we find that the authoritative comment is focused on solving the riddle of the poem, which points to the red fruit as the flesh of the fetus being carried by the pregnant poetic persona. A four-year-old suggestion by a *Genius* user—a length of time that suggests it will never be incorporated into the annotation—offers an alternative reading to "red fruit" as referring to the forbidden fruit of Adam and Eve (fig. 7), an interpretation that addresses the frustrated tone of the speaker of the poem and the resentful description of pregnancy itself. Without these subtleties, Plath's poem becomes merely a riddle to be decoded. While this kind of crowdsourced consensus clearly suits *Wikipedia*'s verifiable and factually based compilation of knowledge about the world, *Genius*'s creation of annotative authority through such a model reproduces the myth of the *right* reading of any text, a myth that is enabled through the strategic placement or effacement of readerly commentary. The result is a digital palimpsest that increasingly obscures the interpretive tensions beneath its surface, producing codified commentaries that declare interpretive authority through their visibility.

To encourage students to consider how the design of such pages influences the reception and interpretation of the writing they contain, we ask them to compare *Genius* to other social annotation sites, such as *Annotation Studio* and *Prism*. Students readily observe how easy it is to add comments to lines and passages in *Annotation Studio*, but they also find the annotation frame to be too crowded, making it difficult to distinguish between and respond to the comments of other annotators. While a variety of interpretations is valued on this site, the price of this textual accumulation is occasionally unreadability, which undermines the purpose of social annotation altogether. On the other hand, a site like *Prism* offers color-coded forms of visual annotation, which limit the range of responses to a given text but also provide visualizations of interpretation, indicating through highlighted text and pie charts the percentage of readers who, for example, viewed particular words or lines in Geoffrey Chaucer's "The Wife of Bath's Prologue" as feminist or sexist. Asking students to create their own *prisms* on this site engages them with the ways in which the placement and restriction of particular modes of responding to the text within the page have significant interpretive implications. As Drucker suggests, "To imagine new intellectual forms of interpretation is also to design the spaces and supports that structure interpretive acts" (*Graphesis* 180). Students must then grapple with the ways in which graphical elements may both represent and produce interpretations, a prismatic dynamic dependent upon the careful placement of writing within a matrix of modes of meaning-making.

Attention to the history of the page and its contested status within digital environments should compel us, we believe, to evaluate the quality of page design on not only its capacity to accommodate multiple modes or to deliver content but also on its degree of modal intensity and complexity, which may invite or discourage readerly and writerly interactivity, circulation, and recomposition. Printed pages saturated with text, like many of our textbooks and student papers (and much of this essay and book), afford writing a high degree of modal intensity and represent meaning effectively, but often do little to encourage multimodal activity or critique. By contrast, the careful and limited intensity of fable text on the Aesopic manuscript page led to the accumulation of multiple interpretations of fables. This in turn led to the revision and recirculation of the fables themselves, even as it also challenged the limits of the printed page. In tracing the transformation of *Pine Point Revisited* to *Welcome to Pine Point*, the remediation of old media encourages users to recreate the audiovisual experience of reading a printed book, a reading event made possible by each user's navigational choices. Even such innovative and interactive webtext designs, multimodally intense and complex though they are, risk the reproduction of certain print teleologies that value the visual and linear representation of knowledge over its production. For websites like *Genius*, which are highly dependent upon readerly contributions, it is imperative to consider, particularly in our teaching, the subtle ways in which stimulating page designs use visual modes to privilege certain kinds of interpretations and limit the agency of future users. Central to this consideration, we conclude, is the nuanced place of writing on the page, its modal intensity, and its increasingly vexed status as a visual object of attention. Until we recognize the page as a space that can both visually represent and produce meaning, alphabetic writing will neither shed its monomodal reputation nor achieve its powerful potential within the multimodally complex world of digital composition.

Note

1. Though absent from *Pine Point Revisited*, *Welcome to Pine Point* pays explicit attention to the tremendous work of Cloutier, who, because of disability, composed his entire Web site through the process of voice input. The audio of his process often serves as the voiceover for *Welcome to Pine Point*.

Works Cited

Bolter, Jay David, and Richard Grusin. *Remediation: Understanding New Media.* MIT P, 2000.

Carruthers, Mary. *The Book of Memory: A Study of Memory in Medieval Culture.* 2nd ed., Cambridge UP, 2008.

Cloutier, Richard. *Pine Point Revisited.* 2015, pinepointrevisited.homestead .com/. Accessed 15 Nov. 2017.

Codex Claustroneoburgensis 1093. [C. mid-fifteenth century], Stiftsbibliothek Klosterneuburg, Austria.

Drucker, Johanna. *Graphesis: Visual Forms of Knowledge Production.* Harvard UP, 2014.

———. "Reading Interface." *PMLA*, vol. 128, no. 1, Jan. 2013, pp. 213–20.

Illich, Ivan. *In the Vineyard of the Text: A Commentary to Hugh's Didascalicon.* U of Chicago P, 1993.

Kress, Gunther. *Multimodality: A Social Semiotic Approach to Contemporary Communication.* Routledge, 2010.

Mak, Bonnie. *How the Page Matters.* U of Toronto P, 2014.

Manguel, Alberto. *A Reader on Reading.* Yale UP, 2010.

Mitchell, W. J. T. *Picture Theory: Essays on Verbal and Visual Representation.* U of Chicago P, 1995.

Nair, Meera. "Annotate the Plot: Using Annotation to Write Better Fiction." *The Current*, 17 Sept. 2014, thecurrent.educatorinnovator.org/resource/ annotate-the-plot-using-annotation-to-write-better-fiction.

Norris, Sigrid. *Analyzing Multimodal Interaction: A Methodological Framework.* Routledge, 2004.

Parkes, M. B. *Scribes, Scripts, and Readers: Studies in the Communication, Presentation and Dissemination of Medieval Texts.* Hambledon Press, 1991.

Pitzer, Andrea. "The Goggles on 'Welcome to Pine Point': Digital Narrative Chases Memory and Loss." *Nieman Storyboard / Nieman Foundation for Journalism at Harvard*, 4 Feb. 2011, niemanstoryboard.org/stories/the -goggles-on-welcome-to-pine-point-digital-narrative-chases-memory -and-loss/.

Plath, Sylvia. "Metaphors." 1959. *Genius*, genius.com/Sylvia-plath-metaphors -annotated. Accessed 4 Oct. 2017.

Ridolfo, Jim, and Dànielle Nicole DeVoss. "Composing for Recomposition: Rhetorical Velocity and Delivery." *Kairos*, vol. 13, no. 2, Jan. 2009, kairos .technorhetoric.net/13.2/topoi/ridolfo_devoss/velocity.html.

Schacht, Paul. "Annotation." *Digital Pedagogy in the Humanities: Concepts, Models, and Experiments*, edited by Rebecca Frost Davis et al., *MLA Commons*, digitalpedagogy.mla.hcommons.org/keywords/annotation/. Accessed 24 June 2019.

Shipka, Jody. *Toward a Composition Made Whole*. U of Pittsburgh P, 2011.

Simons, Michael, and Paul Shoebridge. *Welcome to Pine Point*. National Film Board of Canada, 2011, pinepoint.nfb.ca/#/pinepoint.

Trimbur, John, and Karen Press. "When Was Multimodality? Modality and the Rhetoric of Transparency." *Multimodality in Writing: The State of the Art in Theory, Methodology and Pedagogy*, edited by Arlene Archer and Esther Breuer, Brill, 2015, pp. 19–42.

Vandendorpe, Christian. *From Papyrus to Hypertext: Toward the Universal Digital Library*. Translated by Phyllis Aronoff and Howard Scott, U of Illinois P, 2009.

"Welcome to Pine Point." *Wikipedia: The Free Encyclopedia*, Wikimedia Foundation, en.wikipedia.org/wiki/Welcome_to_Pine_Point. Accessed 21 Nov. 2017.

Wheatley, Edward. *The "Fabulae" of Walter of England, the Medieval Scholastic Tradition, and the British Vernacular Fable*. 1991. U of Virginia, PhD dissertation.

———. *Mastering Aesop: Medieval Education, Chaucer, and His Followers*. UP of Florida, 2000.

"The Wife of Bath's Prologue [Excerpt]." *Prism*, prism.scholarslab.org/prisms/96267e8e-1c3a-11e3-87ad-8ad585206611/visualize?locale=en. Accessed 25 June 2019.

Wright, A. E. *"Hie lert uns der meister": Latin Commentary and the German Fable, 1350–1500. Medieval and Renaissance Texts and Studies*, general editor, Ayanna Thompson, vol. 218, Arizona Center for Medieval and Renaissance Studies, 2001.

Wysocki, Anne Frances. "awaywithwords: On the Possibilities in Unavailable Designs." *The Influence of Gunther Kress' Work*, special issue of *Computers and Composition*, vol. 22, no. 1, Dec. 2005, pp. 55–62.

Yancey, Kathleen Blake. "Made Not Only in Words: Composition in a New Key." *College Composition and Communication*, vol. 56, no. 2, Dec. 2004, pp. 297–328.

The Essay as Form in a Digital Age

Joseph Harris

I think this is a propitious time to teach and write critical essays. I realize the word *essay* can have an introspective and belletristic feel to it, and so I call on the term here with some hesitation. I'm not particularly keen to promote the genre of the memoir or personal narrative, or qualified to do so. Instead, following T. W. Adorno ("Essay"), I hope to make a case for the essay as a more idea-driven sort of writing, centered on interpretation and response. And moving beyond Adorno, I hope to point to some opportunities for expanding the scope of this kind of critical writing in a digital age. Writers can now quote directly from and comment on texts in a wide range of media—print, image, audio, video—and online spaces encourage the give-and-take of intellectual dialogue. I'm not utopian; I don't believe that new digital technologies have fundamentally altered the nature of writing. But I do think they have opened up new possibilities of expression and exchange.

As a way of getting at some of those possibilities, I would like to begin here with Bruce Horner's incisive lead essay of this book, "Modality as Social Practice." Horner is impatient with those who argue for the supposedly transformative effects of multimodality. He is skeptical of claims that the new digital media have created new discursive forms, and he is inclined to view talk about the "affordances" of such media as fussing a distinction without making much of a difference. And he is especially annoyed with the implication that most academic writing is somehow monomodal, and thus that adding images, video, and audio to print texts is a surefire way of improving them. Horner argues that many theorists of multimodality are too quick to accept a view of academic writing as a vehicle for disembodied reason and argument. In such views, academic writing aspires not merely to mono- but to nonmodality. It strives to be transparent. Horner suggests that this flattened view of academic discourse serves as a useful foil for digital theorists, who can then advocate for a new kind of writing that does something else, something more, something "multimodal."

But such views, Horner goes on to argue, overlook the devotion of most print academic journals to a spare but distinctive visual modality. Think of those old intro-to-the-library lectures in which a librarian would hold a copy of an academic journal in one hand and a popular magazine in the other, suggesting to undergraduates that they could actually spot many of the key differences between the two types of publications from across the room. Such comparisons reveal not an indifference to the material form of a text but a near obsession with it. As Horner puts it, we are taught to see "specific features of a text-object [rendered] remarkable and others not." To drive this point home, he refers to the similarly strict conventions of performing classical chamber music—in which seated and somberly dressed musicians play before a still and hushed audience. The goal is to direct our focus to the music itself, much as readers of academic writing are trained to attend to the argument itself rather than to the ways it is laid out on the page (or screen).

The problem, of course, is that there is no such thing as the music or the argument itself. Texts are not abstractions; they are material objects (or performances that take place in real time and space). For Horner, *modality* refers to the ways a text is physically experienced—"visual, aural, olfactory, kinesthetic, etc." Here he echoes the pioneering work of the New London Group, which in its 1996 manifesto on "A Pedagogy of Multiliteracies" identified five "modes of meaning"—linguistic, visual, aural, gestural, and spatial—that writers can now use in designing texts. I think this view is also close to what Hannah Rule is getting at when she argues, in her fine essay for this book, that all meaning is "embodied." It thus makes little sense to imagine some texts as more modal than others (*multi* versus *mono*). All texts are simply modal in different ways.

I find this view compelling, but I suspect I may draw some different lessons from it than Horner does. Here, for instance, is how he brings his essay to a close: "Modality is the site, means, and outcome of our composing practices—what we work with, and on, and rewrite. It is what we compose, and transform, through our practices." Those are strong sentences. But I am struck by how, in them, Horner refers to modality as something that is acted upon—a site, an outcome, what we work with—rather than something that is part of the act of composing. It's almost as if, having defined modality as something that has always already been an aspect of writing, Horner has by the end of his piece lost interest in it as an analytical term. He would like to talk about writing as a social practice instead.

I don't wholly disagree. Indeed, I've written a book, *Rewriting: How to Do Things with Texts*, in which I describe how I go about teaching writing as a social practice (Harris). And, like Horner, I am wary of claims that multimodal composing is new, more, fuller, better. But I think I can share his skepticism while also acknowledging that the modality of a text in part shapes its composing. It is one thing, for example, to prepare a talk for a conference and quite another to draft an article for a journal, even if you pursue similar lines of thought in both. Similarly, writing about film or music online, which allows you to link directly to recordings of the texts you are discussing, differs significantly from writing about film or music in print, which requires you to re-present those texts in words or still images. As the media scholar danah boyd has written:

> The design and architecture of environments enable certain types of interaction to occur. Round tables with chairs make chatting with someone easier than classroom-style seating. Even though students can twist around and talk to the person behind them, a typical classroom is designed to encourage everyone to face the teacher. . . . Understanding the affordances of a particular technology or space is important because it sheds light on what people can leverage or resist in achieving their goals. For example, the affordances of a thick window allow people to see each other without being able to hear each other. To communicate in spite of the window, they may pantomime, hold up signs with written messages, or break the glass. The window's affordances don't predict how people will communicate, but they do shape the situation nonetheless. (10–11)

I'd like to try to agree with both Horner and boyd. Digital environments don't offer writers some sort of transformative release from the confines of print, but they do pose different opportunities of expression for writers to "leverage or resist." Modality shapes, even if it does not determine, our occasions for writing.

Much of what lies behind what Horner has to say, I suspect, is a commitment to teaching academic writing not as a formula for producing texts that pretend to be simply "straightforward, or rational" but as a more dynamic intellectual practice. I share that commitment. Along with him, I feel that rather than abandoning the academic essay as a simple and dull form, we should instead try to teach it as a complex and nuanced one. Indeed, that's the main reason I'm interested in exploring the possibilities of expression in digital spaces. I think that doing so can help us argue for a kind of critical and intellectual writing that aims not so much to produce commodified bits of knowledge as to respond with insight to the work of other writers and artists.

That may strike some readers as a banal goal, but I'm not so sure. Certainly the field I work in, composition, has seen in recent years a number of influential calls for more systematic and disciplined forms of research and writing. In 2005 Richard Haswell made a fierce argument for what he calls RAD ("replicable, aggregable, data-supported") research in composition, suggesting that we need to get "serious about facts" to be seen as a legitimate field of study (219). In 2010 Elizabeth Wardle and Doug Downs published *Writing about Writing*, a textbook that imagines the course in composition as an introduction to the field of writing studies, in which students read research articles in the field and conduct their own apprentice studies of writing. And in 2015 Linda Adler-Kassner and Wardle edited *Naming What We Know*, a sort of encyclopedia of "threshold concepts" for the study and teaching of writing. The overarching goal seems to have been to establish composition as a kind of social science—that is, as an orderly space where knowledge about writing is formed, vetted, and circulated.

What troubles me about all this is a certain note of insistence. Studies should be replicable; the subject of first-year composition should be research in writing; the field should agree upon a set of threshold concepts. This triumphalist strain can be heard clearly in Wardle's influential 2009 article, "'Mutt Genres' and the Goal of FYC: Can We Help Students Write the Genres of the University?" Wardle uses *mutt* as a term of derision, which at first seems odd in an age of hybridity and intersectionality. It turns out, though, that she intends *mutt* to refer not to a mix of genres but to an imitation of one. Her complaint is that too often the aim of first-year composition is merely to teach students to "mimic genres that mediate activities in other activity systems"—which is to say, to write pieces imitating those in the other, more established disciplines in the university, where people do serious work like "report[ing] on their experiments" and "describ[ing] their home visits" (774). According to Wardle, however, the mutts of first-year comp lack any such "transactional purpose" (775). Instead the "argument paper" gets assigned simply to teach students how to argue and, in a similarly circular fashion, the "informative paper" means to teach them how to inform (777).

Which brings us back to *mutt* in its common and derogatory sense. There are the standard breeds, certified by the AKC, and then there are all those other dogs of indeterminate parentage in the shelters and rescues. Similarly, there are "the genres of the university," authorized by the disciplines, and then the improvised motley of exercises in first-year comp. Wardle's response to this situation is that we need to become, literally, more disciplined, through making research in writing the content of first-year composition, which she calls FYC. As Wardle puts it: "I suggest we should no longer ask FYC to teach students *to write* in the university and instead construct FYC to teach students *about writing* in the university" (767).

Note the *should.* Such deontic views of the field seem to leave many writers and teachers out of it, me included. As a writer, I tend to work in the mode of response; my CV lists far more essays like this one than articles reporting on research. And as a teacher, I try to encourage students to compose pieces that don't follow set forms but instead mix reading, observation, and reflection in idiosyncratic ways—very much the sort of mutt writings, I hazard, that Wardle sets herself against. But my view is that what she sees as a problem isn't always one—that it can be exciting to imagine the first-year writing course as a nondisciplinary space. I want to argue for a less technocratic view of teaching composition, to suggest that we value the work we do with students for its own sake, its own present interest, and not simply for how it prepares them to go off and write some other thing, for some other teacher, in some other course.

In saying this, I'm not arguing for turning composition into a course on personal or creative writing. I'm agnostic about what students might actually read and write about; it seems to me that a good writing course can center on almost any subject so long as a teacher gets students invested in working on it. Unlike Haswell or Wardle, then, I have no program for how we should conduct research or construct the first-year course. I simply hope to save some room for people to do intellectual work that is not always closely tied to the knowledge-producing regimes of the academic disciplines, including our own.

And that is what led me to "The Essay as Form" by T. W. Adorno, the noted German philosopher and cultural theorist of the last century. About ten years ago I designed an undergraduate seminar in creative nonfiction for the first time. My hope was to use critical essays by public intellectuals like Rebecca Solnit, Cornel West, Christopher Hitchens, and Barbara Ehrenreich as models of the kind of writing I wanted students to attempt, and so I was disappointed to discover that most anthologies of creative nonfiction fail to offer many (or often any) examples of such work, filling their pages instead almost exclusively with personal memoirs or literary journalism. Trying to get a better sense of how what commonly gets taught as "the essay" had come to occupy such a narrow range, I read Lynn Bloom's empirical study of the most frequently reprinted nonfiction pieces in American literary anthologies. (No surprises here—Orwell, White, Didion, Thoreau, Woolf, King, over and over again.) And in the middle of that dazzling yet depressing piece, I came upon Bloom's glancing allusion—in the middle of a sentence in the middle of a paragraph—to "Adorno's discrimination between essays and articles" (404). So I looked up "The Essay as Form," which Adorno published as the lead chapter of his 1958 *Notes to Literature*. This placement suggests that Adorno saw the piece as a crucial part of his thinking, but the essay was not translated into English until 1984. And outside of what might be called Adorno studies, it has attracted fairly little comment since then. That's too bad, since along with his eccentric piece on "Punctuation Marks" (also in *Notes to Literature*), the essay has much to offer us as teachers of writing.

What Adorno has to say in "The Essay as Form" does indeed hinge on a distinction between *the essay* and something like *the article*—although he doesn't use the term *article*. He begins his piece by decrying a worldview which "[fences] up art as a preserve for the irrational" and "[identifies] knowledge with organized science" (151). The essay, Adorno insists, is neither. Instead he argues:

> The essay, however, does not permit its domain to be prescribed. Instead of achieving something scientifically, or creating something artistically, the effort of the essay reflects a childlike freedom that catches fire, without scruple, on what others have already done. The

> essay mirrors what is loved and hated instead of presenting the intellect, on the model of a boundless work ethic, as *creatio ex nihilo*. Luck and play are essential to the essay. It does not begin with Adam and Eve but with what it wants to discuss; it says what is at issue and stops where it feels itself complete—not where nothing is left to say. Therefore it is classed among the oddities. Its concepts are neither deduced from any first principle nor do they come full circle and arrive at a final principle. Its interpretations are not philologically hardened and sober, rather—according to the predictable verdict of that vigilant calculating reason that hires itself out to stupidity as a guard against intelligence—it overinterprets. Due to a fear of negativity *per se*, the subject's effort to break through what masks itself as objectivity is branded as idleness. Everything is supposedly much simpler. The person who interprets instead of unquestioningly accepting and categorizing is slapped with the charge of intellectualizing as if with a yellow star; his misled and decadent intelligence is said to subtilize and project meaning where there is nothing to interpret. Technician or dreamer, those are the alternatives. (152)

There's much that might be said about this remarkable passage, but I will begin with Adorno's assertion that the essayist is "slapped with the charge of intellectualizing as if with a yellow star." While edgy, I think the comment is apposite. (Because his father was a Jew who converted to Catholicism upon marriage, Adorno was forced to spend the Nazi era in exile in the United States.) According to Adorno, the essayist is suspected of being unproductive, perhaps even parasitic, of overcomplicating things, of questioning and idling rather than doing real work. The essayist's writing fails to conform to an expected pattern, to achieve the simple clarity expected of science, to get things done. The essay is an oddity, a hybrid, a mutt.

But what's key for Adorno is that the essay is always written *in response*: it "catches fire, without scruple, on what others have already done." Contrast this with the RAD research advocated by Haswell and others. An essay aims not to offer "replicable" results but instead to illumine a particular text from a particular angle. And even though essayists may sometimes pursue similar lines of thought in various pieces, their views can't really be "aggregated" like data from scientific studies. Finally, while good essays are indeed "data-supported" in the sense that they must pay close attention to the texts they discuss, we tend to remember them for the ideas and questions they raise rather than for facts they present. The essay does not aim for comprehensiveness. Instead "it says what is at issue and stops where it feels itself complete—not where nothing is left to say."

Let me emphasize: I am not arguing here against the value of RAD research. (Much as I believe Adorno was not arguing against science.) I am arguing against a view that equates such research with the totality of academic or intellectual work.

It is important, though, to keep in mind that Adorno also distinguishes the essay from the work of art. My sense is that he would have disdained much of what is now considered creative nonfiction. He dismisses what he calls "feuilleton journalism" and writing that "chats about people rather than opening up the matter at hand" (154)—referring, I think, to the sort of pieces about political and cultural figures that now appear in magazines like the *New Yorker* or *Atlantic*. He is contemptuous of artist biographies, and he appears uninterested in memoir. And he seems nervous about being misunderstood as simply arguing for some sort of fine writing, going out of his way to mock would-be essayists who substitute "poetic montage" or "the jargon of authenticity" for careful thought (155).

Adorno instead argues for the essay as a commentary on art and ideas, insisting that essayists must always respect "the object itself" of their writing ("Essay" 154). The essayist must thus be more tentative, "yielding," than most writers, since "at every moment [the essay] must reflect on itself" (170). Adorno thus ends up arguing for a kind of intellectual writing that cannot take a prescribed form because it is always questioning the form in which ideas are expressed. This leads him to suggest, in the closing line of his piece, that the essay is always at heart heretical, in that it aims to allow "something [to become] visible in the object which it is orthodoxy's secret purpose to keep invisible" (171).

For an example of what such an essay might look like in our own field, I suggest turning back to Horner's opening piece. What I most admire about Horner's essay is his persistent attempt to unsettle the terms we've grown accustomed to using in talking about digital writing—or as he puts it, in his characteristically modest style, to "consider thinking about how we have been thinking about, well, alphabetic text and multimodal composition." And at the risk of beating a dead horse, I can't see much sense in trying to "replicate" or "aggregate" Horner's thinking in his essay, although I do hope here to reply in some useful form to what he has to say. That is why it seems to me helpful to distinguish the article from the essay. They do different sorts of work. The article reports; the essay reflects and responds. We need places for both in our journals and our classrooms.

Which brings me at last to the question of modality and digital writing. A familiar complaint about much writing on the Internet is that it is frivolous, a waste of time, an ongoing invitation to indulge in pointless self-disclosure or endless, unresolvable debate. That is of course also the complaint about essays. My inclination is to turn such criticisms on their heads, to argue that the appeal of essay writing, both on the Web and on the page, stems from its seeming aimlessness, from its reliance, as Adorno puts it, on "luck and play" ("Essay" 152). Indeed, I suspect that the Internet may now offer more congenial spaces for the essay than does much of the academy. In her early essay on the history of blogging (2000), Rebecca Blood points out that the first "weblogs" were "link-driven sites" whose editors or authors simply listed Web pages they found interesting along with some brief comments about them. The blogosphere, that is, began as an interpretive space. People were writing about texts that interested or provoked them well before they turned to posting about their cats or what they ate for breakfast.

I believe that such amateur spaces of response and interpretation still exist online and that we can make good use of them in teaching intellectual writing. Let me stress again that I am not trying to herald some sort of digital nirvana or to predict the emergence of bold new forms of composition. Actually, my thinking runs in almost the opposite direction. I think that, to return to boyd's terms, we can "leverage or resist" the affordances of the Web to reinvigorate how we teach a form of writing, the critical essay, that has long been part of a dissenting tradition of work in the academy.

Let me offer a few quick examples. To begin with, as I noted earlier, the Web allows writers to embed texts from a wide range of nonprint media—images, audio, video—directly into their own pieces (rather than, say, redescribing a film scene in paragraph form). When done in a perfunctory way, embedding images or clips may merely illustrate or prettify a piece. But when done more thoughtfully, such quotation can spur closer and more detailed analysis than often takes place on paper. In most of my undergraduate writing classes, I now ask students near the end of term to digitize one of the pieces they've written by posting it to a publishing platform like *WordPress* or *Medium*. Most students take pleasure in finding ways to enliven their writing through adding images, clips, and links. But the more interesting moment comes when I challenge them to add to what they've written, to their actual prose, to comment on the new materials they've inserted. I tell them I will be most impressed by those moments when their work with other media leads them to more writing—and thus, hopefully, to closer and more nuanced analysis.

Most students are readily up to that task. Indeed many of the more ambitious go a step further, reorganizing the structure of their pieces to suit the look and feel of the platform they are working on. Some notice, for instance, that it's not so much that online pieces always have shorter paragraphs, but that digital writers often tend to use paragraphs differently—to isolate and intensify certain ideas, say, or to suggest an unexpected break or turn in a line of thought. And so, rather than simply viewing paragraphs as containers (big or small) that you pour words into, many students start to see and use them as marks of punctuation (pilcrows!)—that is, as ways of shifting the stress and rhythm of their writing. Others notice how images can work in similar ways to signal new sections of an essay or mark shifts of direction in their thinking. Still others revisit the ledes of their pieces, realizing that they now need to identify not simply what they are writing about or what they want to argue but also to suggest what sort of reader, having somehow stumbled upon this piece on the Web, might actually want to continue on to read it, and why.

Digital writers can also compose with nonprint media. By this I don't mean giving up writing prose for making videos or podcasts. I mean using the resources at hand. In many of my courses, I ask students to remediate a piece they have composed earlier in the term, to represent all or part of it for a different medium or platform. And so, for instance, one student writer might choose to recast a couple of paragraphs from a post to our course Web site as a series of tweets, or a podcast, or a brief video. Or, conversely, another student might translate a video into a prose essay. The aim is to get students thinking about the affordances and constraints of different writing environments. Some years ago a student writer responded to this assignment in a way that has stuck with me—in part because it did not involve a particularly flashy use of technology. It was the idea, not the technology, that was interesting. Earlier in the semester, this student, Leslie, had written a prose response to Nicholas Carr's criticism of Marshall McLuhan in his 2010 book, *The Shallows*. In brief, while McLuhan laments the loss of warmth and immediacy that he feel accompanies the shift from speech to written text, Carr believes that the analytic control that one gains through writing is well worth the trade. Leslie, however, feels that both theorists underestimate the emotional bond that many readers form with books. Ironically, though, she was disappointed in her ability to evoke that bond in her prose, so a few weeks later she decided to remediate what she had written as a video essay. In the first half of her piece, "I'm Trapped in a Paper Case of Emotion," Leslie records herself as she sits in front of her laptop, quickly summarizing the gist of her argument, even at one point picking up a copy of *The Shallows* and reading from it. She's an engaging and clear speaker, but this part of the video is pretty much just a spoken version of her written response to Carr.

About three minutes into her piece, though, Leslie announces that she is going to test her hunch about the emotional impact of reading. The screen goes blank, and then the following written question appears: "When you were reading the Harry Potter books for the first time, what was your reaction when you read that Dobby the Elf had died?" This question is followed by a series of quick video clips of several of her classmates, the camera held tight on their faces as they speak in sweet, unaffected, and animated ways about how they first reacted to reading that scene. It's not so much what they say as how they say it—their memories of the book and of themselves as readers brimming over before us—that most helps Leslie make the point that sometimes writing actually intensifies the emotional impact of the spoken word. I am also charmed by the irony that it is through recording the expressions and intonations of her friends on video that Leslie is able to make her point about reading. She has switched modes, but she is still working with texts and ideas. I would call her piece an essay.

Of course, the readers of *this* essay will need to trust me on that point. But I hope that difficulty also speaks to my larger argument. If this were a digital essay, I could embed specific moments from Leslie's video into my text and comment directly on them. My readers would then be able to compare their responses to her work with mine. But since this piece is intended for print, I need to rely instead on description and summary. Sure, if a public link to the video were available (unfortunately, in this case, it is not), I could include a URL to the piece in my list of works cited, and my readers could put down the book they are holding in their hands, go to a laptop, type in the link, scroll to the appropriate moments in the video, watch and listen to them, and then return to this book to see what I have to say. But such a process seems much like the one described by danah boyd of using signs and gestures to communicate through a thick glass window. It's possible, but slow and clumsy. Writing on-screen doesn't change the kinds of intellectual work we can do with texts, but it does make it easier to quote and interpret texts from a wide range of media. It also allows writers to draw on an expanded range of media to make their points (as Leslie was able to, and I am not).

But it is actually a changed relationship between writer and readers that strikes me as the most significant difference between writing on the screen and on the page. This becomes obvious in a writing class that asks students to publish work online. For posting an essay on the Web does not feel at all the same thing as submitting a paper to a teacher (whether the piece is actually printed out and handed in on paper, or simply saved and sent to the teacher's electronic drop box). Even if it seems unlikely, other people—at the very least, the other students in the class—might actually read an online piece (if it is not hidden behind the fire wall of a learning management system). And they might respond to it. This is not a difference in modality in the usual sense of the term, but I think it has everything to do with the shift from print to online discourse. Print and digital texts circulate differently. As readers online, we almost always have the option to respond, to talk back. As writers, we need to take that possibility into account.

As teachers, I think we can take advantage of this circumstance. I remember a course on the history of the novel that I took as an undergraduate in the 1970s. The class met on Tuesday afternoons. The professor asked us to write a two-page response (two handwritten pages) to the novel we were reading for each week, and to deliver those pages to his home on Monday evenings. (He lived on campus; I distinctly remember stepping quietly and nervously onto his porch to slip my responses into his mailbox.) In class the next day, he'd begin by returning our papers, with comments written on them in his beautiful hand, sometimes with a section marked to be read aloud in class. (I still recall the pleasure of seeing sentences I had written highlighted for discussion.) And then he would lead us in a discussion of the novel for that week, using the responses the members of the class had written to it.

I loved that course. The sense of being taken seriously as an intellectual has stayed with me since and has shaped the work I've done as a teacher. And there was surely something about the physicality of the process—the porch, the handwriting, the sound of voices reading in class—that contributed to its impact. But yet, it was also an extraordinarily cumbersome procedure, not feasible outside a small class in a residential college, and it was orchestrated almost entirely by my professor, who picked and chose among our responses and scripted our conversation according to what he saw as important or telling.

Compare this with a course in which each week a few students are asked to post responses to a reading on a public Web site. The other students in the class are then required to read the thoughts of these first-readers and post comments on them. The teacher also comments on the first readings—knowing that whatever they say is likely to be read by almost everyone else in the class. And the first-readers themselves can write responses to the responses to their responses. All of this takes place before the class meets as a group to discuss the assigned text, so that when it does, students are in a position to develop and refine what is likely to already be a lively exchange of positions, of statements and counter-statements.

I'm not arguing that this is a new sort of conversation. Quite the contrary. I value such online exchanges precisely because they showcase the moves involved in a kind of critical conversation about texts that many of us have long tried to teach. But in contrast to the class I took as an undergraduate, in which our actual discussion of the novels we were reading took place almost entirely in the fleeting mode of speech, the Web fixes many of the moves of such a critical conversation on-screen, creating a public, written dialogue that students and teacher can together return to and reflect on. In this case, that is, the screen actually makes writing more visible than the page.

Indeed, the critical moves I most want to teach are often best seen in the comments students make on the responses of first-readers—especially if you insist that commenters do something more than merely agree or disagree. I've thus found it useful to require commenters on first readings to both quote directly from the post they are responding to and to quote a different passage from the text we are discussing. They are charged, in other words, with moving the conversation forward, with extending or developing the ideas they are responding to, rather than simply engaging in a point-counterpoint debate. And again, since this conversation is public and online, these comments and replies themselves become a text that you can teach with. Finally, if and when writers are asked to choose a post they have written to rethink and develop, they have a panoply of responses to their work (as well as the work of other writers in the class) to draw upon.

Which leaves me in a somewhat odd position in regard to the questions raised by this volume. I'm not convinced that the digital age has changed writing—at least not in the sense of creating radically new forms of working with alphabetic text. But I do think it has changed the environment for writing—that the Web has encouraged the growth of spaces for comment and response, interpretation and dissent. And so I believe that those of us who are committed to the critical essay need to think hard about what it means to write in those digital spaces.

There is a lovely, multilayered moment in "The Essay as Form" when Adorno quotes Georg Lukács commenting on the ironic modesty of Michel de Montaigne's choice of the word *essay* to describe his writing: "The essayist dismisses his own proud hopes which sometimes lead him to believe that he has come close to the ultimate: he has, after all, no more to offer than explanations of the poems of others, or at best of his own ideas" (157). Such modesty, to think that your ideas might interest someone else! Since the 1960s, the field of composition has taught us how to honor the stories that students have to tell about their lives, and more recently the new disciplinarians of our field have shown us how students can write as apprentice scholars and researchers. Adorno and Lukács point us toward something different, toward the struggles of students to write as intellectuals, to explain their own ideas. The unpredictable form that struggle takes is the essay, and our digital age is an exciting time to teach it.

Works Cited

Adler-Kassner, Linda, and Elizabeth Wardle, editors. *Naming What We Know: Threshold Concepts in Composition Studies*. Utah State UP, 2015.

Adorno, T. W. "The Essay as Form." Translated by Bob Hullot-Kentor and Frederic Will, *New German Critique*, no. 32, Spring-Summer 1984, pp. 151–71.

———. "Punctuation Marks." Translated by Shierry Weber Nicholson, *Antioch Review*, vol. 48, 1990, pp. 300–05.

Blood, Rebecca. "Weblogs: A History and Perspective." *Rebecca's Pocket*, 7 Sept. 2000, www.rebeccablood.net/essays/weblog_history.html.

Bloom, Lynn Z. "The Essay Canon." *College English*, vol. 61, no. 4, Mar. 1999, pp. 401–30.

boyd, danah. *It's Complicated: The Social Lives of Networked Teens*. Yale UP, 2014.

Carr, Nicholas. *The Shallows: What the Internet Is Doing to Our Brains*. W. W. Norton, 2011.

Harris, Joseph. *Rewriting: How to Do Things with Texts*. 2nd ed., Utah State UP, 2017.

Haswell, Richard H. "NCTE/CCCC's Recent War on Scholarship." *Written Communication*, vol. 22, no. 2, Apr. 2005, pp. 198–223.

The New London Group. "A Pedagogy of Multiliteracies: Designing Social Futures." *Harvard Educational Review*, vol. 66, no. 1, Spring 1996, pp. 60–92.

Wardle, Elizabeth. "'Mutt Genres' and the Goal of FYC: Can We Help Students Write the Genres of the University?" *College Composition and Communication*, vol. 60, no. 4, June 2009, pp. 765–89.

Wardle, Elizabeth, and Doug Downs, editors. *Writing about Writing: A College Reader*. Bedford/St. Martin's, 2010.

Styling the Multimodal Classroom: Addressing the Labor of Assessment through the Rhetorical Lexicon of Style

Claire Lutkewitte, Star Medzerian Vanguri, and Stephanie Vie

Despite increased attention to modality in the composition classroom, our approaches to assessing multimodal projects often remain embedded within traditional frameworks that suggest that there are discrete modes and that reward the use of more modes, rather than fewer. Instead, if we indeed look at modality in terms of actions (or "practices," to borrow Bruce Horner's term in this collection), then our assessments of student writing should take into account the stylistic choices our students make when composing. "[I]f style is seen as a composer making choices" (Folk 213), responding to student texts through the lens of style offers a vocabulary for those choices that more generalized rubrics and reflective questioning cannot.

Style is undergoing a revival in composition studies, having held a marginalized place in the field since the 1980s, largely because of its associations with current-traditional rhetoric and syntax in particular. Its marginalization has been based on misconceptions about style and about the history of the discipline of composition studies, as has been argued by Paul Butler and Tom Pace, among others. Pace points out that we have perpetuated the "standard narrative" that "process pedagogy supplanted current-traditional rhetoric, and that process, in turn, was supplanted by social constructionist and critical pedagogy. At every step, the profession pointed to an emphasis on style as a key sign that a particular pedagogy was deficient" (1). Style was too concerned with surface-level correctness, too expressivist, too divorced from context. Butler likewise addresses this disciplinary misremembering, this "selective and biased memory" of style, by identifying the period from the 1960s to the mid-1980s as style's "Golden Age" (7). That style thrived in the process era and was not restricted to mere syntax despite the prevalence of a well-worn narrative linking style with the current-traditional movement and with reductive, decontextualized sentence pedagogies illustrates that more attention to style is warranted as our discipline increasingly acknowledges the multimodal nature of all composition. Thus, our essay encourages a new approach to style and assessment, recasting a persisting and intertwined narrative that style only applies to static, monomodal texts.

Recent scholarship expresses the need to rework style so that it aligns with our current notions of what it means to compose. Collin Gifford Brooke, cautioning against overreliance on print culture, encourages us to "restore the dialectical character of the rhetorical canons" by seeing such canons "as actions, as practices [that] always occur within a particular technological context" (xiii). In treating style as action here, we conceptualize it as dynamic and fluid, adaptable for the multifaceted, nonlinear, and ever-changing nature of modality. So, we attempt to illustrate style's flexibility when we approach modality, picking up T. R. Johnson and Pace's analogy of style as "a kind of bridge by which we can lead our students—and each other—beyond counterproductive binaries" (x)—a bridge that exists between conceptions of traditional, print-based academic writing and multimodal compositions. Given the implied modality of all texts, we don't view using style as applying a traditional, print-based concept to multimodal texts. Instead, we view style as a way to talk about all texts.

Specifically, in this essay, we propose a stylistic approach to composition that prioritizes students' choices and the actions students perform to create those choices. We use Edward Corbett's categories of schemes—balance, order, omission, and repetition—as a framework for teaching and assessing the modality of student work. Within these organizing categories lies a stylistic lexicon that is capable of describing the complex workings of modality, namely the relations between modes. While Horner and John Trimbur, in this collection, offer the term *transmodal* to acknowledge these points of intersection and crossover, we attempt to show how this modal relationality works through the lexicon provided by stylistic schemes. What this essay offers to the existing literature on multimodality and multimodal composition is its explicit focus on the composer's choices (here, a student's) through the lens of style, which we believe is central to both the act and the discipline of composition. This focus deepens existing conversations regarding assessment and even burgeoning discussions of the role of rhetorical canons in composing and assessment. It provides students with specific language they can use to guide and reflect on their composing choices, and, further, it addresses the concerns of faculty members who seek assessment tools that can be applied to all texts.

Why Style Benefits Assessment Practices

Scholarship in composition studies has offered numerous approaches to multimodal composition pedagogy. On one end of the spectrum there is what Dustin W. Edwards calls "transformative work," which repurposes "already-existing materials into new texts for new audiences" (42). He categorizes such work into a typology: assemblage, reappropriation, redistribution, and genre play (47). On the other end of the spectrum there are texts that are created anew.[1] Recent research on teaching and assessing student work that is explicitly named multimodal, however, has had the unintended consequence of intensifying the perceived binary between alphabetic, print-based texts and multimodal texts, once again positioning the alphabetic as primary.

For instance, Michael-John DePalma examines how writers transfer their print-based writing knowledge and skills to other media, finding that using reflective practices, like tracing, helps instructors assess how students rely on their "prior print-based writing knowledge when remediating print-based texts into new media texts" (633). Another study by DePalma and Kara Poe Alexander illustrates that students were successful in relying on print-based knowledge and skills when they worked in multiple modes only when they perceived such work as similar to the work they did in print. When students perceived multimodal work as unlike print-based work, they struggled. In particular, "when students conceived of the task as different yet still attempted to statically apply their print-based rhetorical knowledge and composing practices to aspects of multimodal composing, they faced significant difficulties conceptualizing an audience and negotiating semiotic resources" (185). DePalma and Alexander's solution for helping students is to engage in reflective practices and critical discussions of genre throughout the writing process.

The struggle described by DePalma and Alexander is not unlike the one faced by composition instructors who see print texts and multimodal texts as disparate. But while reflection and critical discussions about genre are undoubtedly important, we suggest instead that instructors look inward to how students' difficulties with assignments might stem from our own teaching practices. Do our teaching practices, for instance, lead students to perceive a binary between alphabetic, print-based texts on the one hand and multimodal texts on the other, a binary that Pegeen Reichert Powell notes in the introduction to this collection is "unproductive and misleading"? Do we treat alphabetic, print-based texts as the foundations for all other texts? Do we erroneously lead students to believe that alphabetic writing will soon take a back seat to, rather than coexisting with, image?

As an alternative, we argue that style is a tool capable of being applied to all forms of composing; seeing style this way can help us both teach and assess student work. In other words, rather than simply transferring notions of style from alphabetic, print-based texts and applying them wholesale to what is different, we assert that style can serve as a framework for composing, broadly conceived. Ultimately, we argue that employing a vocabulary that is explicitly stylistic in our classrooms can create fluid transitions within assignment sequences and result in more valid and accurate assessments of the stylistic qualities of students' compositions.

Schemes Scaffold Assessment with Specificity

Attention to and interest in the rhetorical figures has continued to wane. However, according to Mike Duncan and Star Medzerian Vanguri, "stylistic principles (namely, rhetorical tropes and schemes) are uniquely able to describe phenomena ranging across mediums and modalities in recognition of composition's many forms" (xiii). Tropes and schemes are both considered figures of speech because of their artful deviation: a trope is an unexpected or unconventional use of an element of composition (image, word, or phrase), and a scheme involves a change in a typical order or pattern. Thus, tropes are generally understood to correspond to meaning, schemes to arrangement. Schemes—through which we approach style in this essay—have taken a back seat to the tropes, namely the master tropes of metaphor, metonymy, synecdoche, and irony, "with priority assigned to metaphor as the paradigm of figural as distinct from literal expression" (FitzGerald 46). However, we suggest here that schemes may be more beneficial for pedagogies that approach modality as action because they provide great specificity in describing a composition's form, including the relations between various elements in a composition. For example, balance is dependent on an even number of elements; order requires a sequence of events; omission is identifiable by what is present; repetition necessarily involves multiple occurrences. Rhetorical figures give specificity and nuance to our expectations for student work in a way that simply labeling them as *rhetorical* does not. This essay illustrates the possibilities of a figurative pedagogy.

Again, the figures of speech—schemes and tropes—are characterized by deviation and therefore involve the disruption of convention. Because deliberate deviation involves choice, this stylistic lexicon can encourage students to make choices that are "critically considered and chosen rather than unwittingly followed" (see Horner's essay in this collection) by providing students with language and strategies that encourage and authorize these choices. The relational nature of schemes gives composition instructors an additional advantage when teaching and assessing by allowing them to identify the choices students make. The principles of balance, order, omission, and repetition, when used to communicate expectations to students, reinforce the notion that modality is a matter of actions.

While William FitzGerald speaks of modes (in the sense they can be countable), his words are particularly useful when we juxtapose them with our argument. He notes that "[a] figure-rich pedagogy for today must span performative modes and prepare students to communicate ornamentally across those modes. In this respect, the figures are an untapped resource—a working vocabulary (not an antiquarian catalog) for twenty-first century communication" (54). The working vocabulary we present is composed of the four previously mentioned standard categories of schemes—balance, order, omission, and repetition. They are large umbrella groupings that house under them various stylistic tools available to students, depending on genre and purpose. Our approach to using the categories of schemes as criteria for teaching composition relates to Madeleine Sorapure's concept of the composition of modes, which suggests that we assess the effectiveness with which modes are brought together instead of assessing the individual modes that make up a multimodal composition. In our approach, we see Sorapure's idea of "bringing together" as the actions, and thus the choices students make when composing. Sorapure proposes we use the terminology of the rhetorical tropes of metaphor and metonymy to do so, at the same time acknowledging that this approach does not teach students how to create multimodal texts with specificity. We assert that schemes are helpful stylistic tools for the composing process when named, taught, and reinforced.

These schematic categories help scaffold all assignments and thus allow for semester-long, rather than assignment-specific, formative assessment. Sonya C. Borton and Brian Huot remind us that all assessment involves both formative and summative evaluations. However, when inconsistent criteria are used in classrooms where instructors call one assignment a traditional written assignment and another a multimodal one (thus emphasizing difference), the formative assessment spans only the length of the assignment. Acknowledging this in practice requires a pedagogy and an assessment strategy, Sorapure claims, that focuses on how modes are "brought together or, literally, composed" while drawing upon our discipline's rhetorical undergirding. To illustrate how the categories of schemes can be used as criteria for assessing texts, we will locate them within a first-year composition assignment. The stylistic choices we are unable to showcase here due to the print-based nature of this collection are described and analyzed.

Examining Style in Action through a Multimodal Assignment

The example we present here illustrates work in a first-year composition course with explicit attention (in both the course and the project itself) given to style, schemes, and the principles of balance, omission, order, and repetition. The example is representative of the quality of work produced by students in this first-year composition course and demonstrates how instructors can also think critically about composing in terms of choices and actions. The project, a one-and-a-half-minute video targeted toward college students, begins with a series of four photographs, each of a student standing in a natural pose and smiling at the camera. In every photograph, the student subject stands roughly the same distance from the camera. Each photograph lasts for about three seconds before fading into the next. The song in the background is TLC's "Unpretty." After the series of four photographs, a statement about the cultural devaluing of natural beauty appears in all capital letters in a white, typewriter-style typeface on a black background. The message works as a transition between the sequence of student images and the sequence that follows.

Figure 1. Image from video project showing a photograph of a student on the left and a *Photoshop*-modified version of the photograph on the right

The next series of images places each of the initial photographs next to a *Photoshop*-edited version of the same photograph—the original photograph on the left and the enhanced photograph on the right (fig. 1). In the modified version, the student's face and arms have been thinned out and her neck elongated. Her waist is more defined and her breasts enlarged and lifted. The differences are subtle, and in fact the whole video is a gradual progression of modifications that ultimately ends with over-the-top, and in some cases botched, attempts at cosmetic surgery. The project uses a sequence that builds anticipation for the video's climactic moment. The song's chorus is fitting for the argument of the project, its lyrics declaring, "You can buy your hair if it won't grow / You can fix your nose if he says so." It is played throughout the duration of this series of side-by-side photographs, as it was for the initial photographs, reinforcing the relations between these images and their unretouched counterparts.

As the series of images ends, so does the song's chorus. A new song, Simple Plan's "Crazy," announces the next series of images. Like the previous series, these images are side-by-side before-and-after photographs, but they are of celebrities and professional models rather than students. Stylistically, this set of images is consistent with the last. The new song, a commentary on the social pressures of appearance, reflects a shift from the photographs of students to those of the public figures, yet both sets serve similar rhetorical purposes and are composed similarly on the screen. The images shift from a series of side-by-side unmodified and modified photographs to pre- and post-cosmetic-surgery photographs as the first three verses of "Crazy" play. This portion of the song ends with the line, "If you open your eyes / You'll see that something is wrong." As this line from the song plays, the statement "This is wrong" appears on the screen, in the same all-caps, black-and-white style as before (fig. 2). The statement reinforces the sentiment of the lyrics, as the word *wrong* appears just as it is heard. To demonstrate how the categories of schemes can be used to articulate performance expectations for students and evaluate their work's effectiveness, we offer an analysis broken down by category and further by scheme.[2]

Perhaps most significant to the project's overall organization is balance. Balance, which describes how multiple elements work together for emphasis and equality, is achieved visually in this video through parallelism and antithesis. At the sentence level, parallelism can be created

Figure 2. The last screen of the video project

by similar word or phrase patterns. In this project, balance is created by visual parallelism in which a before-and-after sequence is created by two images' placement next to each other, separated into left and right halves of the screen. This balance makes the composition aesthetically pleasing while reinforcing the project's argument. While the images take up the same amount of space, their parallel structure highlights their differences. The result is an antithesis that draws attention to the parts of the images that have been altered. Students analyzed antithesis in images and in sentences earlier in the semester, and the project employs antithesis to highlight difference and add visual contrast. In determining the effectiveness of the schemes of parallelism and antithesis, the students understood these tools' rhetorical effects so that they could apply the schemes deliberately and strategically.

In the video, balance is also created via *tricolon*, a series of three parallel structures, generally of increasing power. The tricolon created here is made up of the video's three sets of images: the full-screen photographs of students, the split-screen before-and-after photographs of students, and the split-screen before-and-after photographs of models or celebrities (fig. 3). The video is divided into these three parts, and each builds in intensity. As mentioned, the alterations featured in the images become progressively more dramatic, from natural to *Photoshop*-modified, to subtly surgically enhanced to dramatically surgically enhanced or botched. Just as the images build in intensity, so too does the text's implicit argument.

Another principle this project applies is order. As a category of schemes, *order* includes the devices that deviate from typical or expected order. When applied to sentences, this category includes inversions of word order (anastrophe), interruptions that affect the normal flow of the sentence (parenthesis), and placements of similar concepts side by side

Figure 3. Example of tricolon in the video project

(apposition). More specifically, in a sentence using the scheme of apposition, the second of the two adjacent elements serves as an explanation or modification of the first, as in the phrase *my brother John*. Apposition in its visual form is most apparent in this project. The video is a sequence of side-by-side images, the first natural and the second enhanced; the second element is dependent on the first for its meaning and their placement further enhances both elements. In this way, apposition is useful in teaching students order through proximity. While order more generally allows us to treat composition as a kind of visual storytelling, we believe using the term *order* rather than relying on narrative theories gives us access to the more specific schemes within this category that show students how to actually achieve effective sequencing via the relationality of elements.

Schemes of omission are fairly easily recognized in academic writing because their deviation from the rules of traditional academic prose indicate that their use is likely deliberate and chosen for stylistic effect. An ellipsis, an omission of words, might be used to de-emphasize certain material, while asyndeton, an omission of conjunctions between clauses, can be used to create a rhythm that complements the sentence's message or tone. Omission in this project is experienced aurally in the music. The first stanza of the TLC song plays as the first set of images appears in the video. However, the second stanza is skipped and the second set of images is displayed with the song's third stanza, its chorus. The omission is further pronounced by the fact that the image sequences continue uninterrupted even though the song has been modified, the second stanza omitted. This example reinforces the stylistic lesson that omissions can speak as loudly as what is included in a text. The second stanza of the song was deliberately left out so that the second series of images would match up with the lyrics of the chorus, which reinforce explicitly the implicit message of the image sequence. While this aural omission is perhaps the most noticeable example in this text, omission is also useful for teaching and evaluating the design principle of white space and the concept of scope (the project's parameters, limitations, and exclusions).

Lastly, schemes of repetition can describe coherence and cohesion in student work. In this video, repetition is used in the text and images; when text appears, it is always in the same white Courier font on a black background. The first time it is used to make a claim about the cultural devaluing of natural beauty and the second time it is used to leave readers with the judgment, "This is wrong." The stylistic repetition gives each moment equal weight and importance. Repetition also occurs in the photographs: the video begins with a series of single photographs of students before those same images are paired with digitally modified versions. Thus, viewers are exposed to the images twice, having seen the unmodified versions once before the modified versions are viewed. Coupled with the other principles used, such repetition aids in the viewers' understandings of the video's meaning. Consistent timing throughout adds to the cohesion of the overall argument as well. All images are given the same amount of time to be taken in by the viewer, thus creating a deliberately repetitive viewing experience. In terms of pedagogy, framing repetition as a stylistic choice can ease the apprehensions of students who are initially resistant to the concept, as repetition in traditional academic prose is often treated as something to be avoided.

The Labor of Assessment and Style

As mentioned throughout this book, multimodal composition has by many accounts been characterized by a dichotomization of alphabetic, print-based texts and those that involve multiple modes. Much of the current literature on multimodal assessment focuses heavily on a kind of translation or transference of rhetorical frameworks used for alphabetic, print-based materials into a multimodal framework. In a study examining how teachers respond to multimodal work, Emily Wierszewski, for instance, finds that "teachers tend to borrow extensively from existing print-based evaluative criteria as they assess multimodal texts."

On one hand, such transference has been viewed as understandable given the rhetorical underpinnings of our field, a foundation that encourages composers to consider issues of audience, the available means of persuasion, and kairotic timing, among others; as Borton and Huot have argued, "all composing tasks, including multimodal projects, should be informed both broadly and deeply by a rhetorical understanding of composition" (99). Similarly, Elizabeth A. Murray, Hailey A. Sheets, and Nicole A. Williams point out that using rubrics created for alphabetic texts to assess texts that incorporate multiple modes is often a result of necessity. As graduate students who were limited by department-wide rubrics but were yet expected to incorporate digital assignments into their composition courses, these authors illustrate that rubrics that rely on rhetorical frameworks can be successfully adapted for various types of assignments or transferred across different composing situations.

On the other hand, scholars such as Meredith W. Zoetewey and Julie Staggers believe that the digital writing classroom might be better served if we focused on transforming, not simply transferring, the rhetorical criteria upon which we already rely. They suggest we transform concepts like coherence, clarity, and relevance so we can read and evaluate them within a new media framework. Such a transformative approach to assessment addresses Sorapure's concern that "the weakness of a broad rhetorical approach is that it doesn't in itself offer any specific guidance or criteria for handling the multimodal aspects of the composition." Even Jody Shipka's "Statement of Goals and Choices," which asks students to "detail how, why, and under what conditions they made their rhetorical, technological, and methodological choices" (113), might stymie students who lack specific language with which to describe their composing choices. Instead, by explicitly presenting specific rhetorical criteria for assessment through the lens of style, students and instructors alike are given access to a vocabulary that allows us to create and respond to texts with greater specificity and nuance (see Jenna Pack Sheffield's essay in this collection, for example, for a discussion of how students might use the canon of style to strategically compose writing with search engine optimization in mind).

Such qualities are crucial for effective assessment. Without careful scaffolding—the kind that offers specific terms, concepts, and ideas upon which assessors can draw—assessment of all projects can tend toward broad generalizations. Chanon Adsanatham's discussion of student-generated grading criteria for new media assignments raises an important point in any discussion of assessment: in the composition classroom, students should be provided with opportunities to generate, respond to, and refine the criteria by which their compositions will be assessed. However, Adsanatham's study also notes the time-consuming nature of creating and refining such criteria; as he explains, "I had to read each item one-by-one and synthesize it into a comprehensive and coherent document . . . evaluate each benchmark to ensure it was clear, fair and well developed, and . . . clarify/add additional information to certain points" (162). Given the time it takes to create effective assessment criteria (and, additionally, given the amount of time it takes for students to compose), it behooves instructors to have a set of criteria that can be used across multiple genres. This is one of the benefits of the stylistic lexicon we outline here: its terminologies and categories can be used for all sorts of composing practices and projects and can help describe the actions students can employ when composing. When introduced early in the semester and used throughout the course, this stylistic lexicon can support students' reflective awareness of their composing processes.

As our field has increasingly embraced multimodal composition, both as a research subject and as a pedagogical approach, we have focused greater attention on the issue of assessment. From student-generated evaluative criteria (Adsanatham) to Shipka's "Statement of Goals and Choices" to the rhetorical-genre-based rubrics and heuristics created by Cheryl Ball that emerged from her work with the multimodal academic journal *Kairos*, faculty members have a number of options when it comes to prompting students to consider the rhetorical foundations of their composing choices in a variety of settings. What has been missing, though, in our focus on these rhetorical foundations is a balanced attention toward the micro-level stylistic choices that composers make. For instance, in one such *Kairos* webtext, Sherry Rankins-Robertson, Tiffany Bourelle, Andrew Bourelle, and David Fisher present seven grading criteria for a multimodal assignment in an online writing course to help students develop rhetorical awareness. In assessing student work, they contend that a writer must address the intended audience, have a clear sense of purpose, engage in a critical discussion while influencing others, define and evaluate criteria, have sufficient evidence, follow conventions, and organize and utilize graphics effectively. None of these criteria specifically calls attention to style, which can offer a useful vocabulary when invoked explicitly.

In fact most rhetorically based approaches to assessment take a macro-level view, asking students to reflect on "the evolution of the composition from the first to the final draft, commenting specifically on the most critical changes and the effectiveness of these changes in the final draft" (VanKooten and Berkley 162) and to answer questions like "What makes the clip memorable and why?" or "How is ethos utilized?" (Adsanatham 171) and "Please describe the thought process and problem-solving tasks that this assignment required. . . . How did you go about compiling and arranging images, particularly in relation to your music?" (Brooks et al 26). Ball offers two pieces of advice: "(a) Your design should enact your argument, and (b) [t]o come up with that design, think of a visual metaphor for your argument" (72).

These questions are valuable. They prompt authors to articulate choices, to reflect on those choices, and to speak to particular moments in the composing process and the finished piece. Yet such prompts potentially miss an opportunity to allow students to refer to their choices by name. Even Andrew Bourelle, Tiffany Bourelle, and Natasha N. Jones's exploration of how the rhetorical canons can be applied to multimodal technical communication projects focuses only on the macro-level stylistic choices students may make, with student reflections "indicat[ing] that they understood the importance of creating a clear, concise, and easily understandable style in their texts" (316) but not necessarily delving deeply into the stylistic categories we present here in this essay. The authors note that, "from a 21st-century, multimodal perspective, style can refer to how one incorporates sound, images, or design elements to persuade their audience through pathos, logos, and ethos" (316), and we would argue that more detailed discussions of the stylistic schemes detailed in this essay can help work toward this end.

What other proposed approaches to assessing compositions have not yet offered, we believe, is a vocabulary that names the micro-level choices and actions students may take in a rhetorically and stylistically effective way. Though other approaches have offered effective means of assessing the rhetorical choices composers make, these approaches have not sufficiently focused on the stylistic choices—the schemes—that lend specificity to assessment. Style gives us both this language and a rhetorical rationale for its use.

By working from a vocabulary that can describe all texts, all assignments in a course, whether the assignments are print-based or digital, are bound together by the same terms. Style creates curricular coherence, a consistent pedagogy that allows teaching and assessment to work together by scaffolding the concept of composing via the categories of schemes. This curricular coherence is particularly important in an age of mapping curriculum, developing program- or department-level learning outcomes and goals, and making other efforts toward large-scale pedagogical development and refinement in rhetoric and composition. Asking students to return to the same terms, concepts, and ideas multiple times during the semester and multiple times over the course of their college experience offers students the chance to deeply reflect on their choices as composers and to apply what they have learned to new and challenging writing situations.

Perhaps most important, this approach solidifies what we do and teach as composition, not simply writing, by offering a disciplinary coherence that does not position multimodal composing as counter to traditional academic writing but rather sees composing and thus modality as a matter of students' actions. Using the stylistic categories of schemes as a framework for composition courses makes our discipline's rhetorical grounding explicit, consistent, and recognizable in our assessment of students' works.

Notes

1. Edwards and others argue that texts cannot be entirely new, that they must borrow some materials from somewhere; see Kathleen Blake Yancey and Stephen J. McElroy's *Assembling Composition*.

2. Our approach to the categories of schemes is drawn from Corbett's *Classical Rhetoric for the Modern Student* and informed by Chris Holcomb and M. Jimmie Killingsworth's *Performing Prose*. The terminology is presented in great depth in Richard Lanham's *Handlist of Rhetorical Terms*.

Works Cited

Adsanatham, Chanon. "Integrating Assessment and Instruction: Using Student-Generated Grading Criteria to Evaluate Multimodal Digital Projects." *Computers and Composition*, vol. 29, no. 2, June 2012, pp. 152–74.

Ball, Cheryl E. "Assessing Scholarly Multimedia: A Rhetorical Genre Studies Approach." *Technical Communication Quarterly*, vol. 21, no. 1, 2012, pp. 61–77.

Borton, Sonya C., and Brian Huot. "Responding and Assessing." *Multimodal Composition: Resources for Teachers*, edited by Cynthia Selfe, Hampton Press, 2007, pp. 99–111.

Bourelle, Andrew, et al. "Multimodality in the Technical Communication Classroom: Viewing Classical Rhetoric through a 21st Century Lens." *Technical Communication Quarterly*, vol. 24, no. 4, 2015, pp. 306–27.

Brooke, Collin Gifford. *Lingua Fracta: Toward a Rhetoric of New Media*. Hampton Press, 2009.

Brooks, Kevin, et al. "What's Going On? Listening to Music, Composing Videos." *Computers and Composition Online*, Fall 2006, cconlinejournal.org/brooks/composingvideo.pdf.

Butler, Paul. *Out of Style: Reanimating Stylistic Study in Composition and Rhetoric.* Utah State UP, 2008.

Corbett, Edward P. J. *Classical Rhetoric for the Modern Student*. 3rd ed., Oxford UP, 1990.

DePalma, Michael-John. "Tracing Transfer across Media: Investigating Writers' Perceptions of Cross-Contextual and Rhetorical Reshaping in Processes of Remediation." *College Composition and Communication*, vol. 66, no. 4, June 2015, pp. 615–42.

DePalma, Michael-John, and Kara Poe Alexander. "A Bag Full of Snakes: Negotiating the Challenges of Multimodal Composition." *Computers and Composition*, vol. 37, Sept. 2015, pp. 182–200.

Duncan, Mike, and Star Medzerian Vanguri, editors. *The Centrality of Style*. Parlor Press, 2013.

Edwards, Dustin W. "Framing Remix Rhetorically: Toward a Typology of Transformative Work." *Computers and Composition*, vol. 39, Mar. 2016, pp. 41–54.

FitzGerald, William. "Stylistic Sandcastles: Rhetorical Figures as Composition's Bucket and Spade." Duncan and Vanguri, pp. 37–56.

Folk, Moe. "Multimodal Style and the Evolution of Digital Writing Pedagogy." Duncan and Vanguri, pp. 213–37.

Holcomb, Chris, and M. Jimmie Killingsworth. *Performing Prose: The Study and Practice of Style in Composition*. Southern Illinois UP, 2010.

Johnson, T. R., and Tom Pace, editors. *Refiguring Prose Style: Possibilities for Writing Pedagogy*. Utah State UP, 2005.

Lanham, Richard A. *A Handlist of Rhetorical Terms*. U of California P, 1991.

Murray, Elizabeth A., et al. "The New Work of Assessment: Evaluating Multimodal Compositions." *Computers and Composition Online*, 8 Sept. 2009, cconlinejournal.org/murray_etal/index.html.

Pace, Tom. "Part 1: What Happened: The Rise and Fall of Stylistics in Composition." Johnson and Pace, pp. 1–2.

Rankins-Robertson, Sherry, et al. "Multimodal Instruction: Pedagogy and Practice for Enhancing Multimodal Composition Online." *Kairos*, vol. 19, no. 1, Fall 2014, kairos.technorhetoric.net/19.1/praxis/robertson-et-al/index.html.

Shipka, Jody. *Toward a Composition Made Whole.* U of Pittsburgh P, 2011.

Simple Plan. "Crazy." *Still Not Getting Any*, Lava Records, 2004.

Sorapure, Madeleine. "Between Modes: Assessing Student New Media Compositions." *Kairos*, vol. 10, no. 2, Spring 2006, kairos.technorhetoric.net/10.2/coverweb/sorapure/.

TLC. "Unpretty." *FanMail*, LaFace and ArtisaRecords, 1999.

VanKooten, Crystal, and Angela Berkley. "Messy Problem-Exploring through Video in First-Year Writing: Assessing What Counts." *Computers and Composition*, vol. 40, June 2016, pp. 151–63.

Wierszewski, Emily. "'Something Old, Something New': Evaluative Criteria in Teacher Responses to Student Multimodal Texts." *Digital Writing: Assessment and Evaluation*, edited by Heidi A. McKee and Dànielle Nicole DeVoss, Computers and Composition Digital Press, 2013, ccdigitalpress.org/dwae.

Yancey, Kathleen Blake, and Stephen J. McElroy. *Assembling Composition.* NCTE, 2017.

Zoetewey, Meredith W., and Julie Staggers. "Beyond 'Current-Traditional' Design: Assessing Rhetoric in New Media." *Issues in Writing*, vol. 13, no. 2, Spring-Summer 2003, pp. 133–57.

Search Engine Optimization and Its Significance for Alphabetic Composing in Writing Pedagogy

Jenna Pack Sheffield

During my first year as an assistant professor of English, I began working in content strategy for 30SecondsToFly (30STF), an artificial intelligence technology startup. I pursued this role to ensure that my teaching was reflective of current digital writing practices, and while I felt that my background in rhetoric and composition had prepared me for this work, search engine optimization (SEO) was an aspect of the job that came as a surprise. Well before I started at 30STF, I had viewed SEO—"the efforts intended to improve the ranking of a website" in search engine results (Luh et al. 240)—as a simplistic marketing ploy. SEO did not seem to offer much value to me as a writer. Yet, as our SEO expert combed through every newsroom article, requesting changes to the permalinks, headings, image titles, and more, I discovered that SEO requires significant intellectual work. In fact, I found that honing my SEO skills made me a more capable writer and I became determined to integrate lessons about SEO into my writing courses. The research on how—or even if—SEO is being covered in writing courses, though, is scarce.

Some scholarly articles describe how SEO can be employed by editors and publishers to increase traffic to their digital articles (Tornoe); how it can be used by scholars to increase visibility for their research (Beel et al.); how it is used by workplace writers to optimize their work (Killoran; Spinuzzi); and in what ways it is affecting the practices of professional writers, such as journalists (Dick). Yet SEO is not often discussed in relation to the writing that students do in composition courses.

The essays in this edited collection examine the changing role of writing in light of the composition field's turn toward multimodality. In this essay, I suggest that SEO is a concept that writing instructors need to pay more attention to. I argue that SEO is significant for writing pedagogy because it connects to, and allows us to reinforce, many of the values we as instructors already emphasize in our courses; at the same time, SEO requires some new skills and different considerations of writing processes and practices. As other essays in *Writing Changes* do, this essay challenges the commonly posited binary between alphabetic composing and multimodality, showing how SEO, which is primarily an alphabetic composing task, is integral to producing digital texts that circulate online—regardless of the content (video, music, image)—rather than opposed to or separate from other modes.

Snake Oil or Something More: Defining Search Engine Optimization

Put simply, SEO involves an effort to make a Web site (or blog post, or Web article) rank high in search engine results for a set of keywords (Spinuzzi). SEO is important in business settings because companies want their Web sites to appear within the first few results when consumers search for keywords related to their products or services. This high ranking is important because Internet searchers rarely look past the first results page (Deursen and Dijk 398). In fact, a study conducted in 2011 by the professional search engine optimization firm Slingshot SEO found that the first result in a *Google* search receives 18.2% of all click-through traffic ("Beginner's Guide"). The higher a site's ranking, the more people are likely to visit the site and make a purchase. Aside from making money, some companies value SEO because it helps them become thought leaders in their industry online. Independent professionals, contractors, and freelancers also need their Web content to be found—either to alert potential customers to their services or to disseminate industry knowledge. However, SEO is not just for business. Bloggers aim to attract audiences to their sites to initiate conversations or ensure that important information and opinions are made available to the public. Creators of Web sites on special interest topics need their content to get views and incite action. Researchers, too, aim to attract audiences to their articles so they can contribute to their field's collective wisdom. Accordingly, SEO is valuable to a vast majority of writers composing for the screen.

While the value of SEO may be clear, the ways in which it operates are not always so clear. When a search engine user types in a keyword or phrase, each search engine results page—the page listing the most relevant links for the keywords—holds "a series of snippets—clickable links that often include preview text to establish the webpage's relevance to the search" (Gudivada et al. 43). The ranking of a site is based on a complex algorithm, and the algorithm varies based on the search engine (*Google*, *Bing*, etc.). A major purpose of SEO is to adapt a site's content to these algorithms to ensure that the site ranks highly. In other words, the practices involved in achieving the search engine results page constitute SEO.

SEO has often held a bad reputation, which may be why some academics shy away from it. When SEO first became popular, coders and writers often engaged in black-hat, or unethical, SEO tactics to draw in users, such as hiding text and links behind images (Gudivada et al. 45) or creating pages with duplicate content. Black-hat tactics are likely to blame for the impression that SEO is equivalent to "snake oil," as Clay Spinuzzi discusses in his study of the Web services company Semoptco. According to Spinuzzi, SEO as snake oil is the "work of shysters and frauds who . . . have worked to drive traffic to a given site, but not to ensure that the site is actually relevant or useful to the searcher" (365). In other words, SEO can be a trick to draw users to a site. Yet, SEO can be performed well and ethically, and most industry trends are currently promoting quality content over lazy keyword stuffing. When done right, Spinuzzi asserts, SEO involves a complex set of skills such as "identifying relevant keywords, building appropriate content . . . that incorporates those keywords, keeping the content fresh," and building links (113–14). Other humanist academics may, as James Porter notes, shy away from such technical applications because these academics fail to see how they are related to rhetorical competency (211). In the sections that follow, I argue that SEO is intricately connected to rhetorical competency.

Others may equally choose not to address SEO because it is complex and evolving, given that the algorithms are proprietary and often change. Despite the fluidity of the field, SEO practitioners study analytics and can make reasonable assumptions about their SEO tactics based on how their Web content performs after SEO tweaks have been made, and practitioners often then share these assumptions in trade journals and respected blogs ("Beginner's Guide"; *Search Engine Land*; Tornoe). Some researchers study Web pages, looking at characteristics of the pages that tend to rank higher (Zhang and Cabage). This expertise has created a body of knowledge on SEO, meaning that there are tried-and-true strategies, which we can help our students learn.

Search Engine Optimization and Composition Pedagogy

There are a few ways in which SEO can be a valuable concept for us to explore in the composition classroom. One significant value is that it can help students become better writers and researchers. For example, understanding how SEO influences search results can prompt students to critically consider the credibility of online information. Learning some basic optimization principles also benefits students by helping them reach and retain an audience with their public discourse and create an interest network. Important scholarship in the field has been devoted to arguing for students to engage in public writing to understand how to construct "a responsive public" (Wells 329), consider the delivery systems in which writing circulates, and see writing as a means for social change (Mathieu and George). Showing students how to optimize an online text plays an important part in enabling these activities because SEO is a means by which search engines control the texts an audience sees and interacts with. In a similar vein, some of the adjustments writers make to their writing for SEO allow students practice in key concepts such as concision, active voice, and precision.

SEO also plays a practical role in career preparation. In a *CCC* article, "When Writing Becomes Content," published in 2015, Lisa Dush supports the notion that students who are learning to compose for the Web need the ability to write well within a content management system and the ability to optimize writing by applying SEO metadata, noting that these skills signal career preparation to employers (173, 189). The jobs English students pursue, such as content strategist, technical writer, and editor in chief, increasingly require an understanding of SEO. And many of the students we see in first-year business, technical, and digital writing courses are likely to be involved in Web writing at some point in their careers.

SEO is a reality of writing today, but it does not have to be intimidating or unfamiliar. In fact, SEO reinforces the field's values, hearkening all the way back to the canons of rhetoric—invention, arrangement, delivery, style, and memory. In the sections that follow, I describe how SEO connects with the values of composition pedagogy and share ways in which SEO changes the way we think about alphabetic composing, using the rhetorical canons as a framework for that discussion. While the canons originally referred to creating speeches, they have remained "a cornerstone of the study of rhetoric," according to Patricia Bizzell and Bruce Herzberg (3), a cornerstone that is now applied to the writing process. Given the "close pedagogy/theory relationship in the field of Rhetoric and Composition," the canons have been applied time and again to pedagogical research and practice in composition studies (Lauer 120). Scholars and teachers draw upon these canons (Lauer; Kessler; Porter) because the canons, as Kathleen Welch puts it, "form a complete system for generating and analyzing discourse" (270) and, in Kate Kessler's words, they "help writing teachers understand the value of product writing and process writing as we evolve in our practice of post-process pedagogy" (89). Arrangement, style, and invention are used most often in composition textbooks (Welch 270), but scholars have also made compelling arguments for reviving the canons of memory and delivery in the context of the composition classroom (Porter; Brooke). Essentially, I use the canons to drive my discussion of the importance of SEO because they connect strongly with the rhetorical competencies valued in writing courses.

Before exploring these connections, I should note that in this essay, I emphasize on-page optimization (factors such as word choice, heading use, and site speed) versus off-page optimization (external factors like drawing links from other sites) because writers have less control over off-page optimization. Most on-page algorithm factors can be broken down into the concepts of trust—an assessment of the site's authority and reputation—and relevance, or how well the site matches the search query (Killoran 54). Through these factors, search engines determine rankings.

Invention

While classical rhetoric characterizes invention as "the search for persuasive ways to present information and formulate arguments" (Bizzell and Herzberg 3), contemporary scholarship has offered expanded interpretations. Karen Burke LeFevre, for instance, argues that invention is creative and social, and involves making new knowledge rather than just discovering existing knowledge (33). Janice Lauer offers an apt, contemporary summary of invention's relation to writing pedagogy: "Invention provides guidance in how to begin writing, to explore for ideas and arguments, to frame insights, and to examine the writing situation," and invention is the only canon that addresses both content and process (1–2). When applied to the composition classroom, therefore, invention is often associated with prewriting, brainstorming, and applying heuristics to generate ideas.

Keyword Research

The first way in which SEO connects to invention is in relation to generating ideas for an initial writing topic. Just as invention is considered the first of five stages for preparing a communicative act, SEO keyword research is often the first phase of composing Web content, driving the selection of a topic. Conducting keyword research could be seen as a type of invention for students exploring ideas for a Web-based writing assignment. To begin the process, some writers choose to find trending or popular topics. While those topics should relate to the writer's Web site, the writer often begins with no particular keywords or topics in mind; others already have a general topic in mind and begin by determining keywords and phrases relevant to their Web site, product, or service, then testing those keywords through tools such as *Google Ads*'s Keyword Planner, which allows writers to discover other variations of keywords and phrases and analyze the average amount of monthly searches and competitiveness for each ("Beginner's Guide").

Once a writer identifies a primary keyword, the writer is likely to niche down, using tools or brainstorming to identify more specific or related keywords. A writer may move from finding that "diversity" is a trending topic to then using a tool that reveals "advantages of diversity in the workplace" and "age diversity in the workplace" as popular searches, a process that starts to give the writer ideas for focusing. This process can also constitute an idea-generation activity because perhaps the writer does not see the term "workplace inclusion" in the results and decides that writing an article about inclusion would help her carve out a niche topic. Keyword research essentially helps writers identify relevant keywords, but writers must then do the work of identifying what will make their writing unique—hence, another connection to writing studies: having a unique topic or compelling argument matters significantly. For SEO, finding a niche topic has been proven to bump rankings (Tornoe).

Semantic Search

If we are to adopt Lauer's definition of invention as "strategic acts" that provide a writer with "direction, multiple ideas," and "subject matter" (2), initial keyword research constitutes generating subject matter and multiple ideas; what often is considered the next step of SEO preparation—semantic search—can help give writers more direction. Semantic search refers to the idea that search engine algorithms can understand a searcher's intent through contextual meaning (Sanders). Search engines no longer need a keyword match to offer users related content; they can use context to determine the searcher's purpose and provide relevant links.

What does semantic search mean for our students? Employing SEO as an invention strategy means students who are writing for the Web should work to anticipate searches that go beyond a keyword or short phrase and predict the core of the audience's questions on a topic. Essentially, semantic search is driven by the notion of conversation, so writers must guess the kinds of questions their audience might ask—if, for example, the audience members were talking to Siri on their phones—anticipating the purpose and intent of the keywords. Formulating versions of questions, based around keywords, that begin with *what*, *how*, and *why* is a common tip. For instance, while a *Google Trends* search may reveal "Obamacare," "McCain," and "healthcare vote" as common searches, someone speaking to Siri may be more likely to ask a question such as "What are the cons of repeal and replace?" Because search engines can understand the contextual meaning of searches, our student writers, too, need to understand what users want and what contexts may influence a user's search. *Google* draws from items such as a user's search history and location to pull up search results that are most in line with the user's entered keyword or phrase. Writers have to work backward. They may create user personas (fictional representations of your typical Web site visitors) or do interviews with Web site users to learn more about searchers. They may type keywords into the search engine and examine the results to analyze what the engine finds as relevant to that particular keyword search. These practices are where invention takes on the creative, meaning-generating aspect emphasized by LeFevre.

SEO reinforces the composition field's emphasis on invention while encouraging slightly new ways of engaging in the process. Early research into keywords and audience search preferences allows the writer to determine topics the audience cares about, identify missing content opportunities, and provide an understanding of the rhetorical situation. While this may seem formulaic, Lauer argues that intentional heuristic procedures are on a continuum from highly formulaic to "aleatory (trial and error)" (122). Rule-governed formulas, Lauer suggests, can stifle creativity, but aleatory procedures fail to offer guidance. She says all strategies fall somewhere on this continuum, and I would argue that applying SEO as an exercise in invention falls in the middle. Such a practice is formulaic through the deployment of analytics tools to generate ideas; however, creativity begins as writers narrow down and select unique topics aligned to keywords. Even questioning why some keywords are more competitive than others may help student writers discover a compelling focus.

Establishing Ethos

One point that deserves further elaboration is the connection between SEO and ethos, often categorized under invention as one of Aristotle's three artistic proofs. Paul Kemp, in "Aristotle in the Classroom: A Rhetorical Bridge between Literature and Composition," discusses how we teach students to analyze the ethos of a writer by looking at the ways in which authors present themselves as "responsible, knowledgeable figures whose discourses can be trusted" (3). In this way, SEO does not change writing pedagogy; it reinforces our values, although we have some new considerations to account for. Search engines are, surprisingly, beginning to measure a writer's ethos, factoring a writer's credibility into the ranking of an article by identifying patterns.

Writers need to create patterns across the Web to establish our ethos in a way that is recognizable to readers *and* search engines. One pattern search engines can detect is when an author publishes on multiple sites about the same topic, which can establish that author as a thought leader. Writers who add a byline and social media contact information each time they publish an article are helping the search engine contextualize who they are and their credibility. Writers who are knowledgeable on a topic demonstrate their credibility to search engines through their use of industry terminology. Grammatical errors or spelling mistakes can negatively affect algorithms, reducing the writer's authority, and linking out to credible Web sites has been proven to boost rankings related to authority (Patel). We may encourage student writers to consider these practices to build up trust with search engines and, ultimately, readers.

Audience Awareness and Public Writing

The importance of audience pervades all of the canons, but it is during the invention phase that writers are considering who their audience is and what that audience needs to know. When we ask students to write for the public, as Susan Wells notes, the public sphere is always constructed (326). All writers, Wells says, face the difficult task of constructing a responsive public audience. Lisa Ede and Andrea Lunsford describe two traditional approaches to audience in composition pedagogy: audience addressed, in which the audience is a concrete reality whose values and attitudes can be known, and audience invoked, in which the audience is a "construction of the writer" (160–64). Those who view audience as invoked use "semantic and syntactic resources of language to provide cues for the reader," cues that define the audience's role (160). Ede and Lunsford argue that all writers are engaging with audience invoked and addressed. It should be noted that Lunsford and Ede later revisit their argument about audience addressed and audience invoked in "Representing Audience: 'Successful' Discourse and Disciplinary Critique." While they make it clear that they still "resist efforts to characterize audience as solely textual (invoked) or material (addressed)" and "continue to affirm the importance of considering audience in the context of the rhetorical situation" (170), they also note that their original stance failed to explore the ways audience can silence readers and writers and did not fully explore the role of misunderstanding and failure in terms of achieving success when communicating with others (170–75). In many ways, SEO best practices reinforce Lunsford and Ede's perspective on audience. Through keyword research and analytics capabilities, writers are perhaps more capable than ever of discovering their audience's values or interests (audience addressed). At the same time, writers attuned to SEO engage with the audience invoked by using a variety of cues to define the audience's role and participation in the text. As a small example, SEO experts are always encouraging writers to use more headings for SEO because search engines use that information to determine relevance, and also because readers are better able to follow the purpose of the text and, frankly, maintain their attention spans because headings break up content effectively. Importantly, SEO is not just about garnering an audience; it is about, as the SEO marketing company Moz suggests, "getting the right kind of visitors" ("Beginner's Guide"). Many of the strategies described in this essay are used by writers to construct a certain vision of their readers, ensuring their content is found, read, and engaged by the right kind of audience.

While the composition field's values are reflected in SEO's connection to audience, SEO also emphasizes a slightly new audience reality—search engines. In this vein, SEO may also relate to Lunsford and Ede's concerns about silencing readers and writers given that there can be so many different audiences that writers must engage with when their writing becomes public via a search engine. While early SEO writers tended to view the search engine as their primary audience, as search engines continue to judge content more and more adeptly, most SEO practitioners now view users as the primary audience and search engines as a secondary audience. This suggests that writers should focus on content quality first, but as Neil Patel, a *New York Times* best-selling author and top influencer on the Web, suggests, "An SEO copywriter also understand [sic] how Google feels about certain words and phrases." In this way, the search engine becomes audience addressed, as writers try to learn a search engine's preferences. Having these different audiences in mind can help our students engage with the task of writing for multiple audiences—a task we already emphasize in our courses—with the added challenge of considering a digital system as an audience. Along those lines, when addressing audience, writers face a unique challenge in that they must anticipate how their primary audience, Web searchers, will use a search engine. For instance, a search engine user is less likely to search for a company name; users look, instead, for a company type or location (Killoran 56). Consequently, part of constructing a responsive public is anticipating how the audience will be searching for topics.

Arrangement

The second rhetorical canon, arrangement, is concerned with the parts of speech, or now more broadly, the organization or structure of a text. While classical rhetoric was formulaic in its approach to arrangement, contemporary theories still value the concepts but loosen the reign on prescribing one correct approach. Aristotle, for example, said all speeches

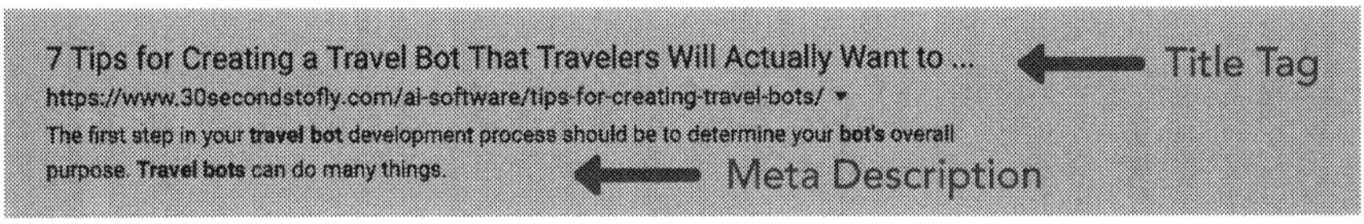

Figure 1. Example of meta description in *Google* search engine results, 6 Jan. 2019

should have four parts—"the introduction, the statement of the issue, the argument, and the conclusion" (Bizzell and Herzberg 5). When compositionists apply arrangement to classroom instruction, it often takes on a looser interpretation of selecting the appropriate organization for a particular text. When applied to new media writing, specifically hypertext, Collin Gifford Brooke describes how arrangement became considered obsolete: because readers navigate texts on the Web on their own, shifting the responsibility for order to the reader (89). Yet, Brooke argues for the centrality of arrangement. Describing arrangement as pattern, he emphasizes arrangement as a process of allowing patterns and relations to emerge among blogs, wikis, and databases.

Keyword Placement and HTML Tags

One way that SEO connects to arrangement is in terms of keyword placement. Simply repeating the same keyword multiple times is not likely to sway an algorithm and could penalize the site, but using related concepts and synonyms can boost an article. Strategically organizing those keywords (arrangement) in the right locations helps with SEO by giving more context to search engines. Industry advice is to embed keywords into specific tags, such as heading tags and meta descriptions. The meta description is "a short description of a page's content" that often serves as the snippet of text beneath a listing in the search engine results page ("Beginner's Guide"). While search engines don't currently use the meta description to rank sites, it is integral to helping readers determine the relevance of the page to their search (fig. 1). Since the meta description describes to readers the content of the page they will click on, using keywords in the description (in a way that flows) helps readers see the relevance of the content and encourages them to click on the content.

Some experts recommend arranging a relevant keyword early in the meta description to ensure it fits in the snippet and helps users understand the page's focus. (The keyword the user searches for appears in boldface in the snippet, which further signals relevance.) Arranging the text so that keywords are located in headings (especially at the beginning of the text) is also helpful for both users and search engines. Search engines use headings to determine the relevance of content, and users are more likely to stay on a page if the content is broken into headings that describe the content directly below the headings. As students begin to learn how to apply heading tags and write meta descriptions (easily done in a content management system without entering into the code), they should also be advised to arrange varied keywords in those sections to help users and search engines identify the text's relevance to the search query. The arrangement of keywords essentially serves as a persuasive tool by convincing Web users, from their initial interaction with the search engine results page to their experience reading the content, that the article they are reading is relevant and will address their concerns.

Content Organization

SEO also reinforces the notion that the arrangement of a text should be driven by context, audience, purpose, and medium. For example, the inverted pyramid structure (a summary toward the beginning of a Web-based article and more specific details toward the end) can enhance an article's SEO. This approach allows writers to grab the audience's attention right away and makes the content prime to be pulled for snippets (McCoy). Search engines such as *Google* have begun to pull featured snippets from a popular article; these snippets appear at the top of search results in response to a user's question (fig. 2). Breaking one's Web writing into numbered lists or bullet points can also make the content more likely to be pulled for snippets. Snippets have high click-through rates, thus enhancing SEO.

The reason why I argue that the arrangement of a text, when optimizing for SEO, should be driven by context, audience, and purpose is partially because strategies such as the inverted pyramid approach are useful only if the content matches the purpose of SEO. A how-to blog post is a contender for a snippet; a long-form op-ed is not the type of content that a search engine would turn into a snippet, and the article's persuasive effect on a reader may suffer if the writer puts the main point at the beginning of the piece. Some SEO experts even recommend that, in terms of arrangement, writers bullet point three or four benefits of the Web page before writing an introduction (Patel), but again, different organizational choices will be enacted based on what the writer determines

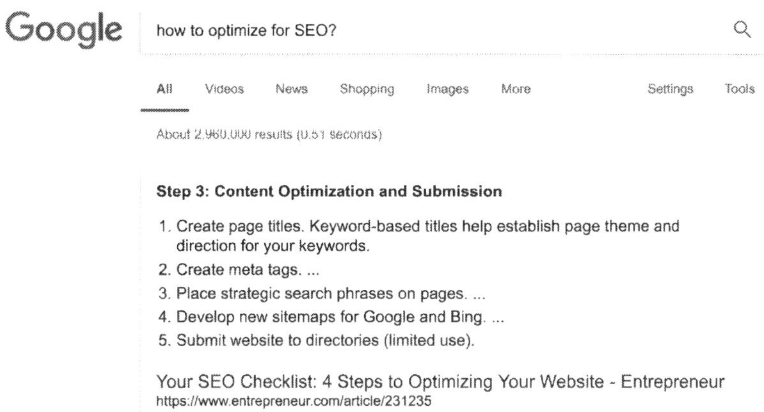

Figure 2. Example of a featured snippet in *Google* search engine results, 6 Jan. 2019

about the audience and purpose of the text. As instructors, we can help student writers make these structural decisions and see the interrelation between attending to SEO and maintaining the quality, integrity, and flow of the piece. While the SEO literature does recognize a shift toward quality content, students should be encouraged to explore the ethical implications of arranging content to enhance optimization. While writers need to compete in the SEO world, when optimization veers too far in the realm of tricking users into visiting a page when the content is not useful to the search, the practice of SEO becomes problematic.

Delivery

In classical rhetoric, delivery referred primarily to aspects such as the speaker's voice or body gestures. As such, twentieth-century writing instruction often failed to attend to delivery. But in his article from 2009, "Recovering Delivery for Digital Rhetoric," Porter argues for reviving discussions of delivery. Porter proposes a theoretical framework for digital delivery consisting of five components: body and identity, distribution and circulation, access and accessibility, interaction, and economics. Two of these aspects of delivery—accessibility and circulation—are relevant to SEO.

Access and Accessibility

According to Porter, accessibility is the "level of connectedness of one particular group of persons—those with disabilities" (216). *Access* is more broadly defined as having connections to computer resources. SEO reinforces certain accessibility best practices. These strategies include writing alternative text that describes images for vision-impaired individuals using screen readers, writing descriptive titles and headings that carefully indicate the purpose of the text directly below the headings, creating transcripts for video content, and writing effective anchor text (the clickable text on a Web page that sends users to the site to which the text is referring). As an example, SEO writers are advised to carefully compose the alt tag so that vision-impaired visitors can understand what is pictured in the image. In terms of delivery, this creates a better user experience, but it also helps with SEO because engine crawlers rely on this information to understand the image's purpose and the connection to the user's search.

To design with access in mind, writers need to consider those with limited access to digital resources. Porter suggests that one important aspect of this process is designing for mobile platforms, given that in many countries mobile phones are individuals' primary means for accessing the Internet. The ability to write for mobile phones is also becoming important for writers who are concerned with SEO, as mobile-friendliness is now an algorithm factor; hence, mobile-friendly composing is an area where delivery and SEO connect. While many writers have little control over site design, there are some strategies for optimizing one's Web-based writing for mobile platforms. These strategies include chunking content by using short paragraphs, lists, and headings; keeping writing concise; making font sizes legible; and compressing images or using different file types to improve page load speed. Some even suggest that making article titles and headings shorter—i.e., short enough to fit on one line—can boost SEO (Tornoe). Delivery, in this sense, comes down to making one's content easy to view and follow on a different medium. These are all relatively manageable strategies that we can teach our students, emphasizing how an alphabetic composing skill, SEO, impacts the accessibility of their discourse.

Circulation

Circulation has to do with the "potential for [a writer's message] to have a document life of its own and be re-distributed without [the writer's] direct intervention" (Porter 214). Porter notes that writers can design their discourse to have a high degree of circulation or limited ciriculation, depending on the writer's wishes (214). SEO essentially serves as a mechanism for effective circulation: writers use SEO to gain a broader audience by helping search engine users discover their articles. The more effective the SEO, the more the Web site or article has a life of its own and can be distributed further without the writer's intervention. As writers go public, they must, as Paula Mathieu and Diana George argue, "understand how public messages do and do not circulate and why it is important to be part of a network of communication rather than imagine that anyone can truly 'go it alone' when it comes to writing that aims to make a difference" (131). In other words, Mathieu and George assert that we have to pay attention not only to composing but also to circulation. When helping students understand SEO as a delivery mechanism, we can guide them toward SEO's power to construct and constrain their audiences and the life cycle of their texts.

Style

The fourth canon, style, has to do with the expression of ideas, or how something is said rather than what is said. In *Style: An Introduction to History, Theory, Research, and Pedagogy*, Brian Ray affirms that style has been defined in numerous ways—in terms of "classical rhetorical devices and amplification of discourse, as the manipulation of punctuation and syntax for rhetorical effect, as risk and deviation from norms, and as voice and authenticity" (7). A primary debate has centered around viewing style as form, meaning, or both. *Style as form* means that style only decorates discourse; *style as meaning*, on the other hand, implies that the use of devices (such as manipulating sentence length and choice of words) affects the development of ideas and their interpretation by an audience (Ray 7). Two aspects of style are particularly relevant to SEO: persuasion and personality, and word choice and readability.

Persuasion and Personality

Perhaps the most important part of adopting a writing style that is optimized for the Web is matching the audience's intent: anticipating the concerns of the audience and using the audience's language and style. Keyword use plays a part in this equation. Writers must use enough keywords to help search engines understand the topic but avoid using keywords so often that the site is penalized for spam. There is not an exact science to this style, but generally, the keyword phrase should flow with the purpose of the text. If writers find themselves using vague pronoun references, those spots might be natural opportunities for inserting keywords. Always aiming to provide value to readers first, writers anticipate the audience's concerns and the ways in which they might phrase these issues, and then style their writing accordingly.

Additionally, SEO-oriented writing is typically persuasive, and most SEO experts recommend writing in a straightforward manner at a moderate reading level, using subject-focused sentences with a conversational tone (Sanders). While straightforward, plain language is the recommended style, a unique, compelling style can make one's writing stand apart from related content. Thus, Web writers must find a tricky balance: using a style that is familiar and comfortable for readers—a style that echoes their readers' questions—while also finding ways to make the writing engaging and distinct. This is perhaps no different than traditional debates about how we teach academic writing. As Ray notes, many teachers find themselves correcting "errors" such as the use of conversational language, humor, or personal stories in academic writing, yet most agree that these principles are not universal and teachers often secretly hope to find some personality in their students' writing (4). Much the same, Patel recommends that SEO-focused writers use humor to excite readers or simplify a controversial topic and emphasizes the importance of personality; yet he acknowledges that straightforward use of keywords and a direct style is more important given that personality can sometimes get in the way of ensuring Web copy is understandable to readers. In essence, while there are small changes in convention when writers consider SEO, the broader value of paying attention to style and connecting it to audience remains the same.

Word Choice and Readability

Word choice, readability, and mechanical correctness are key stylistic concerns for SEO. While rumors have spread that search engines consider a text's reading level in their algorithms, John Mueller, a senior webmaster trends analyst at Google, suggests this may not be the case (Slegg). Yet, he states that a common mistake in Web writing that can impact SEO is when writers talk past the audience; for example, a medical Web site may not show up in search results for its intended audience because the site uses lengthy jargon that the audience would not be searching for (Slegg). If the Web site had been aiming to attract medical professionals, Mueller argues, the search terms would differ and likely be more technically focused. Again, SEO values reinforce the field of composition's emphasis on the interrelation between audience and style. Search engines can detect errors in style, such as AP style, and some SEO experts suggest they have standards for grammar and punctuation. Thus, paying attention to mechanical correctness, another important aspect of style, allows one's writing to have a better chance of getting ranked. If anything, giving students a basic understanding of SEO and its relation to grammatical correctness may allow us to further emphasize that correctness allows writers to establish their credibility.

Optimizing writing for SEO also requires small tweaks to the text, such as anchor text and permalinks. Web writers new to SEO often write vague anchor text such as "article" or "click here," but as Google's "Search Engine Optimization Starter Guide" recommends, anchor text should indicate to readers what type of content they will see if they click on the link, capturing the topic of the page being linked to. This text gives search engines clues about the relevance of the page's content. For student writers, a small task such as composing effective anchor text can highlight the connection between style and purpose. Other SEO style tips abound, such as including specific numbers in headlines, which leads to higher conversion rates, or addressing the audience as *you* for business-to-consumer customers and as *we* for business organizations.

Regarding the form-versus-content debate, SEO seems, at first glance, to merely decorate discourse. Some of the tips appear to be stylistic choices that simply help users understand purpose. However, the stylistic devices we use for SEO are ultimately about retaining an audience, making SEO-as-style integral to form and meaning.

Memory

SEO also has some minor connections to the fifth canon, memory. The above sections have already described how SEO operates, so the essential point to make about memory is that the strategies writers use allow them to—as Brooke remarks about memory—build and maintain patterns across several texts and interfaces; by using metadata to tag and describe texts, writers are establishing patterns, allowing the concepts they write about to take on an "aggregative" quality (162). Web writers are essentially assisting the memory patterns of users when they engage with SEO. When a writer composes the title tag and meta description, for example, that is what the user sees and uses to make decisions about accessing texts when surfing the Web.

Pedagogical Implications

Given the concerns of this edited collection about the changing role of writing in light of the multimodal turn, SEO reinforces the importance of alphabetic writing as a primary means of delivering and circulating messages on the Web. Placing an emphasis on SEO can, in some ways, change the way writers write, beginning with invention. Yet, while SEO has an effect on Web writing, the difference may be one of degree versus kind, as SEO is not a break from our disciplinary expertise. If anything, knowledge of SEO can deepen or enhance the importance of certain values and principles in writing since attaining an audience for one's writing can be a motivating factor for students and professionals alike.

While SEO does not vastly change composition pedagogy values, we can attend to SEO more strategically in our instruction if we want students to understand how SEO contributes to constructing a responsive public, generating ideas, and circulating content. A student in my Writing for Digital Environments course wrote a compelling blog post on the topic of health insurance discrimination against transgender individuals. She was excited about the post; yet, five days after she published it, her article had few visitors and no comments, aside from a few classroom colleagues' required responses. "I guess no one likes my writing," she said to me as she walked into class. The issue was that this student had a vision of her blog post being automatically boosted to the top of *Google*—as if anyone who searched for "health insurance discrimination transgender" would immediately find her post, eagerly read it, and comment. However, a lot of work goes into making one's work visible. There are small and more substantive ways in which we can engage students with SEO to help them understand this important point about the audience and scope of their writing.

At a basic level, instructors may offer class instruction on some of the best practices for optimizing one's writing. Many of the sources cited in this essay are useful starting points for instructors who want to learn.

A lecture on SEO could stem into an activity where students select an interesting keyword as a class, and small groups are assigned to analyze the characteristics of some of the top results—particularly the phrasing of titles, use of headings, application of tags, and the uniqueness of the topic and style. Instructors could then ask students to select the fifteenth page of the search engine results and see if they notice differences in pages that are not as highly ranked. This small activity can work in a first-year writing course because it is an exploration of information literacy. After all, while quality affects SEO, students could find high-quality results on the fifteenth page of results if the writer has no knowledge of SEO and has not optimized the page. This can tie into a discussion of ethics, given that students may discover highly ranked but untrustworthy information.

If instructors ask students to blog or compose Web sites, selecting a site such as *Wix* or *WordPress* makes applying metadata manageable because these sites prompt users to input SEO-targeted information. If we ask students to attend to SEO as they compose in these spaces, we may ask them to demonstrate the work they put into optimizing. Students could be asked to write a reflection about their Web composition, discussing their keyword research, topic, and title selections, their approach to accessibility, mobile optimization, style, and so forth. Because search engine algorithms frequently change, instructors should encourage students to stay up to date on SEO best practices. Effective research skills come to the fore again here, as credibility and timeliness are important when it comes to finding accurate sources on SEO. Putting that work on students can encourage them to question SEO in action.

While it is difficult to keep up with trends in SEO, looking at the concept as an extension of the five canons demonstrates its sustainability and value. If writers compose clear, engaging, well-structured, audience-focused content, they are already optimizing their on-page content; however, extra attention to SEO in writing courses can pay off—figuratively and literally—as a valuable skill for students pursuing digital writing careers, and as an intellectual exercise even for those who are not. SEO is integral to producing digital texts that circulate online, and as such, search-engine-optimized writing is not opposed to or separate from other modes, such as video or music, but instead integral to their circulation. Just as the canons "form a complete system for generating and analyzing discourse" (Welch 270), SEO takes writers through the entire process of inventing, composing, and circulating discourse. We should pay attention to SEO because it helps us do what we have always wanted to do in our courses but also because it achieves new results in new environments in terms of connecting one's writing to readers. Granted, SEO should not completely take over one's approach to writing. For example, many news outlets feel that SEO is applying pressure to the ethical and writing standards that journalists find to be important, and many outlets are therefore refusing to completely bow to demands for more search traffic (Dick 462). Yet, the promising news is that while SEO requires new approaches to alphabetic composing, alphabetic composing, in turn, pushes back—as perhaps the number one rule of SEO is to write quality content.

Works Cited

Beel, Jöran, et al. "Academic Search Engine Optimization (ASEO): Optimizing Scholarly Literature for Google Scholar & Co." *Journal of Scholarly Publishing*, vol. 41, no. 2, Jan. 2010, pp. 176–90.

"The Beginner's Guide to SEO." *Moz*, moz.com/beginners-guide-to-seo. Accessed 1 Apr. 2018.

Bizzell, Patricia, and Bruce Herzberg, editors. *The Rhetorical Tradition: Readings from Classical Times to the Present*. Bedford/St. Martin's, 1990.

Brooke, Collin Gifford. *Lingua Fracta: Towards a Rhetoric of New Media*. Hampton Press, 2009.

Deursen, Alexander J. A. M. van, and Jan A. G. M. van Dijk. "Using the Internet: Skill Related Problems in Users' Online Behavior." *Interacting with Computers*, vol. 21, nos. 5–6, Dec. 2009, pp. 393–402.

Dick, Murray. "Search Engine Optimisation in UK News Production." *Journalism Practice*, vol. 5, no. 4, 2011, pp. 462–77.

Dush, Lisa. "When Writing Becomes Content." *College Composition and Communication*, vol. 67, no. 2, Dec. 2015, pp. 173–96.

Ede, Lisa, and Andrea Lunsford. "Audience Addressed / Audience Invoked: The Role of Audience in Composition Theory and Pedagogy." *College Composition and Communication*, vol. 35, no. 2, May 1984, pp. 155–71.

Gudivada, Venkat N., et al. "Understanding Search Engine Optimization." *Computer*, vol. 48, no. 10, Oct. 2015, pp. 43–52.

Kemp, Paul F. "Aristotle in the Classroom: A Rhetorical Bridge between Literature and Composition." *ERIC*, 2001, eric.ed.gov/?id=ED458624.

Kessler, Kate. "Composing for Delivery." *English Journal*, vol. 95, no. 2, Nov. 2005, pp. 89–96.

Killoran, John B. "How to Use Search Engine Optimization Techniques to Increase Website Visibility." *IEEE Transactions on Professional Communication*, vol. 56, no. 1, Mar. 2013, pp. 50–66.

Lauer, Janice M. *Invention in Rhetoric and Composition*. Parlor Press, 2004.

LeFevre, Karen Burke. *Invention as a Social Act*. Southern Illinois UP, 1986.

Luh, Cheng-Jye, et al. "Estimating Google's Search Engine Ranking Function from a Search Engine Optimization Perspective." *Online Information Review*, vol. 40, no. 2, 2016, pp. 239–55.

Lunsford, Andrea A., and Lisa Ede. "Representing Audience: 'Successful' Discourse and Disciplinary Critique." *College Composition and Communication*, vol. 47, no. 2, May 1996, pp. 167–79.

Mathieu, Paula, and Diana George. "Not Going it Alone: Public Writing, Independent Media, and the Circulation of Homeless Advocacy." *College Composition and Communication*, vol. 61, no. 1, Sept. 2009, pp. 130–49.

McCoy, Julia. "Google's Featured Snippets: How to Get Your Content to Appear." *Content Marketing Institute*, 27 Mar. 2017, contentmarketinginstitute.com/2017/03/google-featured-snippets/.

Patel, Neil. "SEO Copywriting: How to Write Content for People and Optimize for Google." *neilpatel.com*, www.neilpatel.com/blog/seo-copywriting-how-to-write-content-for-people-and-optimize-for-google-2/. Accessed 2 Apr. 2018.

Porter, James E. "Recovering Delivery for Digital Rhetoric." *Computers and Composition*, vol. 26, no. 4, Dec. 2009, pp. 207–24.

Ray, Brian. *Style: An Introduction to History, Theory, Research, and Pedagogy*. Parlor Press, 2015.

Sanders, Alexis. "What Is Semantic Search and What Should You Do about It?" *Moz*, 14 Nov. 2016, moz.com/blog/what-is-semantic-search.

Search Engine Land. Third Door Media, 2019, searchengineland.com.

"Search Engine Optimization (SEO) Starter Guide." *Google Search Console*, static.googleusercontent.com/media/www.google.com/en//webmasters/docs/search-engine-optimization-starter-guide.pdf. Accessed 27 June 2019.

Slegg, Jennifer. "Google's Use of Readability, Reading Level & Vocabulary Metrics in Search Algorithms." *The SEM Post*, 31 Jan. 2018, www.thesempost.com/googles-use-readability-vocabulary-search-algorithms/.

Spinuzzi, Clay. *All Edge: Inside the New Workplace Networks*. U of Chicago P, 2015.

Tornoe, Rob. "The New Era of SEO." *Editor and Publisher*, vol. 49, no. 4, Apr. 2016, pp. 28–72.

Welch, Kathleen E. "Ideology and Freshman Textbook Production: The Place of Theory in Writing Pedagogy." *College Composition and Communication*, vol. 38, no. 3, Oct. 1987, 269–82.

Wells, Susan. "Rogue Cops and Health Care: What Do We Want from Public Writing?" *College Composition and Communication*, vol. 47, no. 3, Oct. 1996, 325–41.

Zhang, Sonya, and Neal Cabage. "Search Engine Optimization: Comparison of Link Building and Social Sharing." *Journal of Computer Information Systems*, vol. 57, no. 2, 2017, pp. 148–59.

Of Writing and the Future: Augmented Reality Composition

Brenta Blevins

Much has been made of the multimodality and multiliteracy capabilities in digital media texts, whether broadly (New London Group; Cope and Kalantzis; Kress, "Multimodality") or by focusing on particular modes, primarily through the visual (George; Hocks; Kress, "'English'"; Selfe, "Toward New Media Texts") and with increasing attention to the sonic (Ceraso; Selfe, "Movement"). As this essay collection emphasizes, however, scholarly conversation about textual modes, particularly in digital composing, can seem to presuppose "a specific, fixed definition of alphabetic print text (a.k.a. 'writing') as distinct from what is termed multimodality" (qtd. from Horner's essay in this volume). My essay seeks to explore how alphabetic writing is intrinsic to new media composing by looking specifically at the emerging medium of augmented reality (AR).

Approaching and following the turn of the twenty-first century, the terms *tectonic shift* and *tectonic change* appear in scholarship to describe the transformation brought by changing digital communication media (Kress, "'English'"; Yancey, "Made"). Responding to the shifting landscape for composing technologies, Kathleen Blake Yancey argued in her Conference on College Composition and Communication (CCCC) Chair's Address in 2004 for conceiving of "composition in a new key" ("Made" 297). With so much ongoing flux, writers are composing in whatever media and genres "will emerge in the next ten minutes" (298). Just over a decade later in his CCCC Chair's Address in 2015, Adam Banks called on writing instructors to consider technology's impact, asking, "What happens to composing when laptop and desktop computers go the way of the typewriter?" (274).

My essay responds to these questions around changing composition technologies by analyzing the emerging digital medium of augmented reality. I explore AR as one case for considering the role of writing when the technological modes of textual production and consumption are undergoing rapid change. In recent years, augmented reality and the perhaps more familiar virtual reality media have increased in availability, offering fresh challenges to composition in a new key. Such evolving communication media have the potential to change the sites of writing, both in terms of production and consumption, providing new ways to test the assumptions and boundaries surrounding writing and the writing classroom.

To consider the current state of digital writing as well as to speculate on writing in future media, I employ the format of an essay to explore how we can prepare for composing in new media through alphabetic writing. Drawing from Joseph Harris's description of the essay in his contribution to this volume, I use the term *essay* to indicate a form of "response" that is also looking at writing "from a particular angle." But I am also using the term *essay* in the sense of *essayer*, "to try." I am trying out an emerging medium and writing here in an attempt to demonstrate the intrinsic nature of alphabetic writing in digital media composition, as it exists now and may exist in the future.

Beyond Binary Oppositions

Much as this collection attempts to complicate the alphabetic-multimodal dichotomy, my exploration of AR composing seeks to challenge a number of other binary oppositions: past-future, old-new, process-product, print-digital, essay-multimedia. In considering the use of AR assignments and projects in my writing classes, I find alphabetic writing intrinsic to, not opposed to or separated from, the multimodal in the digital medium of augmented reality, both in the final AR products and the entire composing process.

Yancey's proposal for a "new key" entails understanding composition as encompassing alphabetic, essayistic projects (i.e., "words on a page") as well as composing with words, images, and audio together ("Made" 298). Yancey thus argues against the dichotomies of print-digital and alphabetic-multimodal in favor of a both-and approach to composition: writing both for print and for digital display, writing both with words and with other means of persuasion. It is in such a both-and approach that we should continue to incorporate emerging media assignments in our writing classrooms. The following sections challenge the binaries associated with composing. As this collection reveals, binaries such as print-digital, alphabetic-multimodal, old-new, past-present, alphabetic essay–digital composition, and process-product fall short when describing the complicated process of composing.

Print-Digital, Alphabetic-Multimodal Binaries

While theorists recognize the alphabetic as multimodal and that no text is monomodal (Kress, "Multimodality"; Shipka, *Toward a Composition*; Ball and Charlton; Rule, in this collection), the phrase *print-based, alphabetic literacy* nonetheless appears frequently in scholarly conversation, demonstrating and reifying the link between the terms *print* and *alphabetic*, often positioned in contrast with digital or electronic writing. As Bruce Horner notes in this collection, social practices and ideologies form "effectively monomodal" perspectives on text, "despite the inherent multimodality of all texts that Kress and others have acknowledged." As this collection observes (Harris; Horner; Rule), attention to paper-based document design, however, points to the ways in which print-based texts are multimodal, such as through the spatial mode in layout designs (Wysocki; Klein and Shackelford). Further, theorists such as Paul Prior ("Moving Multimodality") and Jody Shipka (*Toward a Composition* and "Including") have specifically worked to challenge the binaries of print-digital and alphabetic-multimodal. Avoiding these writing dichotomies helps us see digital composition as supporting the essayistic and illuminates how alphabetic writing is central to digital composition.

Old-New, Past-Present Binaries

Frequently, as Jason Palmeri observes in analyzing the history of multimodal composition and as Pegeen Reichert Powell emphasizes in this collection's introduction, print—and the alphabetic—have become conflated with the past, while digital—and the multimodal—are assigned to the future. As Horner notes in this collection, multimodality's associations extend to "the new, the better, the enriching, and even the liberating . . . understood to be brought about by means of technologies." Kress explains that the "cultural and political dominance of writing over the last few centuries" has contributed both to the erasure of visual elements in printed writing, "making it invisible through its usualness, its 'naturalness,'" and to making "the always existing facts of multi-modality invisible" ("'English'" 70). While the dominance of print once rendered its multimodal features invisible, now new digital media—and the focus on the multimodal—have the potential to render the alphabetic invisible. However, multimodality belongs as much to the past as to the contemporary era—and to the future.

Alphabetic Essays–Digital Compositions Binary

The essay has been caught up in this alphabetic-multimodal binary, as the alphabetic is associated with past and school-based writing and seemingly placed in opposition to multimodal composing. Compositionists remain committed to essayistic composing—as not a rejection but an inclusion in new media composing, as Harris does in his piece for this collection on the essay in the digital era. Douglas Hesse argues for the continued role of the essay in education and larger culture, contending that there is "important value to reading and writing extended, connected texts whose authors manage the double pulls of complexity and order, producing works that convey their status as products of a certain experiential and intellectual nexus, not as objective truth" ("Saving a Place" 47). Hesse emphasizes that he is "emphatically not arguing the essay as the sole or even main genre for writing instruction. I'm arguing that it needs to be in the mix" (47). While Banks calls for the promotion of the essay to "dominant genre emeritus" (272–73), he offers it a place to remain "on campus and in our thinking, teaching, and writing lives," recognizing the essay as "a valuable, even powerful technology that has particular affordances in helping us promote communicative ability, dialogue, and critical thinking" (273).

Neither Hesse's call for the continuation of essayistic composition nor Banks's appeal for the adoption of writing projects beyond the essay are contradictory. Indeed, Hesse notes that Banks's CCCC Chair's Address falls "squarely in the exploratory, celebratory tradition of the essay tradition" ("Re: Video"). Banks's performance, then, is a multimodal essay, meeting his challenge to extend beyond formulaic essay templates while fulfilling Hesse's call for the continued presence of essayistic writing. Said another way, essayistic writing is not strictly limited to print-based text. Indeed, as Harris notes in this volume, with the Web, writers can incorporate nonprint sources to illustrate as well as to analyze. Harris proposes that "we can 'leverage or resist' the affordances of the Web to re-invigorate how we teach a form of writing, the critical essay, that has long been part of a dissenting tradition of work in the academy." Likewise, Santosh Khadka presents a "re-imagination" of essayist coursework that offers "multiple essay forms, multiple writing styles, multiple modes and mediums of writing, and multiple presentation patterns incorporated into it." This multiplicity is additive rather than subtractive and fosters a "shuttling ability" that enables writers "to move back and forth between differing essay forms, discourse styles, writing modes, and/or organization patterns, as the writing situation demands." Writers should be able to switch, then, between writing essays in print, as well as new digital media, and back again.

Process-Product Binary

Discussions of multimodality often focus on labeling and theorizing the final composing product. As my analysis of the augmented reality assignment sequence in the next section shows, and as is common in many writing assignments, composing relies on composing. By this, I mean that writing relies upon prewriting or invention activities that take a variety of writing forms, ranging from freewritings to brainstorms to drafts and ultimately reflection essays. In other words, the entire writing process makes use of multiple writing genres in support of the final product. Prior proposes we look for multimodality not only in specific texts—such as the end product—but also in "chains of genre" that include diagrams, talking notes, planning drafts, annotations, and so forth ("From Speech" 18). While such texts are often occluded by a focus on the end product, they are nonetheless multimodal texts in and of themselves. Thus, multimodality is not merely a quality located in the final product but is present throughout the entire composing process.

An Augmented Reality Composing Assignment

To support my contention that alphabetic writing is intrinsic to digital media, I explore augmented reality specifically through a unit I have used in my first-year writing courses and in my Writing for the Workplace and for Public Audiences class. Analyzing the work in this module reveals that alphabetic writing is integrated throughout AR. As Banks challenges us to think about preparing for composing beyond the computer, AR has already presented us with capabilities for composing using such wearable devices as Google Glass (Tham; Tham et al.; Hall). Much as Shipka has complicated the idea that multimodality is not exclusively the domain of the digital (*Toward a Composition* and "Including"), I consider through AR how the alphabetic is not exclusively the domain of print or traditional media. Instead, emerging new media may help us see what has been otherwise naturalized in the media with which we have long familiarity. The conceptual tendency to focus on multimodality as more than alphabetic print has diminished the awareness of the linguistic throughout digital composing.

Defining Augmented Reality

Augmented reality is the addition of digital text to an audience's surroundings. My definition of AR draws from Paul Milgram and Fumio Kishino's reality-virtuality continuum from 1994, which taxonomizes digital representation technologies. Differentiating technologies based on the user's perception of their surrounding actuality, this continuum situates digital realities by placing reality on one pole and virtuality on the opposite pole. Virtual reality texts immerse the audience in a fully constructed digital text often by relying on head-mounted viewing displays that block the user's visual and auditory perception of their physical environment. Closer to reality and further from virtuality, augmented reality presents users with a combination of text and their surroundings. When users interact with AR, they use a technology, such as smart glasses or a smartphone or tablet screen, that shows the user's actual location overlaid with digital text.

An augmented reality assignment might seem an unlikely presence in a writing classroom. Skepticism about a digital medium's relation with writing is not unfamiliar. For example, although expectations might suggest the contrary, Madeleine Sorapure finds writing integrated into *Adobe Flash* composing. Sorapure contends that this multimodal content technology offers ways to see the "definition of writing stretched and transformed" and identifies four categories—text, image, code, and comment—that define and shape writing (413). Even in the very visual *Flash* medium, Sorapure locates alphabetic text displayed visibly on screen, as well as in the comments *Flash* authors leave in their code. Thus, Sorapure indicates how alphabetic writing is used in one digital environment in both product and process. Examining an authoring technology such as *Flash* means "we can come to a better understanding of the new directions in which writing is moving" (428). I likewise see alphabetic writing in AR and promote continual engagement with changing authoring technologies. In an era of changing media, this understanding of alphabetic writing in both process and product becomes increasingly important.

Augmented Reality Unit

In my class assignments, students design an AR video that an end user triggers to view information about the user's local environment. To support student AR composing, I incorporate in my courses a scaffolded unit on augmented reality. The unit begins with readings on multimodality and multiliteracy and then provides multiple encounters with AR texts. After students become experienced with viewing and analyzing short AR texts in class, they next proceed to analyzing an AR text—in this case, the most popular augmented reality game to date: *Pokémon GO*. In this mobile gaming app, players collect virtual creatures by interacting with on-screen maps while also moving through their physical surroundings. Students apply the class readings on multimodality to identify the modes present in *Pokémon GO*. Although this smartphone game might seem to rely on the visual mode of the smartphone screen, students notice, for example, a range of sound effects and music involving the aural mode, the spatial mode presenting in both the digital depictions of maps and users' experiences in walking through their surroundings, and linguistic text in on-screen messages, menus, status updates, and embedded photographs. This multimodal analysis facilitates attention to the interweaving of alphabetic writing with other modes in augmented reality.

After students complete their AR analyses, the unit next calls for them to author their own AR text. This assignment guides students to create a video about the history of a campus building, addressed to an audience interested in the history of the campus, that draws on the university archives and is triggered by a specific AR software application. To fulfill the assignment, students need to briefly perform library research, create an informative video using the technology of their choice, upload their video to the AR software, and associate a trigger image that will initiate the video in the AR software.

Though some might question the role of a video project in a writing class, the AR project is writing intensive. In contending that multimodal composition is not limited to the digital but also includes more material, nondigital composing, Shipka notes that when she presents multimodal composing in faculty workshops, she's often asked, "Where's the writing?" (*Toward a Composition* 2–3, 140). Likewise, for digital composing, when I hear the question "Where's the writing?" I answer, "Throughout both the composing process and product," as my next section demonstrates.

Where's the Writing?

The augmented reality assignment requires multiple deliverables that ultimately support a video that the audience views in situ on a smartphone or tablet. This assignment sequence simultaneously incorporates and supports both the alphabetic and multimodal, as well as print and digital media, in the final product as well as in the process to build the AR.

After students have become familiar with augmented reality by viewing multiple AR projects and analyzing *Pokémon GO*, the unit next calls on students to design the grading rubric themselves (Adsanatham; Sabatino and Blevins). Students build these rubrics based on their analyses of AR projects and the assignment requirement to create an AR video about the history of a building, site, statue, or other significant object on campus. Students next visit the library's university archives to learn about archival research. They engage in freewriting and brainstorming to determine for which campus subject they want to create AR media. After deciding on their topic, they write up their research notes and create a visual design plan for integrating their research and citations using storyboards (Hocks; Córdova). They workshop these in class and then submit them for instructor feedback. Students write scripts to ensure smooth spoken delivery of their research in their video narration. Throughout this process, students create freewritings, lists, research notes, annotations, design plans and storyboards, scripts, peer-review memos, and more. While none of these texts are visible in their final product, they are all contributors to the completed AR compositions.

Such AR process documents represent "chains of genre," to use Prior's terminology. Multimodality arises, as Prior argues, "not only when a particular text/performance is realized materially in multiple media";

"[m]ore fundamentally, every text, every utterance, is multimodal as it must involve a mix of inner and outer semiotics" ("From Speech" 24). Prior articulates how, through his concept of "mediated multimodal genre systems," we can see multimodality present in more than just specific texts; multimodality is also visible through the process of developing and using these "productive chains of discourse" (28), and in the consciousness of people and externalized artifacts and actions (24). While students' final AR products incorporate alphabetic writing, alphabetic writing also is used throughout the AR process. Shipka emphasizes understanding multimodality less through product and more through process: "To label a text multimodal or monomodal based on its final appearance alone discounts, or worse yet, renders invisible the contributions made by a much wider variety of resources, supports, and tools. . . . [I]t masks the fundamentally multimodal aspects of all communicative practice" (*Toward a Composition* 52).

As I have described elsewhere (Blevins), when their projects function, students' augmented reality assignment products result in AR videos that display on the audience's digital device after the AR software recognizes the physical trigger image—such as a building's identifying sign. These videos incorporate student narration, digital music, and sound effects, as well as various combinations of those audio elements. The project visuals include contemporary photographs and moving images that the students create, as well as digitized historical images downloaded from the library archives, which students crop, arrange, and otherwise adjust for visual display on-screen. Although some projects result in essentially slideshow narrations similar to in-class presentations, other final products function as video essays that feature introductions, substantive content, and conclusions. These projects make claims about a building's or other artifact's importance, the historical significance of campus namesakes, and contemporary, past, and sometimes future campus usage. In their final products, the students take on the role of experts based on their research and personal experience. In doing so, they transition from prospective students who were recently led around the university by campus tour guides to themselves offering guidance about the university and its history and social environment. These AR compositions combine media, modes, and materials to attempt to evoke community and engage their audiences by making connections between campus residents of the past and those in the present.

While alphabetic writing is integral to the AR video process, alphabetic text appears throughout students' AR products: the trigger images and the completed videos. Most videos feature linguistic messages; students purposefully place on-screen words into their videos through titles and required citations, as well as captions, textual emphasis, and quotes. They also embed images that contain alphabetic text, such as video footage and photographs of building signs, engravings, labels, tags, and so forth. Because the AR videos in my courses use visual images to initiate playback in the AR viewing software, the trigger image often contains alphabetic writing, generally through names on signs. Thus, while augmented reality may resemble here a primarily visual medium, it clearly incorporates the alphabetic.

In his famous "The Rhetoric of the Image," Roland Barthes articulates not only how images function rhetorically but also how images and words operate together in combination. While his essay preceded the articulation of multiliteracy, Barthes clearly makes an argument about both visual and multimodal rhetoric. In analyzing a one-page color advertisement of pasta products, Barthes points out that, first, we do not read through language alone, and second, that linguistic messages are present in every image: "as title, caption, accompanying press article, film dialogue, comic strip balloon" (38). Similarly, I find linguistic messages used in my students' videos in both primary text, such as in authored captions, citations, and AR trigger images, as well as through their secondary texts—for example, embedded photographs and graphic images within their videos—that happen to also contain building signs, labels, and so forth.

Although the AR composition might seem primarily concerned with new media, the assignment is an essayistic sequence in both product and process: the AR video, the student-designed rubric, and the reflection essay. Although not in traditional essay format, the AR rubric makes an alpha-numeric argument based on student analysis about the combined attributes a successful AR project has, as well as the baseline features for a minimally effective AR video.

In their completed AR videos, students try out ideas and composing strategies, making claims and offering images and clips that sometimes illustrate and document but other times offer additive analysis and commentary, as Harris (in his essay for this collection) notes in his students' digital essay writing. The AR contends with an audience that is not distant from the textual subject, but is located in the same physical area as the video's topic, offering a potential for extended conversation outside the digital medium. These AR video essays offer a form of writing that demonstrates Khadka's claim that the essay "is not necessarily a static and stilted text form, but . . . capable of accommodating multiple media and discourse styles . . ."

After students complete their videos and test their AR content, they write a reflection essay (Yancey, *Reflection*). This reflection essay prompts students to evaluate their work regarding what they see as strengths, what they see as opportunities for revision, and what they want to remember about composing AR in the future. In other words, students use alphabetic writing to engage in critical reflection about their digital composing process, both in evaluation of past practices and in anticipation of their future composing. In the spirit of the *essayer*, the trying out, this reflection essay provides space for students to describe how they successfully attempted to compose a perhaps unfamiliar argument or in an unfamiliar medium, even if ultimately their work did not produce a functioning AR video or a structure that satisfied them. The reflection essay allows students to recognize their composing processes—for this project and their future writing, whether in this medium or another.

Beyond Augmented Reality

The AR assignment embraces Yancey's challenge to take up composing "not only in words," but, as I have shown here, also in words. However, I would be remiss if I did not address how augmented reality is an emerging medium, and, in both composing and experiencing technologies, AR is subject to rapid change. Ongoing change describes composing in the contemporary context. As Banks contends, "[W]riting, communication, [and] composing, are always technologized" (275), and recent technology change has accelerated.

Deborah Brandt reminds us that literacy has rapidly proliferated and diversified through the twentieth and early twenty-first centuries, and that literacy has not been stable; indeed, she contends that "[l]iteracy is always in flux" (104). I acknowledge here and to my students that AR is a "medium in the making" (Morey and Tinnell 3), one very much subject to flux as an evolving medium. Thus, I engage in explicit conversations with students about how to compose in an unfamiliar medium (whether through the novelty of an emerging or changing medium), such as by engaging in analysis of models, and also prompt students to critically reflect on their composition processes to aid them with their current and future work. Further, I emphasize, as this collection maintains, that alphabetic writing is intrinsic to, not opposed to, these changes. We can draw on our prior experience with writing to compose in an era of evolving communication technologies.

The process focus on the AR assignment supports engagement in active analysis and critical thinking that helps students complete the AR product and plan future compositions. Having students develop their own rubric provides them with facilities in critically analyzing examples and then making determinations about their expectations regarding the products they want to create. As noted previously, a key component of my AR assignment is planning for future media and their resultant change through a seemingly ironic component: the reflection piece. Yancey notes that reflection is not merely a process of looking back:

> Procedurally, reflection entails a *looking forward* to goals we might attain, as well as a *casting backward* to see where we have been. When we reflect, we thus *project* and *review*, often putting the projections and the reviews in *dialogue* with each other, working dialectically as we seek to *discover* what we know, what we have learned, and what we might understand. (*Reflection* 6)

I contend that having students engage in the alphabetic reflection essay helps them prepare for future emerging media as much as composing their new media products in augmented reality. It is through their reflections that they look to the past to look to the future to try out new media and to attempt new ideas and connections.

Toward a Future of Writing

My essay here is not necessarily an argument to teach augmented reality as a specific digital media assignment in all courses, but instead contends that instructors and students alike can prepare for AR composing through familiarity with alphabetic writing. Further, my exploration here serves as a demonstration of the ways in which digital media assignments support alphabetic writing as an integral part of multimodal composing. Incorporation of AR does, of course, prepare students for a particular form of digital composing; as this essay demonstrates, such an assignment sequence also prepares students for composing using alphabetic writing, in both product and process. We remain in the rapid era of change that provoked the New London Group to theorize multiliteracy and Yancey to call for understanding composition in a new "key" ("Made"). Instructors who incorporate AR assignments as an authentic part of their classroom exploration of writing in all its modes, media, and genres can find that their students will engage in not only multimodal and digital writing but also alphabetic writing.

The future of writing is one in which composers must navigate and negotiate between the multiple possibilities available in modes, media, and genres—those that already exist and those that are yet to arise. As such, writers will continue to be called upon to essay, or to attempt, new combinations of mode, media, and genre. Rather than viewing, consciously or unconsciously, alphabetic and digital compositions as dichotomous, we must view the alphabetic and the multimodal as one and the same in both digital and print environments. Much as Barthes noted decades ago in discussing mid-twentieth-century mass media, alphabetic writing is integrated into new media. Students can apply their existing alphabetic writing knowledge in composing new media texts.

In discussing the presence of alphabetic writing in new digital media, I am not making an argument for the direct transfer, per se, of all alphabetic writing skills into new media composing, although I believe, as Dànielle DeVoss and coauthors note, transfer is important (209). However, as Cheryl Ball and coathors observe, transfer of alphabetic expectations into new media composing does not proceed unproblematically. Thus, I join with Michael-John DePalma's call for additional research related to transfer across media, to gain better understanding of how composers engage in transfer across modes and media. Although there is more to study in a changing media environment, I see the continued importance of alphabetic writing and new media composing, much as Harris (in this collection) and Khadka support the continuation of essay writing in digital and multimedia contexts. Thus, I support composing as a both-and-more approach: composing in new media, composing in traditional media, and challenging ourselves to think beyond simplistic dichotomies, whether alphabetic-multimodal, print-digital, or process-product. Recognizing the continuing role of alphabetic writing in new media composing can provide instructors and students alike with awareness of the multiple modes present in digital media in process and product. Further, such recognition may also help instructors and administrators counter concerns related to new media assignments, providing them support to articulate that even when students are developing new media compositions, they are still working with alphabetic writing.

The late age of print (Bolter) in which the screen rises to dominance (Kress, *Literacy*) is an era of media change. While this essay has noted the emergence of more broadly available virtual reality and augmented reality, it remains difficult to predict what new media may arise next. As Banks's 2015 CCCC address reminds, change is inevitable and we should be prepared for how writing changes or does not change when our familiar computers go the way of the typewriter (274). This media flux will spur questions such as, What does a writing assignment look like? How do we teach composing across multiple media? How much writing do we need to see in the final product? How and when do we respond to changing genres and composition technologies? We should be prepared to address those questions because "[t]echnology is what we do, or what we need to do, not just because literacy is always technologized, . . . but because of the big picture technological issues that are always brought to bear on all facets of our lives and work" (Banks 274). We should address those questions to understand the future of writing. If Barthes's examination of the advertisement as a particular genre in the particular medium of the print magazine and my subsequent consideration of the appearance of AR videos can be seen as guides, future new media composing will continue to incorporate alphabetic writing in both product and process. New media provide opportunities to try out not only new composing technologies but also expanded ways to attempt ideas and to explore new possibilities in and about writing.

Works Cited

Adsanatham, Chanon. "Integrating Assessment and Instruction: Using Student-Generated Grading Criteria to Evaluate Multimodal Digital Projects." *Computers and Composition*, vol. 29, no. 2, June 2012, pp. 152–74.

Ball, Cheryl E., and Colin Charlton. "All Writing Is Multimodal." *Naming What We Know: Threshold Concepts in Writing Studies*, edited by Linda Adler-Kassner and Elizabeth Wardle, Utah State UP, 2015, pp. 42–43.

Ball, Cheryl E., et al. "Genre and Transfer in a Multimodal Composition Class." Bowen and Whithaus, pp. 15–36.

Banks, Adam. "2015 CCCC Chair's Address: Ain't No Walls behind the Sky, Baby! Funk, Flight, Freedom." *College Composition and Communication*, vol. 67, no. 2, Dec. 2015, pp. 267–79.

Barthes, Roland. "The Rhetoric of the Image." 1964. *Image-Music-Text*, translated by Stephen Heath, Hill and Wang, 1977, pp. 32–51.

Blevins, Brenta. "Teaching Digital Literacy Composing Concepts: Focusing on the Layers of Augmented Reality in an Era of Changing Technology." *Computers and Composition*, vol. 50, Dec. 2018, pp. 21–38.

Bolter, Jay David. *Writing Space: The Computer, Hypertext, and the History of Writing*. Lawrence Erlbaum Associates, 1991.

Bowen, Tracey, and Carl Whithaus, editors. *Multimodal Literacies and Emerging Genres*. U of Pittsburgh P, 2013.

Brandt, Deborah. *Literacy in American Lives*. Cambridge UP, 2001.

Ceraso, Steph. "(Re)educating the Senses: Multimodal Listening, Bodily Learning, and the Composition of Sonic Experiences." *College English*, vol. 77, no. 2, Nov. 2014, pp. 102–23.

Cope, Bill, and Mary Kalantzis. *Multiliteracies: Literacy Learning and the Design of Social Futures*. Routledge, 2000.

Córdova, Nathaniel I. "Invention, Ethos, and New Media in the Rhetoric Classroom: The Storyboard as Exemplary Genre." Bowen and Whithaus, pp. 143–63.

DePalma, Michael-John. "Tracing Transfer across Media: Investigating Writers' Perceptions of Cross-Contextual and Rhetorical Reshaping in Processes of Remediation." *College Composition and Communication*, vol. 66, no. 4, June 2015, pp. 615–42.

DeVoss, Dànielle, et al. "The Future of Literacy." *Literate Lives in the Information Age: Narratives of Literacy from the United States*, edited by Cynthia L. Selfe and Gail E. Hawisher, Lawrence Erlbaum Associates, 2004, pp. 183–210.

George, Diana. "From Analysis to Design: Visual Communication in the Teaching of Writing." *College Composition and Communication*, vol. 54, no. 1, Sept. 2002, pp. 11–39.

Hall, Ralph P. "Teaching Using Google Glass and Apps." *The Journal of Interactive Technology and Pedagogy*, 2 June 2014, jitp.commons.gc.cuny .edu/teaching-using-google-glass-and-apps/.

Hawisher, Gail E., and Cynthia L. Selfe, editors. *Passions, Pedagogies, and Twenty-First-Century Technologies*. Utah State UP / NCTE, 1999.

Hesse, Douglas. "Re: Video of Banks' Talk?" *WPA-L Listserv / Arizona State University*, 25 Mar. 2015, 1:19 p.m., lists.asu.edu/cgi-bin/wa?A2=ind1503&L=WPA-L&F=&S=&P=488844.

———. "Saving a Place for Essayistic Literacy." Hawisher and Selfe, pp. 34–48.

Hocks, Mary E. "Understanding Visual Rhetoric in Digital Writing Environments." *College Composition and Communication*, vol. 54, no. 4, June 2003, pp. 629–56.

Khadka, Santosh. "(Teaching) Essayist Literacy in the Multimedia World." *Composition Forum*, vol. 32, Fall 2015, compositionforum.com/issue/32/essayist-literacy.php.

Klein, Michael J., and Kristi L. Shackelford. "Beyond Black on White: Document Design and Formatting in the Writing Classroom." *Writing Spaces: Readings on Writing*, edited by Charles Lowe and Pavel Zemliansky, vol. 2, Parlor Press, 2011, writingspaces.org/klein-schackleford--beyond-black-on-white.

Kress, Gunther R. "'English' at the Crossroads: Rethinking Curricula of Communication in the Context of the Turn to the Visual." Hawisher and Selfe, pp. 66–88.

———. *Literacy in the New Media Age*. Routledge, 2003.

———. "Multimodality." Cope and Kalantzis, pp. 179–200.

Milgram, Paul, and Fumio Kishino. "A Taxonomy of Mixed Reality Visual Displays." *IEICE Transactions on Information and Systems*, vol. E77-D, no. 12, Dec. 1994, pp. 1321–29.

Morey, Sean, and John Tinnell, editors. *Augmented Reality: Innovative Perspectives across Art, Industry, and Academia*. Parlor Press, 2017.

The New London Group. "A Pedagogy of Multiliteracies: Designing Social Futures." *Harvard Educational Review*, vol. 66, no. 1, Spring 1996, pp. 60–92.

Palmeri, Jason. *Remixing Composition: A History of Multimodal Writing Pedagogy*. Southern Illinois UP / NCTE, 2012.

Prior, Paul. "From Speech Genres to Mediated Multimodal Genre Systems: Bakhtin, Voloshinov, and the Question of Writing." *Genre in a Changing World*, edited by Charles Bazerman, et al., The WAC Clearinghouse / Parlor Press, 2009, pp. 17–34, wac.colostate.edu/docs/books/genre/.

———. "Moving Multimodality beyond the Binaries: A Response to Gunther Kress' 'Gains and Losses.'" *Computers and Composition*, vol. 22, no. 1, Dec. 2005, pp. 23–30.

Sabatino, Lindsay Ann, and Brenta Blevins. "Initiating Multimodal Training: Faculty Development for Creating and Assessing Assignments." *Designing and Implementing Multimodal Curricula and Programs*, edited by J. C. Lee and Santosh Khadka, Routledge, 2018, pp. 125–38.

Selfe, Cynthia L. "The Movement of Air, the Breath of Meaning: Aurality and Multimodal Composing." *College Composition and Communication*, vol. 60, no. 4, June 2009, pp. 616–63.

———. "Toward New Media Texts: Taking Up the Challenges of Visual Literacy." *Writing New Media: Theory and Applications for Expanding the Teaching of Composition*, edited by Anne Frances Wysocki et al., Utah State UP, 2004, pp. 67–110.

Shipka, Jody. "Including, but Not Limited to, the Digital: Composing Multimedia Texts." Bowen and Whithaus, pp. 73–89.

———. *Toward a Composition Made Whole*. U of Pittsburgh P, 2011.

Sorapure, Madeleine. "Text, Image, Code, Comment: Writing in Flash." *Computers and Composition*, vol. 23, no. 4, 2006, pp. 412–29.

Tham, Jason Chew Kit. "Wearable Writing: Enriching Student Peer Review with Point-of-View Video Feedback Using Google Glass." *Journal of Technical Writing and Communication*, vol. 47, no. 1, Jan. 2017, pp. 22–55.

Tham, Jason, et al. "Glass in Class: Writing with Google Glass." *The Journal of Interactive Technology and Pedagogy*, 26 Apr. 2016, jitp.commons.gc.cuny.edu/glass-in-class-writing-with-google-glass/.

Wysocki, Anne Frances. "The Multiple Media of Texts: How Onscreen and Paper Texts Incorporate Words, Images, and Other Media." *What Writing Does and How It Does It: An Introduction to Analyzing Text and Textual Practices*, edited by Charles Bazerman and Paul Prior, Lawrence Erlbaum and Associates, 2003, pp. 123–63.

Yancey, Kathleen Blake. "Made Not Only in Words: Composition in a New Key." *College Composition and Communication*, vol. 56, no. 2, Dec. 2004, pp. 297–328.

———. *Reflection in the Writing Classroom*. Utah State UP, 1998.

Part Three

Modality and Writing Program Administration

Positioning Writing: An Analysis of Textbook Arguments about Multimodality

Hilary A. Sarat-St. Peter and Elizabeth G. Allan

Many instructors employ textbooks to facilitate, organize, and expand students' literacy practices. In a 2006 survey on integrating multimodality into the college writing classroom, a majority of writing instructors reported using a textbook to "support the teaching of multimodal composition" (Anderson et al. 64). Now, more than a decade later, we ask which of these textbooks has persisted in multiple editions and whether the most recent updates might reveal a shift in the composing practices that are explicitly and implicitly recognized and rewarded. How do these textbooks sponsor (Brandt, "Sponsors" and *Literacy*) the production of alphabetic text, image, music, and video? To what extent have the "dynamic relationships" among modes (New London Group 80) changed across multiple editions of these textbooks? We found that even as the textbooks in our sample include multiple modes and media, they also regulate and constrain students' use of those media. For instance, although alphabetic text is itself multimodal (Palmeri 9), most of the textbooks we analyzed created an implicit binary between alphabetic and nonalphabetic modes. Our findings shed light on the complex role that textbooks play in sponsoring multimodal composing practices—a role that students and instructors might endorse, subvert, or resist in the context of the college writing classroom.

About Sponsorship

As Deborah Brandt has defined them, *sponsors* are "any agents, local or distant, concrete or abstract, who enable, support, teach, model, as well as recruit, regulate, suppress, or withhold literacy—and gain advantage by it in some way" ("Sponsors" 166). The sponsors of literacy include human agents, such as teachers, as well as a variety of resources including books, clubs, texts, toys, and writing tools (Brandt, "Sponsors"; Cushman). Sponsorship's most overt function is supportive; sponsors serve as "delivery systems" that bring literacy to the public (Brandt, "Sponsors" 167). Sponsors also deliver the "ideological freight" that people must accept in exchange for access to literacy—just as sports teams that receive corporate funding wear a corporate logo on their jerseys (168). Because literacy is a "profit-bearing resource" (Brandt, *Literacy* 191), sponsorship is regulatory. Sponsors compete for the opportunity to commodify, constrain, and control literacy. However, despite sponsors' agendas, many readers and writers are adept at using literacy in "subversively liberatory ways" (Brandt, "Sponsors" 168). Thus, the concept of sponsorship provides an "explicit and substantive" link between literacy and economic opportunity (169); it is at once enabling, ideological, regulatory, and subversive.

About the Multimodal Turn

Although it may not use the term *sponsorship*, scholarship about the multimodal turn does illuminate the delivery systems that present multimodal composition to students. For example, our present sociocultural milieu supplies tools and practices for multimodal composition. Kathleen Blake Yancey argues that the proliferation of multimodal platforms has brought about the "creation of a writing public" on a massive scale that parallels the emergence of a literate public in previous centuries (298). Gunther Kress highlights two key technological shifts related to multimodality: the "medium of the screen," which integrates multiple modes of representation, and the particular prominence of image within that medium (6). Such large-scale changes permeate local communities differently and unequally (Selfe). The sociocultural systems that deliver multimodality interact in diverse and unpredictable ways with specific readers and writers.

As composition studies has tracked these large-scale changes, many scholars have identified the ideological freight delivered by the theoretical terms we use to talk about multimodality. Cynthia Selfe and Gail Hawisher use the term *multimodal literacy* to signal the "enormous importance" of multimodal reading and writing practices (1). However, as Pegeen Reichert Powell argues in this collection, the term *multimodal* is problematic because it evokes a "progress narrative" (citing Palmeri). The term *literacy* is similarly troublesome. Since it evokes a "bundle" of assumptions derived from alphabetic text, characterizing multimodality as *literacy* obscures "other possibilities . . . for expressing our relationships with and within technologies" (Wysocki and Johnson-Eilola 349). Claire Lauer notes that some composition instructors prefer *multimedia*, a "gateway term" that allows them to "interface in familiar ways with their students and those outside of academia" (226). The multimodal turn has yet to establish a stable vocabulary; it recycles and appropriates an eclectic variety of terms that ship diverse ideological freight.

The pedagogically diverse college writing classroom (Fulkerson 655) is perhaps the most strategically designed system for delivering current literacy practices to readers and writers. Multimodal composition pedagogies, including innovative ways to evaluate multimodal work, have evolved alongside students' existing multimodal composing practices (Ball, "Designerly," "Assessing"; Gee; Selfe and Hawisher). Noting that some multimodal writing pedagogies treat visual media as mere supplements to the written word, Diana George has advocated pedagogies that promote visual media as technologies for meaning-making in their own right (32). Similarly, Selfe has called for heightened attention to aurality in the teaching of writing. Such inventive pedagogical practices resist an alphabet-centric conceptualization of multimodal literacy—a "*words-plus* model of multimodality," in which multiplying media becomes merely redundant (Allan 237).

As multimodal composition pedagogy evolves, we would expect textbooks' sponsorship role to change as well. Textbooks dance an "intricate quadrille" with instructors, students, and cultural contexts (Connors 178). Despite the ubiquity of textbooks, they are undertheorized artifacts that occupy an "equivocal status" in writing-related disciplines (Gale and Gale 4). Like all delivery systems, textbooks are problematic artifacts; they simultaneously enable, influence, constrain, and regulate the literacy practices that they sponsor. Even textbooks that claim to put forward "expansive notions" of the writing process often constrain students' writing practices (Knoblauch 244). According to Aubrey Schiavone, textbooks' assignment prompts regulate students' writing practices by encouraging "the production of [alphabetic] text and the consumption of visual and multimodal artifacts" (359). In a survey by Daniel Anderson and coauthors on integrating multimodality into the writing classroom, sixty percent of writing instructors reported using textbooks to teach multimodal writing, yet only nineteen percent of respondents were "very satisfied" with the textbooks they used (76). This dissatisfaction, we argue, is rooted in the complex sponsorship that these textbooks exert in the context of pedagogically diverse college classrooms.

Method

To investigate how textbooks sponsor multimodal writing, we analyzed a sample set of textbooks identified as resources for multimodal writing pedagogy in the survey by Anderson and his coauthors. We excluded handbooks and trade publications, books that have no later editions, and books that are no longer offered as "new" by the publisher or by major booksellers. The resulting sample set included the following:

Everything's an Argument (3rd edition, 2004, by Andrea Lunsford and John Ruszkiewicz; 7th edition, 2016, by Lunsford, Ruszkiewicz, and Keith Walters)

Seeing and Writing 2 (2nd edition, 2003) and *Seeing and Writing 4* (4th edition, 2010) by Donald and Christine McQuade

IX: Visual Exercises (1st edition, 2004, CD-ROM, by Cheryl E. Ball and Kristin L. Arola) and *Writer/Designer* (1st edition, 2014, by Arola, Jennifer Sheppard, and Ball, which includes *IX: Visualizing Composition 2.0* by Ball and Arola—the 2nd edition of *IX: Visual Exercises*, which was published separately in 2010)

We refer to each textbook by title and edition number in the discussion below.

We examined how each textbook recognizes and rewards composing practices such as the production of alphabetic and nonalphabetic texts. Independently, we used descriptive coding to analyze sample passages from textbooks. After comparing preliminary results, we collaboratively developed analytical codes, which we then applied iteratively through the constant comparative method (Hesse-Biber and Leavy).

We began by analyzing prefatory material addressed to instructors to identify the authors' theoretical perspectives and the arguments the textbooks make about various composing practices. These explicit and implicit arguments reveal the ideological freight that the textbooks deliver along with writing instruction. We compared the instructor-focused arguments with the arguments made in the introductory chapters or prefaces addressed to students. We then analyzed each edition's table of contents to determine how the textbook positions alphabetic text in relation to image, music, and video. The organizational structure of each edition reveals the extent to which the textbook both encourages and regulates multimodal composing—by consigning nonalphabetic modes to special sections or chapters, for example.

Finally, we selected key instructional passages that explicitly invite students to produce multimodal texts and compared them to instructional material that calls for alphabetic writing. We analyzed how each textbook signals the relative value of alphabetic and nonalphabetic texts.

Delivering Ideological Freight: Textbooks' Explicit and Implicit Arguments

The sections that follow describe themes that emerged from our analysis of prefatory material, such as progress narratives, arguments that justify the inclusion of nonalphabetic modes, and the use or disuse of widely recognized terminology.

Seeing and Writing, *2nd and 4th Editions*

The prefaces to *Seeing and Writing* (2nd and 4th editions, both by McQuade and McQuade) introduce and explicate the textbook's overarching theme: the "interrelationship between the verbal and the visual" (ix). The preface to the second edition includes sixteen passages related to this theme. These passages present two interconnected arguments about multimodality: the explicit argument that seeing and writing are separate but related processes, and the implicit argument that seeing is a means to effective writing. The preface reads: "The second edition of *Seeing and Writing* strengthens our commitment to helping students improve their analytic and compositional skills by treating seriously the connection between the verbal and the visual in today's culture" (vii). By focusing on the visual at the expense of other modes (e.g., sound, video) and by positing a binary relation between the verbal and visual, *Seeing and Writing* reinforces the persistent assumption that monomodality is possible. Other passages expand upon this binary, instrumental relation. "Seeing" is closely related to the process of analyzing the "images, photographs, paintings, sculptures, cartoons, as well as cultural artifacts" and other multimodal resources included in the textbook (ix). However, the purpose of such analytical exercises is to "provide engaging prompts" for the production of "essays" and other alphabetic text genres (ix).

The preface to *Seeing and Writing* exhibits only minor changes from the second to the fourth edition. The preface to the fourth edition is shorter (six versus fourteen pages) and is presented in a smaller font; it also includes comic-book-style profile pictures of the authors (xi). The preface explicates the textbook's objective ("to give seeing and writing equal attention") and reiterates its core argument that careful seeing (analyzing the visual materials provided) is instrumental to writing (vi). Schiavone, who also analyzed *Seeing and Writing 4*, calls this the "consume-in-order-to-produce approach," which she views as more linear than binary (365).

In comparison with the preface to the second edition, the preface to the fourth edition calls more attention to its student-friendliness. The bulk of the preface provides an overview of revisions to the textbook suggested by teachers and students. Nine passages highlight the "rhetorical variety" of visual and verbal materials as a means of "engaging" students (vii)—thus making the implicit argument that multimodality is student-friendly.

Everything's an Argument, *3rd and 7th Editions*

The prefaces to both editions of *Everything's an Argument* (3rd and 7th editions) justify the inclusion of multimodal materials and frame these materials in terms of the textbook's thematic focus: argument. The third edition positions alphabetic text and other modes in a commutative partnership in which multiple modes offer "diverse" opportunities for analyzing and crafting arguments (Lunsford and Ruszkiewicz vii). The preface to the third edition includes seven passages related to multimodality, most of which highlight the "visual arguments" and other "visual media" included in the edition, conflating multimodality with the visual (vi–vii). These passages enumerate the affordances of including visual media, which are characterized as "fresh" and "student-friendly," offering opportunities for students to "recognize and respond to a more diverse range of arguments" (vii). The visual materials included in the third edition represent progress, appeal to students, and connect the textbook to a rhetorical tradition (vi).

The arguments about multimodality presented in the preface to the seventh edition are more diverse, numerous, and explicit. The preface includes twenty passages related to multimodality, many of which highlight the edition's "enhanced attention to media" (Lunsford et al. vii). Notably, the edition has dropped the qualifier *visual* from the term *media*, implicitly expanding the concept of multimodality beyond the visual. One recurring theme that appears in sixteen of these twenty passages is diversity; the edition includes "texts of every kind" (ix), capturing "rhetorical opportunities students encounter across a range of media, both in and out of school" (vii). Related to diversity is the theme of progress, which appears in nine passages. By diversifying the included materials, the edition has "advanced our game," thus "keeping up" with cultural and political changes (vii).

IX: Visual Exercises *CD Cover (1st Edition)*

The cover of the *IX: Visual Exercises* CD includes prefatory material that is geared toward an audience of instructors. The title explicitly emphasizes the visual, and the cover reinforces this association by highlighting "visual rhetoric," "visual elements," and "helping students visualize" (Ball and Arola). The remainder of the CD cover makes three arguments about multimodal pedagogy. The first is an explicit argument that instruction in visual rhetoric requires multimodal delivery, "because there are things you just can't do in a book." The text's "illustrated definitions," "interactive assignments," and other multimodal instructional materials are presented as a more effective way to teach visual rhetoric. Ironically, despite drawing attention to the constraints of traditional textbooks, the CD cover argues that *IX: Visual Exercises* "can be packaged with any Bedford/St. Martin's textbook."

Writer/Designer *(Including* IX: Visualizing Composition 2.0*)*

Compared to the other textbooks we analyzed, *Writer/Designer* by Arola, Sheppard, and Ball provides the most explicit rationale for multimodal pedagogy. At least twenty passages of the preface present at least ten distinct arguments about multimodality. Two arguments recur with particular frequency and intensity: instructors require expert guidance to teach multimodal composition, and multimodal composing consists of strategies that can be taught to students. The first argument is evident in eight passages that name the textbook's theoretical influences, which include the New London Group (vi–vii), Lev Vygotsky's concept of scaffolding (viii), and Michigan Technological University's first-year writing program (vii).

The second argument is evident in eleven passages detailing the "guidance and activities" that *Writer/Designer* provides for students, including multimodal assignments, analytical heuristics, and "process-focused activities" (viii). The preface notes that the bibliography contains "further rationales about the value and significance of multimodality" (v).

Table 1 summarizes the arguments about alphabetic text and multimodality that we found in our data set. These arguments represent the ideological freight that the textbooks deliver in exchange for literacy. We discovered three major trends in the arguments regarding the positioning of alphabetic and nonalphabetic modalities across all textbooks and editions. First, most of the arguments focus on justifying the inclusion of nonalphabetic modes. The textbooks in our sample ask students and instructors to value nonalphabetic modes and recognize their role within

Table 1. Arguments about Alphabetic Text and Multimodality, by Textbook

	Seeing and Writing (McQuade and McQuade)	
Edition	2nd (2003)	4th (2010)
Argument(s)	Seeing is a means to effective writing	Seeing is a means to effective writing Visual materials are student-friendly
	Everything's an Argument (Lunsford and Ruszkiewicz)	
Edition	3rd (2004)	7th (2015)
Arguments	The term *argument* includes visual media Visual media are student-friendly	The term *argument* includes media of every kind Nonalphabetic modes are student-friendly Multimodality represents progress
	IX: Visual Exercises (Ball and Arola) and *Writer/Designer* (Arola et al.)	
Edition	*IX: Visual Exercises* (2004)	*Writer/Designer* (including *IX: Visualizing Composition 2.0* [2014])
Argument(s)	Instruction in visual rhetoric requires multimodal delivery	Instruction in visual rhetoric requires multimodal delivery Multimodal composing can be taught to students Instructors need expert guidance to teach multimodal composing

the college writing classroom. Second, the textbooks reveal disagreement regarding whether to frame nonalphabetic modes in widely recognized terms (such as *text*, *argument*, and *media*), or to assert that nonalphabetic modes require new approaches to teaching and writing. Such disagreement suggests uncertainty about the degree to which textbooks must evolve along with the multimodal turn. Finally, the prefaces to each edition perpetuate the progress narrative by equating the inclusion of nonalphabetic modes with advancement. Featuring more modes and media enables the textbooks we analyzed to appeal to instructors' perceived need to keep up with the "rise in literacy standards" (see Brandt, "Sponsors" 173).

Positioning Alphabetic and Nonalphabetic Modes: The Organizational Structure of Multimodal Writing Textbooks

The sections that follow outline findings from our analysis of each textbook's organizational structure, including the extent to which each textbook integrates or separates alphabetic and nonalphabetic material.

Seeing and Writing, *2nd and 4th Editions*

The organization of McQuade and McQuade's *Seeing and Writing 2* reflects the textbook's premise that seeing and writing are separate but interconnected processes. The edition consists of ten themed, chapter-like sections, including an introduction for students and two appendices. The first three main chapters present an array of verbal and visual materials related to themes from contemporary American culture (vii). The final two chapters ("Reading Icons" and "Challenging Images") and appendices ("On the Theory and Practice of Seeing" and "On Reading Verbal and Visual Texts") explicitly highlight the visual mode. In addition to these mode-specific chapters, each chapter of the textbook incorporates "features" (recurring subsections) designed to produce meaningful juxtapositions of visual and verbal media (xi). These subsections include photographic chapter dividers, "paired verbal and visual texts" (xi), and a "visualizing composition" feature in each chapter (e.g., 54). Although these features present visual and verbal content within each chapter, the two types of content remain clearly demarcated, thus implying a need to distinguish between alphabetic and nonalphabetic texts.

Much like the second edition, *Seeing and Writing 4* is organized into ten main sections including an introduction, seven chapters, and two appendices. However, this edition reflects two major changes: the removal of two chapters devoted to specific modes and media, and the addition of two chapters focused on American culture: "Confronting Class" and "Taking a Stand" (493–682). The two appendices remain largely unchanged, and the section on "How This Book Works" now offers a visual overview of the textbook's features (xii). New features include "Responding Visually," which consists of special prompts that "offer opportunities to create visual compositions in response to certain selections" (xii). Here, the word *certain* reveals an attempt to position, differentiate, and limit students' use of the visual mode. While most of the prompts in the textbook require students to respond verbally, only "certain selections" call for a visual response (xii).

Everything's an Argument, *3rd and 7th Editions*

Even as *Everything's an Argument* incorporates multimodality-related content, the organization of the third edition constructs a clear separation of content related to alphabetic text and other modes or media. All overt instruction about composing multimodal arguments is contained within one section, entitled "Stylish Argument" (Lunsford and Ruszkiewicz 283). This arrangement relegates multimodality to style. Within the "Stylish Argument" section, three chapters cover specific modes and media: "Visual Arguments" (301), "Spoken Arguments" (338), and "Arguments in Electronic Environments" (331). These chapters include instruction about analyzing and producing arguments in their respective modalities, as well as discussion of sociocultural issues such as "Achieving Visual Literacy" (309). The third edition intersperses visual examples throughout each chapter (e.g., 8); however, apart from these three mode-specific chapters, the book offers little guidance about analyzing and producing multimodal arguments.

The seventh edition reflects an attempt to more fully integrate multimodality-related content throughout the textbook, although much of this instructional content remains consigned to separate chapters and passages. The number of mode-specific chapters is reduced from three to two, and these chapters are in different sections of the textbook. A chapter on "Multimodal Arguments" covers the analysis and production of multimodal arguments (Lunsford et al. 361), while another chapter on "Visual

Rhetoric" covers appeals to logos, pathos, and ethos in visual media (330). Moreover, even the non-mode-specific chapters include subsections that address themes related to multimodality. For example, a recurring feature on "Considering Design and Visuals" appears in each of five chapters covering specific genres of argument: fact-based (164), definitional (197), evaluative (223), causal (255), and proposal (286). However, chapters and passages dedicated to specific modes are always clearly labeled as such, and the rest of the textbook incorporates little multimodality-related content other than the visual examples that adorn the text. Part four on "Research and Arguments" focuses exclusively on alphabetic text and makes no specific mention of multimodal, visual, or spoken arguments (377–503).

IX: Visual Exercises *(CD)*

The organization and design of Ball and Arola's *IX: Visual Exercises* fully integrates alphabetic text with other modes and media. The CD-ROM includes a digital table of contents, which appears in the interface as a grid of nine terms (or pairings of terms) that link to the exercises. The terms themselves capture phenomena that appear across a range of modes and media. Only two of the terms on the grid denote specific modes. The term *text* connotes alphabetic writing, whereas the term *color* connotes visual modes and media. The remaining terms on the grid are relatively mode-neutral: *emphasis* and *contrast*, for example. Moreover, the design of the table of contents reinforces a fluid interrelation between the verbal and visual modes; moving the cursor over the terms rolls them into images. The grid design suggests traditional alphabetic reading patterns for English: left to right, and top to bottom. However, the introduction invites students to "jump in anywhere" and work through the exercises in any order. Thus, the CD edition also gestures toward nonlinear exploration and student autonomy.

Writer/Designer *(Including* IX: Visualizing Composition 2.0*)*

Writer/Designer is organized into eight chapters, each of which covers a stage in the process of completing a multimodal project. Three of the chapter titles include the word *multimodal*, and the rest of the chapter titles employ mode-neutral terms such as *project* and *design*. Content from *IX: Visual Exercises* is presented in the first two chapters as alphabetic text, screenshots, and links to e-pages. Along with explicit support for completing multimodal projects, each chapter provides an array of multimodal examples, including a case study that serves as an extended example of concepts introduced in the chapter. Notably, *Writer/Designer* does not separate academic writing and research from multimodal composition. Even citation conventions are framed as designed artifacts that apply to texts of all types. For example, the "Designing Your Citations" section of the "Working with Multimodal Sources" chapter includes the e-page "How to Cite a Cereal Box in MLA Style" (Arola et al. 70). Each chapter also provides prompts, including a "write/design" assignment (e.g., 19) and a "Process!" exercise (e.g., 6).

Table 2 summarizes our findings about the organizational structure of textbooks in our data set. The structure of each edition reveals how

Table 2. Organizational Structure, by Textbook

	Seeing and Writing (McQuade and McQuade)	
Edition	2nd (2003)	4th (2010)
Organizational structure	Consigns nonalphabetic modes to separate chapters	Incorporates more mode-neutral chapter themes Prompts students to respond visually to "certain" readings
	Everything's an Argument (Lunsford and Ruszkiewicz)	
Edition	3rd (2004)	7th (2015)
Organizational structure	Consigns nonalphabetic modes to a special section Relegates multimodality to style	Disperses mode-specific sections and chapters throughout the textbook Relegates visual rhetoric and multimedia arguments chapters to "Style and Presentation" Excludes nonalphabetic writing from chapters on academic writing and research
	IX: Visual Exercises (Ball and Arola) and *Writer/Designer* (Arola et al.)	
Edition	*IX: Visual Exercises* (2004)	*Writer/Designer* (including *IX: Visualizing Composition 2.0* [2014])
Organizational structure	Includes a multimodal table of contents Teaches mode-neutral concepts relevant to writing	Thoroughly integrates alphabetic text with other modes and media Integrates multimodality into chapters on academic writing and research

the textbook positions alphabetic and nonalphabetic modes. Many of the textbooks we analyzed limit nonalphabetic modes to specific chapters and sections. While they cover an ever-expanding repertoire of modes and media, these textbooks also regulate and withhold multimodality by treating the modes as discreet and nonoverlapping phenomena. Even the most recent editions of *Seeing and Writing* (3rd edition) and *Everything's an Argument* (7th edition) relegate nonalphabetic modes to supplementary special chapters and "certain" situations. These constraints are particularly surprising in light of prefatory arguments about the vital and intrinsic role that nonalphabetic modes play in writing. Our findings, therefore, independently substantiate Schiavone's observation that, in many textbooks, "theories posit the importance of teaching students to produce visual and multimodal compositions, while the practices encapsulated in textbook prompts tend to promote the consumption of multimodal compositions more so than their production" (359). In contrast, *Writer/Designer* and *IX: Visual Exercises* employ a more inclusive organizational structure that integrates or models multimodality in every chapter. However, as the next section reveals, such inclusion comes at the expense of a detailed treatment of alphabetic text in its own right.

Supporting Multimodal Writing: An Analysis of Instructional Materials

The sections that follow introduce findings and themes that emerged from our analysis of each textbook's instructional materials.

Seeing and Writing, *2nd and 4th Editions*

In addition to readings and images, *Seeing and Writing 2* provides overt supportive instruction for the analysis of visual and verbal texts (*seeing*) and for alphabetic composition (*writing*). This support consists of explanatory passages, annotations, and marginal notes that frame the examples, as well as prompts for further reflection and writing. The first chapter exemplifies this support structure. Early in the chapter, readers encounter a full-spread print of Joel Sternfield's *Warren Avenue at 23rd Street* (McQuade and McQuade 10–11). A caption models some observations about the image, and then asks, "How do [these observations] compare with your own observations?" (11). The section that follows introduces heuristic questions for analyzing visual and verbal texts (e.g., "What do I notice? And why?" [9]), and the next section describes the process of writing up the findings of the analysis as an alphabetic text essay (24–26). Although the edition presents seeing and writing as separate processes, readers are encouraged to "cross-train" by paying attention to visual and verbal strategies (2).

Seeing and Writing 4 resembles *Seeing & Writing 2* in its presentation of overt instructional support, including visual and verbal texts, writing prompts, and explanatory passages. For instance, the introduction to students includes the Sternfield print, a caption soliciting observations, and similar writing prompts—with the addition of a sample student response to the image (10). What has changed is that the fourth edition emphasizes the *writing* part of the title by providing detailed descriptions of the writing process and by explaining the supportive role that *seeing* plays in that process. One feature that exemplifies this change is the addition of comic-book-style representations of the writing process throughout the edition. The first page of the fourth edition consists of an elaborate, fold-out comic that tells the story of a college student whose multisensory observations become the basis for a college paper; another comic depicts the brain as a machine that inputs images and outputs printed pages (2). This comic, despite its visual presentation, privileges the production of alphabetic text as the end goal. Although the comic represents seeing and writing as "inextricably bound" (3), it also positions seeing as a multimodal process and writing as exclusively alphabetic.

Everything's an Argument, *3rd and 7th Editions*

The instructional materials presented in the third edition of *Everything's an Argument* employ a linguistic lens to help students recognize, analyze, and create effective multimodal arguments. The first chapter frames a variety of everyday phenomena—including "clothes," "foods," and the media students consume—as "texts [that] make nuanced, sometimes implicit arguments" (Lunsford and Ruszkiewicz 4). The remaining chapters invite students to interact with such texts in the same way that they interact with the printed page. For example, the chapter on "Visual Arguments" instructs students to "read" an image to discern the "message" (307). Because language serves "as a metaphor for everything else" (Wysocki and Johnson-Eilola 360), the verbal mode retains subtle primacy. Many of the prompts and exercises presented at the end of chapters invite students to analyze visual examples and then write an alphabetic text "report" (328) or "paragraph" (25) about their findings. Once again, these prompts and exercises privilege the production of an alphabet-centric product.

The seventh edition offers more encouragement for students to create their own multimodal arguments, arguing that multimodal composing will prepare students to meet audience expectations: "Readers today expect the arguments they read to include visual elements, and there's little reason not to offer this assistance if you have the technical skills to create them" (Lunsford et al. 166). Although this passage grants students permission to use any "technical skills" they may have (166), the seventh edition offers little overt *instruction* about multimodal composing. While *Everything's an Argument* offers a rhetorical approach to writing, the textbook frames the design of visual elements as technical (see Horner, this collection), not rhetorical. Audience expectations are subordinated to the technical skill of the student writer. Moreover, the edition constrains students' choices. In the "Considering Format and Media" sections of each genre-specific chapter's "Guide for Writing," students are warned that instructors "may specify that you use a particular format and medium" (e.g., 114); if no modality is specified, students are directed to work through boilerplate heuristic questions about format, medium, and visual elements (e.g., 114). The student's preferences rank last, minimizing the potential impact of a student's choice to pursue a multimodal project.

IX: Visual Exercises *(CD)*

The nine exercises presented in the CD prepare students to use many different modes and media (e.g., text, image, sound, animation), but they focus primarily on the production of visual elements. Each exercise provides overt instructional support, including multimodal examples, analytical heuristics, and assignment prompts for the creation of multimodal works. The term *text* plays a paradoxical role. On one hand, the CD edition uses a textual lens to describe many modes and media, including "artwork such as paintings and sculptures, literary works such as poems and novels, musical compositions, and multimodal works such as this

CD-ROM" (Ball and Arola). On the other hand, the CD edition devotes little attention to text in the traditional sense of written words. For example, the opening screen for the exercises on "Text & Purpose" concentrates on "purely visual" texts. After a brief mention of typography and typeface, the exercise on "Element & Contrast" focuses exclusively on the use of color in photography.

Writer/Designer

The instructional materials presented in *Writer/Designer* foreground multimodality not just as a timely or an interesting phenomenon but as a conceptual lens for understanding writing in general. A sidebar labeled "Are All Texts Multimodal?" in the first chapter makes the explicit claim that even a doctoral dissertation could be considered multimodal because it conveys meaning through a variety of "elements" including alphabetic text, images, and the design of the page (Arola et al. 3). Despite such an inclusive approach to multimodality, some passages frame long-form alphabetic text as deficient or inferior to more overtly multimodal compositions. The commentary on several screenshots of Web sites in the second chapter, "Analyzing Multimodal Projects," calls much more attention to the visual elements than to the strategic use of alphabetic text (20–39). The third chapter compares a scholarly book, composed primarily in alphabetic text, with a "media-rich, interactive Prezi" that "adds visual, spatial, and gestural meaning" (43), implying that the *Prezi*'s multimodal design is superior to traditional writing.

Table 3 summarizes themes and patterns that we discovered in each textbook's instructional materials. The textbooks that we analyzed reveal two general instructional approaches. The first approach invites students to apply what they already know—their existing strategies, skills, and vocabulary—to multimodal writing. *Seeing and Writing* teaches students to analyze visual artifacts and produce written essays, resonating with Schiavone's observation that most writing textbooks adopt a consumption-oriented approach to multimodality (372–73). *Everything's an Argument* encourages students to think in verbal terms about multimodal arguments and to draw upon existing skill sets to create multimodal works. The second approach challenges, reframes, and disrupts students' existing knowledge. *IX: Visual Exercises* upends established definitions of *text* by linking the term with nonalphabetic writing, whereas

Writer/Designer encourages students to see all writing (even academic writing and research) as multimodal.

As Brandt reminds us, writing instructors are "conflicted brokers between literacy's buyers and sellers" ("Sponsors" 183). Textbooks are, first and foremost, literacy commodities sponsored by the companies that publish them. In many ways, the authors who write them, the instructors who teach with them, and the students who learn through them are subject to the institutional sponsorship of the publishing industry. The

Table 3. Themes and Patterns in Instructional Materials, by Textbook

	Seeing and Writing (McQuade and McQuade)	
Edition	2nd (2003)	4th (2010)
Instructional approach	Instructs students in the analysis of visual works and the production of alphabetic text Encourages students to cross-train in visual and verbal modes	Foregrounds and explains the writing process Incorporates more visual media (e.g., comics) into explanatory passages
	Everything's an Argument (Lunsford and Ruszkiewicz)	
Edition	3rd (2004)	7th (2015)
Instructional approach	Instructs students to apply verbal reading and writing strategies to multimodal arguments	Encourages students to use existing technical skills to produce multimodal arguments Enumerates constraints on students' choice of mode
	IX: Visual Exercises (Ball and Arola) and *Writer/Designer* (Arola et al.)	
Edition	*IX: Visual Exercises* (2004)	*Writer/Designer* (including *IX: Visualizing Composition 2.0* [2014])
Instructional approach	Employs a textual lens for understanding many different modes and media Devotes little attention to text in the traditional (i.e., alphabetic) sense	Employs a multimodal lens for understanding writing in general Demonstrates little separation of alphabetic text from other modes, even in passages about academic writing and research

arguments textbooks make to justify the inclusion of multimodal content and the promotion of multimodal composing on the grounds that multimodality is timely and engaging also serve the publishers' interests: new editions are promoted as necessary to keep up with the times, and student-friendly texts are more likely to sell. These arguments commodify multimodality by, as Horner observes in this collection, "ascribing specific effects to abstracted modalities," thus ignoring the concrete social practices that imbue certain texts with timeliness or promote audience engagement.

Despite the proliferation of digital textbooks and online supplements, publishers also have a vested interest in sponsoring the consumption and production of alphabetic texts. Yet the persistence of alphabetic writing as the dominant mode in the majority of these textbooks—*Writer/Designer* being the notable exception—also indicates that institutional sponsorship of alphabetic writing in a given local context sometimes overshadows the opportunities for multimodal composition that the textbooks offer. Nevertheless, these textbooks provide both direct instruction and heuristic models for multimodal composing that students (and instructors) may choose to appropriate for their own purposes (see Brandt, "Sponsors" 178–79).

Schiavone argues that textbooks should be "taken up mindfully" in light of their affordances, constraints, and limitations (377). In fact, we know very little about how end users take up textbooks, whether mindfully or not. More research is needed to determine which textbook resources are (not) actually used—and why. Do instructors and students divert these resources to compose multimodal texts for their own purposes? To what extent do students and instructors subvert the ideological freight that textbooks deliver? The answers to these questions will shed further light on the sponsorship and appropriation of multimodal writing textbooks and on their evolving role in the college writing classroom.

Our research does indicate, however, that like many other aspects of the multimodal turn, the popular multimodal writing textbooks that we analyzed fail to conform to a linear progress narrative. They make diverse arguments, assume diversiform and evolving organizational structures, and offer a rich variety of instructional materials and approaches. They enable and constrain students' use of nonalphabetic modes, and they disagree regarding the extent to which established alphabetic practices extend to nonalphabetic and multimodal texts. By packaging multimodality and positioning writing in such disparate ways, these textbooks exert complex sponsorship of composing practices in the context of the college writing classroom.

Works Cited

Allan, Elizabeth G. "Low-Tech / Low-Verbal Multimodal Assignments in First-Year Writing: Beyond a 'Words-Plus' Model of Multimodality." *Journal of Global Literacies, Technologies, and Emerging Pedagogies*, vol. 3, no. 1, July 2015, pp. 236–49, joglep.com/index.php/archives/volume-3-issue-1/.

Anderson, Daniel, et al. "Integrating Multimodality into Composition Curricula: Survey Methodology and Results from a CCCC Research Grant." *Composition Studies*, vol. 34, no. 2, 2006, pp. 59–94. *JSTOR*, www.jstor.org .stable/43501658.

Arola, Kristin L., et al. *Writer/Designer: A Guide to Making Multimodal Projects.* Bedford/St. Martin's, 2014.

Ball, Cheryl E. "Assessing Scholarly Multimedia: A Rhetorical Genre Studies Approach." *Technical Communication Quarterly*, vol. 21, no. 1, 2012, pp. 61–77. *ProQuest*, doi:10.1080/10572252.2012.626390.

Ball, Cheryl E., and Kristin L. Arola. *IX: Visual Exercises*. Bedford/St. Martin's, 2004. CD-ROM.

———. "Designerly ≠ Readerly: Re-assessing Multimodal and New Media Rubrics for Use in Writing Studies." *Convergence*, vol. 12, no. 4, 2006, pp. 392–412. *SAGE Journals*, doi:10.1177/1354856506068366.

———. *Visualizing Composition*. Bedford/St. Martin's Press, 2nd ed., 2010, ix. bedfordstmartins.com.

Brandt, Deborah. *Literacy in American Lives*. Cambridge UP, 2001.

———. "Sponsors of Literacy." *College Composition and Communication*, vol. 49, no. 2, 1998, pp. 165–85. *JSTOR*, doi:10.2307/358929.

Connors, Robert J. "Textbooks and the Evolution of the Discipline." *College Composition and Communication*, vol. 37, no. 2, May 1986, pp. 178–94. *JSTOR*, doi:10.2307/357516.

Cushman, Ellen. "Elias Boudinot and the *Cherokee Phoenix*: The Sponsors of Literacy They Were and Were Not." *Literacy, Economy, and Power: Writing and Research after* Literacy in American Lives, edited by John Duffy et al., Southern Illinois UP, 2014, pp. 13–30.

Fulkerson, Richard. "Composition at the Turn of the Twenty-First Century." *College Composition and Communication*, vol. 56, no. 4, June 2005, pp. 654–87. *JSTOR*, www.jstor.org/stable/30037890.

Gale, Xin Liu, and Fredric G. Gale. Introduction. *(Re)Visioning Composition Textbooks: Conflicts of Culture, Ideology, and Pedagogy*, edited by Gale and Gale. State U of New York P, 1999, pp. 3–13.

Gee, James Paul. "Opportunity to Learn: A Language-Based Perspective on Assessment." *Assessment in Education: Principles, Policy and Practice*, vol. 10, no. 1, 2003, pp. 27–46. *Taylor and Francis Online*, doi:10.1080/09695940301696.

George, Diana. "From Analysis to Design: Visual Communication in the Teaching of Writing." *College Composition and Communication*, vol. 54, no. 1, Sept. 2002, pp. 11–39. *JSTOR*, doi:10.2307/1512100.

Hesse-Biber, Sharlene Nagy, and Patricia Leavy. *The Practice of Qualitative Research*. SAGE, 2006.

Knoblauch, A. Abbey. "A Textbook Argument: Definitions of Argument in Leading Composition Textbooks." *College Composition and Communication*, vol. 63, no. 2, Dec. 2011, pp. 244–68. *JSTOR*, www.jstor.org/stable/23131584.

Kress, Gunther. *Literacy in the New Media Age*. Routledge, 2003.

Lauer, Claire. "Contending with Terms: 'Multimodal' and 'Multimedia' in the Academic and Public Spheres." *Computers and Composition*, vol. 26, no. 4, Dec. 2009, pp. 225–39. *Science Direct*, doi:10.1016/j.compcom.2009.09.001.

Lunsford, Andrea A., and John J. Ruszkiewicz. *Everything's an Argument*. 3rd ed., Bedford/St. Martin's, 2004.

Lunsford, Andrea A., et al. *Everything's an Argument*. 7th ed., Bedford/St. Martin's, 2016.

McQuade, Donald, and Christine McQuade. *Seeing and Writing 2*. Bedford/St. Martin's, 2003.

———. *Seeing and Writing 4*. Bedford/St. Martin's, 2010.

The New London Group. "A Pedagogy of Multiliteracies: Designing Social Futures." *Harvard Educational Review*, vol. 66, no. 1, Spring 1996, pp. 60–92.

Palmeri, Jason. *Remixing Composition: A History of Multimodal Writing Pedagogy*. Southern Illinois UP / NCTE, 2012.

Schiavone, Aubrey. "Consumption, Production, and Rhetorical Knowledge in Visual and Multimodal Textbooks." *College English*, vol. 79, no. 4, Mar. 2017, pp. 358–80, www.ncte.org/journals/ce/issues/v79-4.

Selfe, Cynthia L. "The Movement of Air, the Breath of Meaning: Aurality and Multimodal Composing." *College Composition and Communication*, vol. 60, no. 4, June 2009, pp. 616–63. *JSTOR*, www.jstor.org/stable/40593423.

Selfe, Cynthia L., and Gail E. Hawisher. *Literate Lives in the Information Age: Narratives of Literacy from the United States*. Lawrence Erlbaum Associates, 2004.

Wysocki, Anne Frances, and Johndan Johnson-Eilola. "Blinded by the Letter: Why Are We Using Literacy as a Metaphor for Everything Else?" *Passions, Pedagogies, and Twenty-First-Century Technologies*, edited by Gail E. Hawisher and Cynthia L. Selfe, Utah State UP / NCTE, 1999, pp. 349–68.

Yancey, Kathleen Blake. "Made Not Only in Words: Composition in a New Key." *College Composition and Communication*, vol. 56, no. 2, Dec. 2004, pp. 297–328. *JSTOR*, doi: 10.2307/4140651.

Facebook Posts, *Twitter* Hashtags, and *Snapchat* Stories: Changing Conceptions of Writing in a Social Media Landscape

Stephanie Vie

The Pew Research Center began examining social media trends in the United States in 2005; since then, Pew recorded the massive rise of Americans using social media to share everything from images and news stories to personal narratives and more. In 2005, only five percent of American adults used at least one social media platform, but in 2019, seventy-two percent used social media, and often more than one tool ("Social Media"). And this is not just an American phenomenon: a report on global social media from July 2019 notes that the number of social media users worldwide advanced to over 3.5 billion, and forty-six percent of the world's population now uses social media monthly (Kemp, "Global Social Media Users"). The United States' social media penetration of seventy-two percent is closely followed by East Asia (seventy percent), South America (sixty-six percent), Central America (sixty-two percent), and Northern Europe (sixty-seven percent), among others (Kemp, "Digital 2019").

With this global shift, what constitutes writing in an age of social media has changed—from *Facebook* posts to *Twitter* hashtags, *Pinterest* pinboards to *Snapchat* stories. I argue it is important to consider how social media—and social media writing—impacts composition pedagogy. Indeed, both students and faculty members frequently don't consider social media communication to be writing at all, yet a great deal of valuable writing occurs on social media platforms. This writing is both digital and multimodal, crucial concepts considered in this book. As Pegeen Reichert Powell articulates in her introduction to this collection and as other contributors reinforce, communication has always been multimodal; instead, what is important is which practices are given value and which practices are considered unimportant, particularly for classroom pedagogy. Thus, as Reichert Powell notes, "What we can begin to do, without resorting to or appealing to the writing-versus-multimodality binary, is to be mindful about what practices are valued and rewarded in various contexts and to allow for shifting priorities across various writing and teaching situations." Bruce Horner, also in this collection, reinforces that multimodality is intimately connected to practices: "Modality is the site, means, and outcome of our composing practices—what we work with, and on, and rewrite."

This essay responds to these calls invoking questions about multimodal practices by describing (drawing on data from my grant-funded research) different ways that social media writing practices are recognized and rewarded, and also marginalized, in writing studies. The results show that institutional context is crucial and that faculty members' orientations toward technology in general and social media specifically play key roles. Finally, positionality in the hierarchy of academia—as well as narratives about others' experiences within those hierarchies—hold considerable weight for faculty members when they decide whether or not to rely on social media in their pedagogy.

Social Media, Social Network Sites: Working Definitions

I pause here to offer working definitions of *social network sites* and *social media*; while it is beyond this essay's scope to fully delve into the nuances of these terms, I offer working definitions to guide the discussions that follow. As Caleb T. Carr and Rebecca A. Hayes assert, "[T]here is no commonly accepted definition of what social media *are*, both functionally and theoretically" (46). However, several definitions offered by prominent social media scholars have been broadly cited and accepted. The 2007 definition by danah boyd and Nicole B. Ellison is foundational to discussions of social media today: "Social network sites [are] web-based services that allow individuals to (1) construct a public or semi-public profile within a bounded system, (2) articulate a list of other users with whom they share a connection, and (3) view and traverse their list of connections and those made by others within the system" (211). Charles Steinfield, Nicole Ellison, Cliff Lampe, and Jessica Vitak draw on boyd and Ellison's definition and note that beyond these foundational precepts, social network sites are widely different (116). Social network sites fit within the larger umbrella term *social media*, as all social network sites will be some form of social media, but social media can include technologies that sometimes do not fulfill boyd and Ellison's definition (e.g., blogs, discussion forums). Carr and Hayes offer their own accessible definition of social media as "Internet-based channels that allow users to opportunistically interact and selectively self-present, either in real-time or asynchronously, with both broad and narrow audiences who derive value from user-generated content and the perception of interaction with others" (50). In this essay, I rely on both Carr and Hayes's and boyd and Ellison's definitions to ground my discussions of how writing instructors understand social media and social network sites in their pedagogy.

Further, the relation between social media and multimodality surfaced in several participants' quotes in my study. Just as the definitions of social media or social network sites vary, the inclusion of multimodal elements in social media varies; in *Researching Language and Social Media*, the authors contrast the "primarily verbal resources of technologies like email," for example, with "the integration of visual and audio-visual elements in social network sites like Facebook" (Page et al. 16). While this collection points out that all communication is multimodal, I stress here that as digital technologies, social media have a wide range of potential channels of communication—textual, visual, audiovisual—and elements such as nonverbal communication, linguistic elements, and formatting elements. Multimodality is often thought erroneously as only that which is digital and new, as many contributors to this collection explore.

Similarly, while social media are indeed digital, they are not new. Early applications such as the University of Illinois's *PLATO* system offered instant messaging and chat rooms, among other technologies, in the 1970s. Even early social media that readers of this collection might be more familiar with (*AOL Instant Messenger, Yahoo! Messenger, SixDegrees .com*) were all launched in the 1990s. Additionally, social networking sites may be wholly online, digital, and multimodal, but social networking has taken place offline for as long as humankind has been communicating person to person (see, for example, Mark Granovetter's articulation of strong and weak ties among individuals in social networks, both offline and online). This aligns with Horner's point in this collection that when multimodality is considered "more" (that is, offering something more), it is conflated with "what is different, better, and new." Much like this collection argues that multimodality is not new and not always digital, I point out here that social media are not new and social networking is not always digital—but both are always multimodal. And the faculty members' responses offered later in this essay illustrate that faculty members' incorporation of social media in the classroom is not different or new; we simply often lack the awareness or understanding of how social media may be defined, thus preventing us from seeing that we have already been using social media pedagogically for many years.

Study Overview

This essay's research data are drawn from a grant-funded study of faculty members nationwide, which showcases how writing studies is beginning to connect academic practices to everyday literacies and digital multimodal composition practices. I conducted research with over seven hundred writing instructors about their attitudes toward and pedagogical uses of social media. I later detail the methods guiding my data collection and offer results and discussion that connect to this collection's overall focus on considering "the ways that writing is intrinsic to, rather than separate from, new media and digital communication" (Reichert Powell, this volume). This study does not approach social media in writing instruction today as a disruption of or a departure from its focus on writing; instead, the study sees classroom social media use as yet another digital writing genre that, by virtue of its global ubiquity in people's lives, merits sustained academic attention and inclusion in writing pedagogy. This discussion is an entry point into conversations about what constitutes writing in an age of nearly ubiquitous multimodal composition practices through social media technologies.

This essay shows that, increasingly, faculty members incorporate social media into their classrooms to teach rhetorical principles, to communicate with students, and to increase student engagement. Yet it also illustrates that some faculty members articulate an artificial divide between words and social media, or between the writing process and social media, or between adequate preparation for postgraduate workplace activities and social media. That is, for such faculty members, there is an artificial distinction between social media writing and academic writing that places the latter on a pedestal, believing it to be the right type of writing to prepare students for classroom work and beyond. The former is viewed instead as a fun distraction; in this artificial distinction, social media writing (which is already multimodal writing) is not a means with which to assist students in writing practice.

My aim here is to explode this artificial dichotomy and argue that social media writing is an untapped resource for composition instructors interested in continued examinations of writing in a digital age. One critical element is that social media writing is already a part of the writing classroom by virtue of the fact that most American students currently compose in social media—and bring those composing practices and experiences to the writing classroom, whether or not instructors explicitly teach about or with social media. Students' previous experiences with social media composing inform the ways they think about writing, rhetorical awareness, voice and tone, multimodal composing, and other elements relevant to the teaching of writing. Attempting to artificially distance social media writing from the writing activities and genres that occur in today's composition classroom is erroneous.

What is crucial, though, is the careful, reflective thought process that should go into constructing any successful writing class, the kind that asks instructors to structure writing courses in such a way that learning outcomes are met and that students gain experience in and exposure to various genres and forms of writing and, whenever possible, take into account twenty-first-century literacy practices. While social media is already influential in writing pedagogy by virtue of ubiquity, pushing toward greater reflective thought is key. Thus, faculty members should be aware of and participate in ongoing conversations regarding central themes that impact the teaching of writing in a digital multimodal world: the role of privacy and surveillance in maintaining or breaking down academic hierarchies, for example, or the influence of data mining tools and practices when participating in social media as a writer, or even the challenges of engaging in activist, political, or other publicly visible markers of identity in social media as an academic.

Social Media in Writing Studies

To set the stage for the discussion of my study's data, I first briefly review scholarly analyses and pedagogical explorations of social media in writing studies. In doing so, I illustrate that, while the field's history of multimodal composition (as Jason Palmeri explores in *Remixing Composition*) is long-standing, its attention to social media writing as a form of digital multimodal composition is more recent. Social media is still a somewhat unorthodox subject in the composition field, though it has gained interest among digital rhetoricians, computers and writing scholars, and technical and professional communicators, among others. Yet the field's ongoing interests in topics like writing transfer, labor and assessment, and writing program administration indeed align with social media writing. Social media and their use to compose, to write, to share, and even to teach are not separate from conversations about labor, transfer, administration, and assessment; however, those connections have, for the most part, not yet been explicitly articulated in the field's leading journals.

Scholarship on social media in rhetoric and composition has largely appeared in digital multimodal journals such as *Kairos*, *Enculturation*, and *Computers and Composition Online*, as well as print journals concerned with technological issues, like *Computers and Composition*. Early scholarship focused on emergent (at the time) sites like *Facebook* and former juggernauts such as *Myspace* (see Balzhiser et al.; Maranto and Barton; Vie, *Engaging Others*, "Digital Divide"). As social media proliferated and academic interest grew, cross-platform research emerged that built on earlier explorations of one or two social media platforms (Buck; Williams), although scholars continued to also deeply analyze communication practices in individual social media platforms (Jones; West) and among specific populations, such as multilingual and developmental writers (DePew).

Technical and professional communication also showed interest in social media scholarship in major journals such as *Technical Communication Quarterly* (which featured a special issue on social media in 2014), the *Journal of Business and Technical Communication*, and *Business Communication Quarterly*, among others. Studies in these journals looked at the use of social media in disaster communications (Bowdon; Potts), in the classroom (Dyrud; Kimme Hea; Verzosa Hurley and Kimme Hea), in the community (Dadurka and Pigg), and in knowledge work and the workplace (Ferro and Zachry; Lam and Hannah; Pigg; Stolley). Scholars advised optimal pedagogical practices for teaching and learning with social media (Daer and Potts). And as textual features such as hashtags became more critical in understanding the viral reach of social media writing, authors like Joel Penney and Caroline Dadas investigated the rhetorical role of such features in digital activism.

Finally, a call for more empirical research and data-driven scholarship relying on quantitative and qualitative methods extended through composition scholarship broadly. Some scholars responded by enumerating various ways that social media could provide new methodological approaches for composition research (Wolff). Others, like Sarah Beth Hopton and R. Mitchell Parry, describe methods appropriate for working with big data in social media, such as their use of a text classification pipeline to mine and categorize a nonprofit organization's *Facebook* page to best respond to a community's needs. Jenna Pack Sheffield and Amy C. Kimme Hea explore how longitudinal research in social media allows researchers to consider methodological elements such as building a community, sharing study data, understanding analytics, conducting usability testing, and constructing identity. Such discussions move scholarship on social media beyond analyses of writing and literacy in individual or multiple platforms to instead focus more broadly on theory-building related to methodological approaches appropriate for digital technologies like social media.

This essay continues to intervene in the aforementioned call for greater empirical and data-driven scholarship on social media by bringing the former together with the field's demonstrated interest in teaching and learning with social media. In the next section, I describe my study's methods before moving into the results and discussion.

Methods

My study of 786 writing instructors in the United States aimed to explore instructors' attitudes toward and uses of social media, in the classroom and in personal everyday use. It describes their uses of—or choices not to use—social media pedagogically. Drawing on a mixed-methods framework, the study offered participants opportunities to communicate both challenges and benefits of social media and pedagogy through the survey and optional follow-up interviews. The study was approved by the University of Central Florida Institutional Review Board in 2015 and the survey was distributed in 2015 and 2016, with follow-up interviews, data analysis, and interpretation in 2016. In this essay, I focus on only the survey results and not the follow-up interviews; while the interviews added depth to the survey responses by allowing the faculty members to talk through their social media practices, the survey gave respondents ample spaces to elaborate on their responses.

Research Questions

The following research questions guided this study:

> For faculty members in the United States teaching writing, rhetoric, and composition in higher education today, how does social media play a role in their pedagogy?

What benefits overall might social media have for teaching within the disciplines of writing, rhetoric, and composition at the undergraduate level in the United States?

For those faculty members who choose not to use social media in their pedagogy, what factors go into that choice?

What challenges might affect the adoption of social media for pedagogical purposes in higher education in the United States at the undergraduate level?

Sample Pool

The sample pool included faculty members at accredited institutions of higher education in the United States who were currently teaching or who had taught at least one undergraduate course in writing, rhetoric, or composition between 2012 and 2014. A Qualtrics survey was disseminated through a variety of channels frequented by writing instructors, including social media and professional e-mail lists. This survey was not limited to faculty members who already used social media or were favorable toward their use; I explicitly recruited instructors who did not use social media, or who had used them but quit, through direct e-mails. These e-mails invited the instructors to complete the survey and pass the link along to department colleagues.

Survey

The twenty-nine-question survey was designed to prompt quantitative as well as qualitative responses; depending on their responses, participants would see some or all of the possible questions. Question types included categorical questions, multiple-choice questions (i.e., eliciting quantitative data), and short-answer questions (i.e., eliciting qualitative data). Categorical questions asked for age, employment status, Carnegie classification of the respondent's institution, and position type. Multiple-choice questions included questions consenting the participants and ensuring they fit the sample pool. The remaining seven multiple-choice questions were either yes/no responses (e.g., Would you be interested in or willing to use social media in your teaching in the future?) or responses from a limited list (e.g., Which of the following social media technologies have you used in your teaching?). The ten short-answer questions either asked participants to respond to a set question (e.g., How do you think your students feel about your teaching with or their learning about social media? Why?) or to further elaborate on a multiple-choice question (e.g., Could you explain further your responses in the previous question, "What are some of the challenges of teaching with social media in writing, rhetoric, and composition classes"?). Finally, several questions presented participants with a Likert-type 0–10 scale (e.g., Are you likely to continue teaching with or about social media in the future? 0=not at all likely, 10=extremely likely). Quantitative results were automatically tabulated in Qualtrics and qualitative data were coded using grounded theory methods (detailed below) for emergent patterns and themes.

Survey Respondent Population

Initially, 786 faculty members voluntarily consented to complete the survey. After consenting and meeting sample-pool requirements, 749 remained. Most faculty members were between twenty-five and thirty-four years old (n=247), with the second largest population between thirty-five and forty-four (n=244) and the third between forty-five and fifty-four (n=118). The population dropped off from there, with a combined total of 111 participants over fifty-five years of age (see fig. 1). Of the respondents, 721 described their employment status (see fig. 2). Most were assistant professors (n=182), graduate teaching assistants or associates (n=146), associate professors (n=112), or adjunct faculty members (n=99). The "other" category allowed faculty members to describe a par-

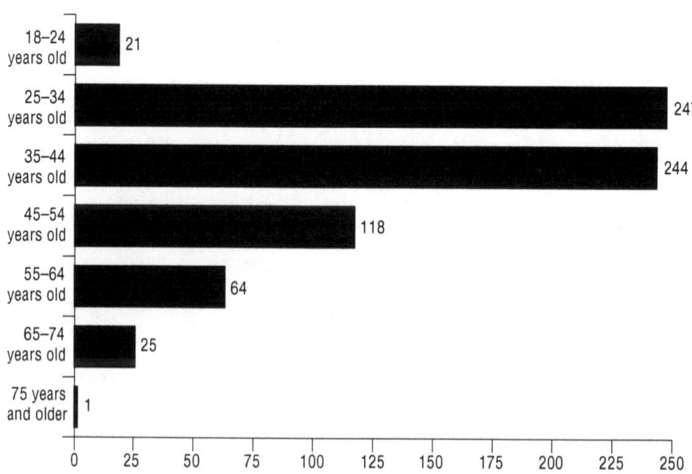

Figure 1. Age of study participants

ticular situation not captured adequately in the demographic categories provided.

Finally, the responses to the Carnegie (institutional) classification (n=721) showed that most respondents taught or had taught at a doctoral-research university (n=396) or a master's-granting university (n=149; see fig. 3). Baccalaureate-granting institutions (n=72), two-year or associate's-granting colleges (n=68), baccalaureate institutions

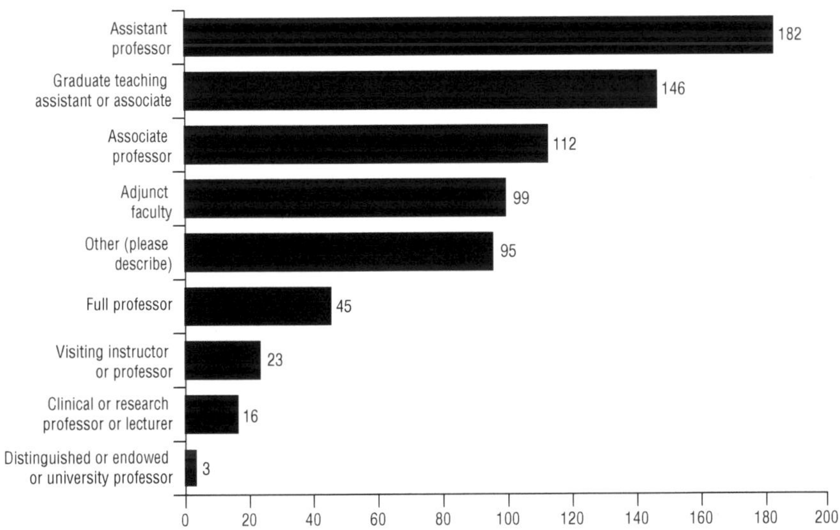

Figure 2. Employment status of study participants

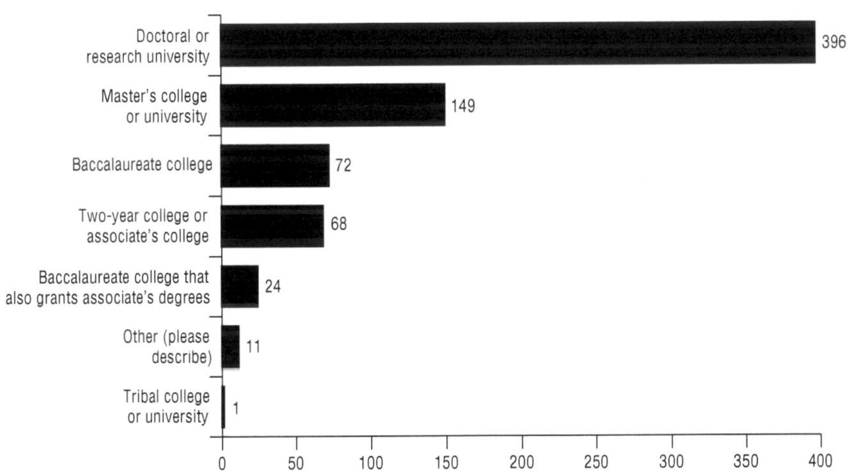

Figure 3. Carnegie institutional classification of study participants

also granting associate's degrees (n=24), and tribal colleges or universities (n=1) rounded out the responses. Again, the "other" category allowed for unlisted institutional types to be reported (n=11), which were hand-coded.

Data Analysis

Quantitative survey results were automatically placed into a readable format by Qualtrics, creating various data visualizations such as bar or pie charts. The qualitative survey responses and follow-up interviews were coded using grounded theory (Glaser and Strauss), an approach that asks researchers to remain open to categories that emerge in vivo from the data themselves; while initial coding categories are possible (e.g., privacy, time, labor), many more fine-grained coding categories emerged as I worked with the data.

I used *ATLAS.ti* coding software to code survey and interview data. I began by using preliminary coding categories developed from previous literature on social media (i.e., privacy, time, labor). Next, I expanded the previous codes and deepened them by incorporating codes that emerged in vivo from the data (e.g., relevance, rigor, learning outcomes, and institutional barriers). Rigor, for instance, was used to label responses where faculty members expressed concerns about social media being (or not being) scholarly or academic. I used the same codes to categorize the follow-up interviews, where additional codes emerged (e.g., abandonment, access, stalking, scaffolding, value). A full list of major codes that emerged from the data is available in the appendix below. In the next section, I present survey trends that relate in some way to multimodality or multimodal composition as well as writing practices.

Results and Discussion

Some of the results of the survey are provided in greater detail in my 2015 article, "What's Going On? Challenges and Opportunities for Social Media Use in the Writing Classroom"; the article discusses, for instance, the various social media technologies instructors use, the challenges they face, and the benefits they perceive from social media use. Within the scope of this essay, however, I focus on the participants' responses that attend to multimodality and multimodal writing in particular to explore further how faculty members perceive the connection between social media and classroom practices as well as their own academic practices.

Many faculty members who responded to the survey understood social media writing as a digital form of multimodal composition, but were divided as to whether or not they wanted to include social media writing in their teaching. Those who responded that they would not be interested in or willing to include social media in the teaching of writing were offered the chance to expand on their response, and some invoked multimodality as part of that decision. One, for example, expressed a preference for other genres of multimodal composing that would be preferred: "Mostly just that I can only fit so much into the curriculum and I'd prefer to expand in the realm of multimodal/digital writing in broader terms (audio and/or video essays) than via social media." In this response, audio and video essays are depicted as "broader" multimodal writing genres than social media, which presumably then is read as a narrower genre (albeit also digital and multimodal).

Others placed their responses within an oppositional context, responding to the idea that writing should best be practiced through what Hannah Rule describes in her essay in this collection as "a standard-issue academic research essay—composition's ur-genre" (citing Ball and Charlton) rather than through something digital. "My courses are to prepare students for writing in the classroom and in the workplace," noted one faculty respondent, implying that a focus on social media would not prepare students for writing in either rhetorical context, despite (as noted in research cited earlier in this essay) the increasing prevalence of social media platforms in today's workplaces. Indeed, Jari J. Jussila, Hannu Kärkkäinen, and Heli Aramo-Immonen note that "social media can be utilized to identify new business opportunities and new product ideas, to deepen relationships with customers and to enhance collaboration not only inside but also between companies and other parties" (606).

Finally, another respondent claimed that social media were "not relevant to actual writing that requires invention, drafting, and revision," suggesting that social media writing would not draw on any of these familiar moments in the writing process—likely an intriguing concept for any social media marketer engaged in creating a digital marketing strategy, or a customer service representative considering how to respond to an irate customer tweeting about a problem. Today, greater numbers of customers expect companies to have an active social media presence and to respond to customer service inquiries, particularly problems, through social media; fifty-six percent of customers have a more favorable view of companies that respond to customers on social media (Patterson 12).

Those, however, who responded to the survey in ways that illustrated a favorable response to social media more often invoked social media as a multimodal practice worthy of inclusion in the classroom. These faculty members clearly connected a pedagogical use of social media with efforts to explicitly embed multimodal composition into writing pedagogy. Some remarked, like one respondent, that social media are a natural fit with twenty-first-century literacy practices. Another respondent noted the difficulty—as did others—in determining which digital tools were to be included in the umbrella term *social media* and which were not included:

> I had trouble in this survey defining "social media" for myself and distinguishing it from multimodal composition in general. My use of social media falls into four general categories: 1) as a collaboration tool (*Google*); 2) as a source of examples of arguments in multimedia forms; 3) as a publishing and sharing platform for student work; and 4) (via *Skype*) as a way to conference with and tutor students when I can't meet with them in person. On one level, social media seems to function for me as a facilitation tool for teaching multimedia composition, in similar ways that *Box* or *Word* annotations do. On the other hand, it inevitably becomes the subject of composition as well as the vehicle.

In reflecting on this faculty member's concern that it is difficult to distinguish "[social media] from multimodal composition in general," though, I believe that the respondent is making a crucial point: that academia frequently seems to laud social media as a new and different thing, separate in some way from multimodal composition (or writing). But instead of seeing social media as separate—much like the authors of the essays included in this collection aim to illustrate that alphabetic writing is multimodal, not separate from multimodality—we should approach social media as simply another form of multimodal writing that already is a part of our pedagogy and our practice. Depending on how one defines social media (especially if capaciously), then faculty members who rely on tools like *YouTube*, *Skype*, wikis, and blogs are already engaging with social media in their teaching—my research ("What's Going On") as well as others' has shown that these are highly popular tools for classroom practice.

I wish to leave readers with the following three important points:

Social media are not really new. They have been with us since the early days of bulletin board systems, MOOs and MUDs, *Usenet*, instant message clients, and blogs. Even social media platforms most familiar to us (e.g., *YouTube*, *Facebook*, *Twitter*, *Instagram*, *Reddit*) are not particularly new anymore. The first *YouTube* video was uploaded in 2005; *Reddit* also began in 2005. *Facebook* was founded in 2004, *Twitter* created in 2006, and *Instagram* launched in 2010.

Social media tools are already a part of most of our teaching practices. We just don't consider them as such. Every writing instructor who asks students to connect in a course management system, who shows a *YouTube* video in class and holds a class discussion around it, who has students reflect in a blog, whose students look things up in *Wikipedia* before starting their essays is using social media in her or his pedagogy. To be sure, there is a difference between critical, intentional use of social media in writing pedagogy that willingly labels itself as such and social media use that is somewhat happenstance. But even those faculty members who described themselves in the survey as nonusers of social media might be surprised upon reflecting further about the technological tools they teach with that social media have—by virtue of their ubiquity in our global society—already slipped in the door and become part of that classroom. What is necessary next are continued conversations explicitly articulating social media as part of writing practice in our field.

Social media push us to consider critical conversations related to social practice. There is a long history of scholarship attending to the role of technological interfaces and algorithms (see, for example, Arola, "Design" and "Indigeneous Interfaces"; Beck; McGee and Ericsson; Gurak; Selfe and Selfe). Such scholarship asks us to consider how the technologies with which we compose are coded in ways that shape our experiences and abilities to compose. *Facebook*, for instance, has come under fire for its alleged role in influencing the 2016 presidential election in the United States; CEO Mark Zuckerberg testified in April 2018 before Congress about user privacy and data protection. *Facebook*, like other social media, has long been critiqued for its role in surveilling users and sharing their data with third parties, and even experimenting on users without informed consent (see Kramer et al.). Horner describes in this collection how "we can have students question the spaces in which they encounter those pages—being read or written—and what might account for those experiences, what alternative spaces might be claimed for those encounters, and what conditions shape the spaces available and their availability." Indeed, social media in the writing classroom offer substantive ways to have students reflect on the role of these tools in social practice, including written reflections on the interfaces and algorithms that shape their daily lived experiences as composers in social media sites.

Thus, social media are already with us. Just as there is no form of monomodal writing, there is no divorcing social media from multimodal composition, or any composition for that matter. As a result, a faculty member's response such as this one—"I feel the same way about social media that I do about multimodality. I'll teach it, but it takes away from time spent on words, time that I deeply value"—is shown to be a false dichotomy. Neither social media nor multimodality take classroom time away from words. What matters is the purpose for those words, the careful reflection and thought that asks faculty members to decide whether and why social media would be the appropriate form for their purposes, in the same way that the faculty members would reflect on a writing assignment's length, audience, and other rhetorical constraints. The key is being deliberate about one's practice and considering, as Horner remarks in his essay for this volume, the "representations of modality/ies—what people think about modality/ies—[and how they] act on practices and are one of the factors of change." It is crucial that the field of writing studies continues to engage in conversations around academic hierarchies, practices, standards, and the role that social media play in both supporting and exposing ruptures in those hierarchies and practices. By mistakenly assuming that social media writing is not already part of the writing classroom, the field misses out on valuable opportunities to exercise agency and take responsibility for writing these changes in our classrooms and programs.

Works Cited

Arola, Kristin L. "The Design of Web 2.0: The Rise of the Template, the Fall of Design." *Computers and Composition*, vol. 27, no. 1, Mar. 2010, pp. 4–14.

———. "Indigenous Interfaces." Walls and Vie, pp. 209–24.

Balzhiser, Deborah, et al. "The Facebook Papers." *Kairos*, vol. 16, no. 1, Fall 2011, kairos.technorhetoric.net/16.1/praxis/balzhiser-et-al/.

Beck, Estee N. "Sustaining Critical Literacies in the Digital Information Age: The Rhetoric of Sharing, Prosumerism, and Digital Algorithmic Surveillance." Walls and Vie, pp. 37–52.

Bowdon, Melody A. "Tweeting an Ethos: Emergency Messaging, Social Media, and Teaching Technical Communication." *Technical Communication Quarterly*, vol. 23, no. 1, 2014, pp. 35–54.

boyd, danah m., and Nicole B. Ellison. "Social Network Sites: Definition, History, and Scholarship." *Journal of Computer-Mediated Communication*, vol. 13, 2008, pp. 210–30.

Buck, Amber. "Examining Digital Literacy Practices on Social Network Sites." *Research in the Teaching of English*, vol. 47, no. 1, Aug. 2012, pp. 9–38.

Carr, Caleb T., and Rebecca A. Hayes. "Social Media: Defining, Developing, and Divining." *Atlantic Journal of Communication*, vol. 23, no. 1, 2015, pp. 46–65.

Dadurka, David, and Stacey Pigg. "Mapping Complex Terrains: Bridging Social Media and Community Literacies." *Community Literacy Journal*, vol. 6, no. 1, Fall 2011, pp. 7–22.

Daer, Alice R., and Liza Potts. "Teaching and Learning with Social Media: Tools, Cultures, and Best Practices." *Programmatic Perspectives*, vol. 6, no. 2, Fall 2014, pp. 21–40.

DePew, Kevin Eric. "Social Media at Academia's Periphery: Studying Multilingual Developmental Writers' Facebook Composing Strategies." *The Reading Matrix*, vol. 11, no. 1, Jan. 2011, pp. 54–75.

Dyrud, Marilyn A. "Social Networking and Business Communication Pedagogy: Plugging into the Facebook Generation." *Business and Professional Communication Quarterly*, vol. 74, no. 4, 2011, pp. 475–78.

Ferro, Toni, and Marc Zachry. "Technical Communication Unbound: Knowledge Work, Social Media, and Emergent Communicative Practices." *Technical Communication Quarterly*, vol. 23, no. 1, 2014, pp. 6–21.

Glaser, Barney G., and Anselm L. Strauss. *The Discovery of Grounded Theory: Strategies for Qualitative Research*. Aldine Publishing, 1967.

Granovetter, Mark S. "The Strength of Weak Ties." *American Journal of Sociology*, vol. 78, no. 6, 1973, pp. 1360–80.

Gurak, Laura J. *Cyberliteracy: Navigating the Internet with Awareness*. Yale UP, 2001.

Hopton, Sarah Beth, and R. Mitchell Parry. "Measuring the Validity of Algorithms to Automatically Categorize Facebook Content." *SIGDOC Conference '16: Proceedings of the 34th ACM International Conference on the Design of Communication*, Sept. 2016, pp. 1–5.

Jones, John. "Switching in Twitter's Hashtagged Exchanges." *Journal of Business and Technical Communication*, vol. 28, no. 1, 2014, pp. 83–108.

Jussila, Jari J., et al. "Social Media Utilization in Business-to-Business Relationships of Technology Industry Firms." *Computers in Human Behavior*, vol. 30, 2014, pp. 606–13.

Kemp, Simon. "Digital 2019: Global Digital Overview." *Datareportal*, 31 Jan. 2019, Kepios, datareportal.com/reports/digital-2019-global-digital-overview.

———. "Global Social Media Users Pass 3.5 Billion." *We Are Social*, 17 July 2019, wearesocial.com/blog/2019/07/global-social-media-users-pass-3-5-billion.

Kimme Hea, Amy C. "Social Media in Technical Communication." *Technical Communication Quarterly*, vol. 23, no. 1, 2014, pp. 1–5.

Kramer, Adam D. I., et al. "Experimental Evidence of Massive-Scale Emotional Contagion through Social Networks." *Proceedings of the National Academy of Sciences of the United States of America*, vol. 111, no. 24, June 2014, pp. 8788–90.

Lam, Chris, and Mark A. Hannah. "The Social Help Desk: Examining How Twitter Is Used as a Technical Support Tool." *Communication Design Quarterly Review*, vol. 4, no. 2, Mar. 2016, pp. 37–51.

Maranto, Gina, and Matt Barton. "Paradox and Promise: MySpace, Facebook, and the Sociopolitics of Social Networking in the Writing Classroom." *Computers and Composition*, vol. 27, no. 1, Mar. 2010, pp. 36–47.

McGee, Tim, and Patricia Ericsson. "The Politics of the Program: MS Word as the Invisible Grammarian." *Computers and Composition*, vol. 19, no. 4, 2002, pp. 453–70.

Page, Ruth, et al. *Researching Language and Social Media: A Student Guide*. Routledge, 2014.

Palmeri, Jason. *Remixing Composition: A History of Multimodal Writing Pedagogy*. Southern Illinois UP / NCTE, 2012.

Patterson, Bill. "Global State of Multichannel Customer Service Report." Microsoft, 2015. PDF.

Penney, Joel, and Caroline Dadas. "(Re)tweeting in the Service of Protest: Digital Composition and Circulation in the Occupy Wall Street Movement." *New Media and Society*, vol. 16, no. 1, 2014, pp. 74–90.

Pigg, Stacey. "Coordinating Constant Invention: Social Media's Role in Distributed Work." *Technical Communication Quarterly*, vol. 23, no. 2, 2014, pp. 69–87.

Potts, Liza. *Social Media in Disaster Response: How Experience Architects Can Build for Participation*. Routledge, 2013.

Selfe, Cynthia L., and Richard J. Selfe. "The Politics of Interface: Power and Its Exercise in Electronic Contact Zones." *College Composition and Communication*, vol. 45, no. 4, 1994, pp. 480–504.

Sheffield, Jenna Pack, and Amy C. Kimme Hea. "Leveraging the Methodological Affordances of Facebook: Social Networking Strategies in Longitudinal Writing Research." *Composition Forum*, vol. 33, Spring 2016. *ERIC*, files.eric.ed.gov/fulltext/EJ1092004.pdf.

"Social Media Fact Sheet." *Pew Research Center Internet and Technology*, 12 June 2019, Pew Research Center, www.pewinternet.org/fact-sheet/social-media/.

Steinfield, Charles, et al. "Online Social Network Sites and the Concept of Social Capital." *Frontiers in New Media Research*, edited by Francis L. F. Lee et al., Taylor and Francis, 2013, pp. 115–31.

Stolley, Karl. "Integrating Social Media into Existing Work Environments: The Case of Delicious." *Journal of Business and Technical Communication*, vol. 23, no. 3, 2009, pp. 350–71.

Verzosa Hurley, Elise, and Amy C. Kimme Hea. "The Rhetoric of Reach: Preparing Students for Technical Communication in the Age of Social Media." *Technical Communication Quarterly*, vol. 23, no. 1, 2014, pp. 55–68.

Vie, Stephanie. "Digital Divide 2.0: 'Generation M' and Online Social Networking Sites in the Composition Classroom." *Computers and Composition*, vol. 25, no. 1, 2008, pp. 9–23.

———. *Engaging Others in Online Social Networking Sites: Rhetorical Practices in MySpace and Facebook*. 2007. U of Arizona, PhD dissertation.

———. "What's Going On? Challenges and Opportunities for Social Media Use in the Writing Classroom." *The Journal of Faculty Development*, vol. 29, no. 2, May 2015, pp. 33–44.

Walls, Douglas, and Stephanie Vie, editors. *Social Writing / Social Media: Pedagogy, Presentation, and Publics*. Parlor Press / The WAC Clearinghouse, 2017.

West, Sara. "Yik Yak and the Knowledge Community." *Communication Design Quarterly*, vol. 4, no. 2B, June 2016, pp. 12–21.

Williams, Bronwyn T. *Shimmering Literacies: Popular Culture and Reading and Writing Online*. Peter Lang, 2009.

Wolff, William I. "Baby, We Were Born to Tweet: Springsteen Fans, the Writing Practices of *In Situ* Tweeting, and the Research Possibilities for Twitter." *Kairos*, vol. 19, no. 3, Spring 2015, kairos.technorhetoric.net/19.3/topoi/wolff/index.html.

Appendix: Codes That Emerged from the Survey Data, Ordered by Number of Occurrences

Code	Occurrences
Pedagogy	629
Twitter	280
Facebook	270
Privacy	154
Academia	92
Resistance	92
Professional	84
Audience, audiences	82
Blogs	78
LinkedIn	78
Time	78
Conversations	76
Identities, identity	67
Personal	65
Training	62
Value	60
Connected	57
Support	55
Public	53
Remediation	52
Access	51
Professionalism	48
Consequences	44
Network, networking, networks	43
Critical	42
Research	41
Choices	38
Pseudonym	38
Multimodal	36
Technology	36
Instagram	35
Challenge	34
Rhetorical	33
Activist	32
Hashtags	32
Students	32
Data	31
Definition	31
Context	30
Tumblr	30

The *Coastal Composition Commons*: Considering Flexibility, Delivery, and Valuation in a Badging Initiative

Denise P. Paster and Alan J. Reid

The field of composition defines *writing* in broad terms as it situates texts across modalities (Alexander and Rhodes; Kress; Palmeri; Selfe; Shipka), and calls for multimodality in the composition classroom are not new. Kathleen Blake Yancey explained in her CCCC address in 2004 that "[t]he literacies that composers engage in today are multiple. They include print literacy practices (like spelling) that URL's [sic] require; they include visual literacy; they include network literacy" (302). And she encouraged instructors to embrace such multiplicity in the writing classroom. As a field, we have embraced multiplicity by adopting expansive definitions of literacy and making multiple literacies and modalities central to our work. That many teachers of writing still assign alphabetic essays doesn't undercut the value of our expansive sense of either literacies or modalities but instead stresses the connectivity that exists between communicative practices and the forms they take.

An example of this movement between modalities can be seen in our first-year writing program at Coastal Carolina University, which is anchored by a digital badging platform that serves as a fourth credit hour in what are traditionally three-credit-hour courses. The badging program has fielded more than 115,000 submissions from students since its inception in 2014. Though the digital badge system primarily calls for students to compose and submit alphabetic texts, it does so while simultaneously embracing a digital aesthetic in its composition, design, and delivery of instruction. And in doing so the system suggests that a binary does not need to exist between print and digital literacies, but that evolution (in teaching and in student production) can take place across modalities in ways that stress rhetorical considerations of affordances. The digital badging initiative suggests, then, that alphabetic and multimodal texts are not necessarily functioning in opposition but that the pedagogical and production practices central to the badging program work in cooperation to enhance both teaching and learning.

A Digital Badging Initiative

In the fall of 2014, Coastal Carolina University fundamentally shifted the way composition is taught to first-year students by launching a digital badging program named *Coastal Composition Commons*. In this essay, we contextualize this pedagogical initiative by describing the program and detailing how it came into existence, but we also question what this specific programmatic approach suggests about trends in teaching writing with emerging technologies. The badging program, which was designed to support students as they enter the university setting as readers and writers while urging faculty members to consider the potentials of teaching writing using networked platforms, draws on the digital distribution of multimodal instructional materials. To earn a badge, students work through digital modules that scaffold writing moves central to our first-year composition classes (as articulated by our student learning outcomes) and submit text-based artifacts, which are either accepted or denied by their instructors. To examine this pedagogical exchange on both micro (institutionally bound) and macro (as we turn to the composition field) levels, we question what this particular use of emerging technologies suggests about our programmatic assumptions regarding teaching, writing, and instructional technology itself.

A digital badge, as defined by the Humanities, Arts, Science, and Technology Alliance and Collaboratory (HASTAC), is "a validated indicator of accomplishment, skill, quality, or interest that can be earned in many learning environments" ("Digital Badges"). In this sense, instructors using the *Coastal Composition Commons* issue digital badges to first-year writing students as a way of recognizing their demonstrated writing competencies. The iconography of a well-designed digital badge should convey the issuer of the badge, the larger institution with which the badge is associated, and the individual skill that is being certified. Figure 1 shows, as an example, the Quoting badge earned by students at Coastal Carolina University. In addition to the information displayed aesthetically, a digital badge contains metadata that, when unpacked, reveal layered information such as the timestamp for when the user submitted for the badge, the artifact that was submitted for evaluation, and when the badge was approved and by whom.

The badges central to our programmatic initiative are taught in both of the first-year classes that make up our composition program (Composition, and Composition and Critical Reading) and draw on multiple modalities to deliver content. The *Coastal Composition Commons* is a stand-alone Web site (ccc.coastal.edu) hosted on a *WordPress* platform using the *BadgeOS* and *Credly* plug-ins. First-year writing students are directed to earn a specific badge by their instructors. To do so, students visit the Web page for the designated badge, where they encounter alphabetic text, images, and (in many cases) embedded videos that provide instructional content related to that particular badge. This content consists of uniform sections that emphasize the *what*, *why*, and *how* of the writing move. For example, the Quoting badge is structured around the following headings: "What Is a Quotation?," "Why Do We Quote?," "What Does Quoting Look Like?," and "Okay, So How Do I Quote?" Each badge requires that students read, view, and often listen to the instructional content and then compose digital artifacts based on an assignment to be assessed for proficiency of that skill. Each writing assignment asks students to move through three steps: responding (often to an embedded text), writing (to show that they understand and can enact the skills and strategies central to the badge), and reflecting (to support the development of metacognitive understandings). Students compose their submissions in word processing software and upload them as pdfs, which are then read and either approved or denied by the instructor.

The eight badges in the Composition course and seven badges in Composition and Critical Reading speak directly to the student learning

Figure 1. The anatomy of a digital badge

outcomes for each course, and they shape the way writing is taught in this context and how assessment is directed. In this way, the badges have been designed to serve two functions: first, they make the student learning outcomes more visible to students and faculty members, emphasizing the outcomes' centrality to first-year composition at Coastal Carolina University, and second, they ensure all students receive direct instruction on these key concepts, ideally eliminating gaps in instruction. Indeed, many of the faculty members who participate in our annual assessment comment on the productivity of recentering on these directives, which can otherwise become secondary as we work through a semester. Within our department, we often speak of the ways in which the badges provide our writing program the benefits of unification without standardization. Many of our instructors have become expertly skilled at weaving badges into the larger structure of their courses, and they take a variety of approaches in terms of when and how they draw on these programmatic pedagogical materials. Although the content of these badges remains unchanged during the semester, our instructors maintain their individual freedoms by deciding when and how they will incorporate badges into their courses. However, a natural sequencing has emerged organically from the badge collective: during a typical fall semester, the majority of instructors will lead with the Wordsmithing and Shifting Styles I badges as a way of fostering audience awareness in student writing. A second wave of badges arrives toward the middle of the semester, which includes (most often in the following order) Shaping a Thesis, Paragraphing, Summarizing, Paraphrasing, and Quoting. Nearly all instructors reserve the Synthesizing badge for the final few weeks of the semester, when students are composing papers grounded in secondary research. It is perhaps not a coincidence that the difficulty level and acceptance rates of these badges are correlated, or that instructors mostly choose to introduce softer badges earlier in the semester when their students are new to the badging system. Still, there seems to be a natural rhythm to the composition classroom, as the badge program has revealed.

Digital Badges, Faculty Engagement, and Shared Authorship

In addition to teaching the skills and strategies that we have named as central to students' successful development as writers, as a program and as an institution—through the articulation of the core outcomes associated with first-year writing—the badges also suggest a particular ideology of language as they embody a pedagogical stance, as all instructional materials do. Some badges are overtly designed to model, for both instructors and students, a specific perspective toward language and linguistic diversity. These badges, named Shifting Styles I, Shifting Styles II, and Wordsmithing, embrace the spirit of "students' right to their own language" (CCCC) as they invite students to see language, writing, and dialect in terms that resist a prescriptive approach to correctness. By stressing the rhetorical nature of communication, the shifting scenes of literacy, and the political implications of privileging correctness, these badges help our writing program resist the focus on conventions that can still be found in some writing courses. In this way, the content of the badges shapes our program and ensures that students are exposed to a common set of strategies and perspectives regarding language—perspectives that value a diverse set of literacy practices. In a program where writing is taught by a combination of tenured, tenure-track, and contingent instructors from a variety of backgrounds, the consistency promoted by the badges helps establish a common set of practices.

This move toward consistency was a collaborative undertaking as we composed badges in-house; because Alan built the badging site from the ground up and because Denise coordinated the authoring of badges, this program remains our own. We retain the freedom to make changes to the badging program when and how we want and can do this with considerable ease. This allows us many affordances, but it primarily positions us to revise our badges in response to a variety of programmatic concerns, questions, and successes. For example, if our annual assessment shows that we need to do more to teach synthesis, we can revise the Synthesizing and Synthesizing II badges; if we want to do more to define the distinctions between our two first-year composition courses, we can do so through the badges; or if we want to respond to a new concern that arises, we are free to create a new badge—as we did in response to the revision to MLA documentation style in the handbook's eighth edition. Because we own these badges, we are free to rethink and revise them in light of the ecology of goals and concerns that shape our program. In fact, we have engaged in some degree of revision every year since the badges have been designed. During some moments, this has meant that badges have been added, sample texts have been substituted out, or, most recently, patterns emerging from the badges themselves (we did not initially use a template when writing them) have reshaped all existing badges. The ways in which we have constructed the *Coastal Composition Commons* allow us to be responsive, and this seems to be of great pedagogical and programmatic significance.

By creating the content for all of these badges ourselves, by composing the texts in house, we also offer all the instructors working in our program opportunities for shared authorship. While not every instructor teaching in our first-year writing program has contributed to a badge, we created frequent opportunities for input as we developed the program. For instance, to decide upon badge topics, we hosted workshops where instructors worked in small groups and generated ideas on how to shape the badges. At subsequent workshops, we shared preliminary badge content and collected feedback. We also continue to invite faculty members from all ranks to help compose and revise badges, and a significant percentage of those teaching in our program have played active roles in this production process. While this distributed authorship has helped position the *Coastal Composition Commons* as a community initiative, the success of this approach depends on the work individual instructors do as they weave these badges into their courses.

The Material Realities of Teaching with Digital Badges

When the use of these badges was instituted in the fall of 2014, a fourth, digitally based credit hour was added to both Composition, and Composition and Critical Reading. And in doing so, the instruction, application, and evaluation of the badges sought to extend both the scope and experience associated with these first-year classes. In material terms, the addition of this credit hour addressed some issues common to the teaching of composition in many institutional settings: with a tenure and tenure-track teaching load of 4-3, and a teaching load of 5-5 for non-tenure-track faculty members, our instructors were asked to teach many sections of composition and work with many students (our composition classes are capped at twenty students). The addition of the badges, and the additional credit hour they carry, reduced these teaching loads, bringing non-slotted teaching by faculty members down to a 4-4 load. The trade-off, quite a significant one, is that these instructors were asked to teach fewer classes but in fundamentally different ways and were required to use a newly developed Web site to teach, no matter how comfortable they were with navigating emerging technologies. This transition proved to be especially challenging for instructors who were unfamiliar or uncomfortable with instructional technologies.

Since the fall of 2014, we have required that instructors of Composition and Composition and Critical Reading teach at least six badges in each course and that they make these badges worth between eighteen and twenty-four percent of students' final grades, to reflect the additional credit hour. This means that an instructor teaching four full sections of a composition course and assigning six badges (and many instructors voluntarily assign all eight of the badges) receives at least 480 additional student submissions per semester that require assessment. This staggering number does not account for the multiple attempts many of our faculty members allow their students to submit as students work to demonstrate the skills and understandings needed to earn a badge. In addition, these badges initially called for a serious reconsideration of course design and assignment sequencing. During the first few semesters, many instructors assigned the badges as extraneous activities; many did not cover the badge-specific content explicitly in class or dedicate time for students to review drafted submissions during class meetings. This led to frustration: instructors were frustrated with the quality of student work, and students were frustrated with the additive assignments. Instructors in our program successfully combatted these frustrations by integrating the badges into their course design—by reshaping the completion of badges as benchmarks within broader assignments, reshaping badge assignments so they spoke in explicit ways to the existing assignments, and allowing students to use and rework some of the material generated for badges in subsequent assignments. This rethinking demanded much labor from our instructors and in many cases it seemed productive for this kind of course redevelopment to happen on an individual level. While we have many shared materials, such as a customized text titled the *Coastal Writers' Reference*, a default textbook, sample syllabi, and shared assignment ideas (which are made public during frequent teaching workshops and on a digital resources page), the process many instructors worked through on their own as they decided how to make the *Coastal Composition Commons* work for them and their teaching was and continues to be fruitful. This is the kind of labor, though, that often remains invisible as individual instructors' teaching is evaluated, especially by students.

This labor, however, isn't unique to our programmatic approach. Any curricular shift that speaks to current composing practices demands time and attention. In her 2004 CCCC Chair's Address, Yancey called on the field to make digital literacies central to our classes, pointing to the shifts brought about by the development of the Web and networked platforms for communication. When commenting on the writing publics supported by digitization, she says, "[U]nlike what happens in our classes, *no one is forcing this public to write*. There are no *A*'s here, no Dean's lists, no writing teacher to keep tabs on you" (300), and as designers of a programmatic badging initiative, we realize that our use of emerging technologies could potentially miss the mark for the kind of motivated writing Yancey describes. As we teach with the *Coastal Composition Commons*, we do keep tabs; keeping tabs, in fact, is a significant aspect of teaching with badges, as earning a badge functions as a core benchmark in our classes. Yancey's point that "[w]hatever the exchange value may be for these writers—and there are millions of them, here and around the world—it's certainly not grades" seems to anticipate the early reaction to badges at Coastal Carolina (300–01). It quickly became apparent to us that the badges themselves, and the demonstration of understandings and skills they recognize, were not valuable in and of themselves. The exchange value—a valuation Yancey positions firmly within the scope of the classroom—was not enough to either justify or situate the work called for by these pedagogical modules. The valuation came, for students and instructors alike, once the badges were woven into a larger class curriculum in ways that showcased their usefulness. Like Yancey suggests of the writing composed, shared, and circulated in digital public spaces, the badges accrued value when they began "to operate in an economy driven by use value" (301).

When we launched the *Coastal Composition Commons*, we knew we were asking a lot of our faculty members by rerouting the focus of their composition classes. Even if the core skills and strategies highlighted by the badges were already central to their teaching, instructors still had to rethink their courses and how they were embedding the badges' concepts in their teaching. Instructors also had to learn to navigate the *Coastal Composition Commons* site itself, and while it was designed around concerns for usability (and underwent rounds of usability testing) we realized this was a lot to ask of already overworked faculty members. We also realized that our diverse group of instructors was not uniformly comfortable with teaching with technologies. For a handful of instructors, this was the first time they had made an instructional technology (beyond a learning management system) central to their teaching. We needed the digital delivery system the *Coastal Composition Commons* provides but knew the digitized nature of the Web site would present challenges for some instructors.

Circulation, Exchange, and Valuation

Our initial challenges with the badging site were warranted, though, as the site offers so much potential for the shared construction and delivery of pedagogical practice. While the site offers flexibility and variability for instructors, for students it offers a more uniform experience in terms of exchange and reception of their writing. Yancey comments on the expanded possibilities for distribution and circulation commonly associated with digitized spaces explicitly as she points to the shortcomings of traditional classroom exchange:

> In contrast to the reading public nearly two centuries ago, the "real" reading public of school is solitary, the teacher whose reading consists of print text delivered on the teacher's desk. In contrast to the development of a writing public, the classroom writer is not a member of a collaborative group with a common project linked to the world at large and delivered in multiple genres and media, but a singular person writing over and over again—to the teacher. (309–10)

Like the composition classroom context Yancey points to, the *Coastal Composition Commons* draws on a system of exchange that positions the instructor as a reader. Student submissions to the badging site can only be read and accredited by instructors: once posted, a submission can be searched by a user with instructor rights (all instructors can see all submissions), read and commented on by that instructor (in a commenting box or on the document itself, which can then be reuploaded), and either approved or denied. Students cannot view other student submissions, and the compositions they produce for this site are not collaborative.

In general and in many educational contexts, texts are moving in new ways due to emerging technologies. David Sheridan, Jim Ridolfo, and Anthony Michel explain, "Just as important as technologies of production are technologies of reproduction and distribution. . . . A standard personal computer can distribute millions of copies of a web page without incurring additional cost" (811). While large-scale distribution of texts was difficult to achieve in the past, and was in many cases reserved for those with special skills and knowledge as well as vast material resources, digital technologies are making such distribution possible for the nonspecialist, and therefore for the students we teach in college composition classes. In this shift that Sheridan, Ridolfo, and Michel see as furthering the democratic project, the possibility for texts to move in larger and less limited circuits becomes realized, and as a result, we need to think about how this transition to "many-to-many, not one-to-many" technologies should invite greater consideration of delivery and distribution in composition courses (811). While we agree that teachers of writing need to focus on the movement of student texts and ask how such movement might reshape the ways in which we think about production as it broadens our view of this process to include the ways in which texts travel, we find value in the determined circulatory paths central to this badging initiative as they support a pedagogical practice that favors programmatic consistency.

In his article "Composition and the Circulation of Writing," John Trimbur, too, calls the field to consider the ways writing circulates. He argues that

> neglecting delivery has led writing teachers to equate the activity of composing with writing itself and to miss altogether the complex delivery systems through which writing circulates. By privileging composing as the main site of instruction, the teaching of writing has taken up what Karl Marx calls a "one-sided" view of production and thereby has largely erased the cycle that links the production, distribution, exchange, and consumption of writing. (189–90)

To further his point and show how the movement of writing is neglected in many composition classes, Trimbur turns to typical classroom practices that limit considerations of delivery. He says that "although student writing does indeed circulate and take on the symbolic exchange value of academic credit, the directions 'trade papers with a partner' or 'hand in your paper' indicate the limits of the circuit in the intimate space of the classroom" (195). The *Coastal Composition Commons* has, in effect, expanded this "intimate" classroom space and extended it to a programmatic level. But this, in some ways, is innovative at least in terms of delivery of both instruction and in archival potential. As a program, we are establishing shared ways of framing instruction and have created innovative approaches to assigning and collecting student work even as we restrict the paths of exchange student texts can navigate. We have reified the "symbolic exchange value of academic credit," but we have digitized this process in terms of collection, evaluation, and the sharing potential of an earned badge. While we initially expected students would share their earned badges over social media, we have seen little evidence of this; it turns out that students are not enthusiastically sharing their badges on their *LinkedIn* profiles.

Despite this lack of earned-badge posting, we have created a system that supports an increase of valuation for student texts in terms of use and exchange. Paying attention to the limited movement of student texts, Bruce Horner, in *Terms of Work for Composition: A Materialist Critique*, states, "[S]tudent writing is evaluated as a commodity while being produced and distributed in ways that guarantee its lack of exchange value: it is clearly authored by and for institutions, not the individual writer, and has an extremely limited range of circulation" (50). Because student writing is location-bound (as it is by our badging system), Horner sees this writing as devalued—seen only in terms of the grade for which it can be exchanged. As creators of a badging system, we see the danger of an overemphasis of exchange. But here is where the badging system as a function of pedagogical delivery helps us sidestep an unproductive valuation of the economy of grading and grades. As instructors stress the centrality of the badges to the larger ongoing inquiries in a composition course—as is enacted when they build badges into a larger sequence of assignments—the functionality of badge submissions is extended. As instructors and students see the usefulness of how the badges introduce the moves central to much of the writing asked of us in academic contexts, the badges resist the strict economics of exchange as they accrue more perceived value.

We turn to the functions of use and exchange here to suggest that, in many ways, this programmatic initiative is doing exactly what it was intended to do: extend the scope and reach of a particular composition program in ways that help unify students' experiences without standardizing those experiences, as the program positions teaching as a community undertaking through shared authorship. This is a project grounded in concerns of production and distribution. When building this system, our goal was to construct a widely usable platform for instruction that would not only enrich student learning but that would also support faculty development in concrete ways. What is also suggested, though, is that we need to resist a binary approach to print and digital composing practices by locating value in initiatives that draw on both mono- and multimodal practices. Thus, the alphabetic texts students are asked to compose as they complete badge submissions do not undercut the utility of this program; instead, assignments stress the fluidity that exists across production practices.

When we first designed the *Coastal Composition Commons*, we assumed its value would come from the badges students earned. Badging systems, falsely, have become associated with motivation. Earning a badge, some believe, provides a jolt of motivation through the promise of an extrinsic reward. Samuel Abramovich, Christian Schunn, and Ross Mitsuo Higashi show that it is not the makeup of badges that motivates but rather the background of the learner (218). In our experience, though, the badges central to our initiative resist the traditional function of badging itself as a system of recognizable exchange. The badges have become significant, for students and instructors alike, in light of their pedagogical affordances and the ways in which they function in, with, and through the larger textual ecology of the class. Students find the badges useful because the badge assignments teach the moves called for by other writing tasks and in other settings; instructors find the badges helpful in terms of their sequencing potential. Indeed, the valuation of our badges begins and ends within our institutional boundaries. Though the badges are tied to specific learning outcomes, their value speaks to a more holistic sense of application that privileges fluidity in how badges are assigned and drawn upon.

The value of the badges, then, is tied to the flexibility they provide for instructors. In terms of production, we can alter and add to the badges at any time. In addition, the badging system is a shared undertaking: all teachers in our program are invited to revise and add badges. In terms of distribution, flexibility is also key. The badges are being woven into classes in richly diverse ways and are taught when and how each individual instructor sees fit. The core value of this approach depends, then, on its digital nature—the flexibility it allows as we create and disseminate the badges. As Yancey says, "[W]e have committed to the screen for administrative purposes" as we host these program-wide pedagogical tools on a digital space that ensures flexibility in terms of its production and reproduction (307). The badge site also acts as a repository and digital archive for student work. As teacher-researchers, the program presents rich potential. Currently, two of our linguistics professors—Becky Childs and J. Daniel Hasty, who coauthored the Shifting Styles I and II badges—are analyzing student responses to the badges and questioning the linguistic stereotypes students bring to class. Tracing the responses as students move from their first to second semester, Childs and Hasty are questioning the ideologies central to how writing is taught at our university (see Childs).

Fluidity, Affordance, and Modalities

While our current approach—which asks students to compose alphabetic texts delivered directly to their instructors—could be seen as a shortcoming, we argue, instead, that the *Coastal Composition Commons* presents a snapshot of a programmatic initiative that functions across modalities. As we have argued, the badging initiative redefines *in-house* as a territory constructed by the badging site itself and asks both instructors and students to spend a fair amount of time engaging with the learning outcomes, as materialized on the badging site. Our hope is that the badging Web site showcases the potential of this kind of digital space to prepare students for the kinds of composing commonly called for by the many screens we read, write, and compose on, for, and with. As instructors initially drafted badges using *Google Docs*, some experienced the potentials of such shared spaces for the first time. In addition, many of the badges include links to readings that question the intersections of technologies and literacies (pieces written by scholars like danah boyd and Nicholas Carr). We also hope these readings encourage our faculty members to theorize digitality with students and design assignments around such lines of inquiry. Denise recently completed a textbook, *Writing Moves*, with coauthors Eleanor Kutz and Christian Pulver, that furthers this initiative: the book supports students as they both study the world of contemporary composing and write for digital environments (Kutz et al.).

The *Coastal Composition Commons* positions technology as central to the teaching of writing in our program. This, in programmatic terms, seems significant. In addition to creating a shared language around the teaching of writing (a language that echoes but also moves beyond our student learning outcomes), the program also positions digital reading, composing, and responding (to the badges themselves and to student submissions) as common activities for writing students and instructors. This technology functions across modalities and stresses the ways in which print and digital literacies are in conversation with one another. The *Coastal Composition Commons* resists an approach grounded in either single or multiple modalities. While the pedagogical work of the badging site is currently delivered across modalities and student work is primarily alphabetic in nature, the site itself (and the flexibility it provides) ensures responsiveness as both teaching and composing practices shift. We are constantly searching for ways to evolve, and the *Coastal Composition Commons* allows us to grow with our program, with our faculty, and with our students.

As digital reading, writing, and responding become more central to our program, we are making use of this moment in ways that underscore the true potentials of digital interfaces in terms of both emerging literacy practices and their relational potential. Currently, Alan is piloting an approach to embedded social annotation on the *Commons* site that fundamentally reshapes the goals central to the badging initiative. Using the social annotation tool *Hypothes.is*, an interface is layered on every Web page which allows users to highlight and comment on the digital text. This tool invites students to respond to texts on the site itself and to archive the reading responses—the questions, connections, and realizations—that emerge as they engage a text while making such responses publicly visible to their instructors and peers. This strategy embraces Web 2.0 sensibilities, creating a larger sense of possibility for formal and informal learning environments. While few instructors in our program currently use this approach, it stresses the potential of digital sites and underscores the responsiveness of large-scale initiatives built in such spaces. Unlike the original use of the *Coastal Composition Commons* site, this social annotation initiative engages in the kinds of twenty-first-century learning strategies called upon across settings and contexts by encouraging learners to become more active and collaborative in their literacy practices.

Many teachers of writing are doing innovative work that points to the changing nature of production as we move into more networked and linked spaces as readers and writers, and as designers and community participants. The work central to the *Coastal Composition Commons* exemplifies one programmatic approach that takes advantage of many affordances associated with digital spaces through the design of multimodal pedagogical materials that are being shared across a first-year writing program. This approach focuses on the creation and distribution of a digitized set of teaching materials and practices, while it asks that students compose alphabetic texts delivered to their instructors. Instead of reifying the binary often located between alphabetic and multimodal texts, though, we suggest that this initiative stresses fluidity in modalities as well as in composing practices in larger terms. We hope our work shows the productivity of using various modalities (and calls for modalities) to address a variety of users' needs and purposes. The *Coastal Composition Commons* has allowed us to produce something impossible in print: a responsive, collaboratively written, digitally shared curriculum meant to be used in highly flexible ways by a large number of users (instructors and students alike). That students are not asked to compose multimodal responses as they earn badges does not undercut the innovation of this approach; instead it shows that we as digital composers (instructors and students) move across modalities in light of our rhetorical purposes. We hope this case study is read as indicative of the promise of digitally anchored programmatic initiatives in light of the fluidity they can support. Like the student writers we work with, we need to consider the affordances associated with contemporary sites of composing and take advantage of their potentials.

Works Cited

Abramovich, Samuel, et al. "Are Badges Useful in Education? It Depends upon the Type of Badge and Expertise of Learner." *Educational Technology Research and Development*, vol. 61, no. 2, 2013, pp. 217–32.

Alexander, Jonathan, and Jacqueline Rhodes. *On Multimodality: New Media in Composition Studies.* Conference on College Composition and Communication / National Council of Teachers of English, 2014.

CCCC (Conference on College Composition and Communication). "Students' Right to Their Own Language." *Conference on College Composition and Communication*, NCTE, 1998–2019, prod-ncte-cdn.azureedge.net/nctefiles/groups/cccc/newsrtol.pdf. Originally published in *College Composition and Communication*, vol. 25, no. 3, Sept. 1974.

Childs, Becky. "Student Voice and Linguistic Identity: Digital Badging as a Tool for Retention of First Year and First Generation Undergraduates." *Journal of English Linguistics*, vol. 46, no. 3, 2018, pp. 186–98.

"Digital Badges." *HASTAC*, www.hastac.org/initiatives/digital-badges. Accessed 6 July 2019.

Horner, Bruce. *Terms of Work for Composition: A Materialist Critique*. State U of New York P, 2000.

Kress, Gunther R. *Multimodality: A Social Semiotic Approach to Contemporary Communication*. Routledge, 2010.

Kutz, Eleanor, et al. *Writing Moves: Composing in a Digital World*. Fountainhead Press, 2017.

Palmeri, Jason. *Remixing Composition: A History of Multimodal Writing Pedagogy*. Southern Illinois UP / NCTE, 2012.

Selfe, Cynthia L., editor. *Multimodal Composition: Resources for Teachers*. Hampton Press, 2007.

Sheridan, David M., et al. "The Available Means of Persuasion: Mapping a Theory and Pedagogy of Multimodal Public Rhetoric." *JAC: A Journal of Composition Theory*, vol. 25, no. 4, 2005, pp. 803–23.

Shipka, Jody. "A Multimodal Task-Based Framework for Composing." *College Composition and Communication*, vol. 57, no. 2, Dec. 2005, pp. 277–306.

Trimbur, John. "Composition and the Circulation of Writing." *College Composition and Communication*, vol. 52, no. 2, Dec. 2000, pp. 188–219.

Yancey, Kathleen Blake. "Made Not Only in Words: Composition in a New Key." *College Composition and Communication*, vol. 56, no. 2, Dec. 2004, pp. 297–328.

Making the Case: Implementing Multimodality in Undergraduate Major Programs in Writing and Rhetoric

Rory Lee

> We have a broad field writing major. We're attempting to tell as complete a story about writing as we possibly can in this major. Obviously, it would never have been responsible or complete to tell a story of writing that wasn't multimodal. But now it jumps up every morning and whacks us on the head with a club, and there would be guilty consciences all around if we tried ignoring it.
>
> —Undergraduate major program representative

Over the past decade, the field of rhetoric and composition has devoted significant scholarly attention toward both the practice of multimodality (e.g., Alexander and Rhodes; Anderson et al.; Kress; Lauer, "Contending" and "What's in a Name"; Lutkewitte; Morrison; Palmeri; Selfe, "Movement"; Sheridan et al.; Shipka) and the development of undergraduate major programs in writing and rhetoric (variably named; e.g., Balzhiser and McLeod; Giberson et al.; Giberson and Moriarty; *Writing Major*; Weisser and Grobman). However, few have explored the intersections between the two. In this collection, Derek Owens and Tara Roeder trace the rise of the term *writing studies*, which began to replace *composition* to describe the field, as well as the ways the term gained momentum alongside the multimodal turn even though *writing studies* does not capture the capaciousness implied by composition and multimodality. Nonetheless, *writing studies* does signal a move beyond the universal first-year course. And if the multimodal turn does represent more accurately our field's contemporary understanding of and approach to writing and rhetoric, then we as a field need to inquire into the ways that undergraduate major programs, both old and new, have designed and implemented curricula that extend beyond alphabetic writing and attend to multimodal composing practices.

As evinced through my 2013 survey of nineteen undergraduate major programs in writing and rhetoric, multimodality is becoming a common curricular feature (Lee). That said, and as is perhaps expected, the curricular incorporation of multimodality varies across undergraduate major programs, and one reason for such variance is the extent to which multimodality is emphasized within the major. Said another way, the implementation of multimodality looks different for a major that makes multimodality a priority than it does for a major that makes multimodality one focus among many. Furthermore, the degree to which an undergraduate major program values or implements multimodality could be contingent on multiple factors, such as faculty buy-in, departmental and institutional resources, programmatic funding, faculty expertise (or lack thereof), programmatic goals and outcomes, faculty availability, and other departmental or institutional constraints.

To explore in greater detail the way curricula attentive to multimodality are diversely designed and implemented within undergraduate major programs in writing and rhetoric, I conducted case studies of three major programs in particular, ones located in different geographical regions of the United States, offered at different institutional types, and containing different levels of multimodal activity. The first was an undergraduate major program with *low* multimodal activity offered at a RU/VH (research university with very high research activity) located in the Northwest. The second was a program with *medium* multimodal activity offered at a private Master's/L institution (master's college or university, larger program) in the South. The third was a program with *high* multimodal activity offered at a DRU institution (doctoral/research university) in the Midwest.

To determine whether a major program exhibited low, medium, or high multimodal activity, I relied on the data collected from my aforementioned survey, which was completed by a program representative for each major. More specifically, I used data indicating how many faculty members implement multimodal instruction, how many required courses offer multimodal instruction, and how frequently multimodal texts are created in classes marked for multimodal instruction. That said, I want to underscore that the designations of low, medium, and high are intended to be descriptive rather than evaluative. Put otherwise, *high* is not a designation that is inherently better or that other undergraduate major programs should aspire to, nor is *low* to be considered inadequate or an indictment of a program's curricular implementation of multimodality. This framework is merely an attempt to illuminate the different degrees to which multimodality as a way of thinking and composing is reflected within a major. Moreover, and as Bruce Horner argues in this collection, multimodality—and specifically the countability of modes—should not be perceived as better than monomodality and the absence of multiple modes, especially since, as Jody Shipka and others have noted, there is no such thing as a monomodal text. Instead, we should think of multimodality as the intrinsic status of all texts and as a means to highlight the presence of, and collaboration between and among, multiple modes. In addition, we should consider the number of modes as well as the privileging of certain modes to be symptomatic of the social and rhetorical practices imbued within and informing a particular genre and the genre's corresponding rhetorical situation.

I completed the case studies by interviewing two faculty members per participating undergraduate major program: the program representative who responded previously to my survey, and a faculty member who teaches multimodality in the major. I also collected curricular materials: for example, syllabi, assignment prompts, and assessment rubrics. The set of questions for both interviewees worked deductively, starting with the curricular inclusion of multimodality in the program as a whole and working toward that individual's pedagogical practices regarding multimodality. In what follows, I share and interpret the data collected from these three case studies. To begin, I provide general information about each major; then, I articulate how all three programs define, teach, assess, and support multimodal composing. In so doing, I talk across the programs to synthesize points of convergence and departure and explicate the circumstances that can foster or constrain multimodal activity.

Programmatic Overviews

The undergraduate major program in writing and rhetoric with low multimodal activity—offered at the RU/VH institution located in the Northwest—is housed within an English department that offers an English major with three concentration options: literature, writing, and English teaching.[1] For this case study, I focused on the writing option, which was established in the fall of 2011. The English department has two hundred to three hundred students on average majoring in English, and one hundred to two hundred of them select the writing option. This case study includes just one interview with the program representative, as I was unable to secure another interview; the other faculty members were concerned about their lack of expertise in multimodality. While this is unfortunate given the methodological design of my study, it does justify and deem accurate the categorization of low for this major's level of multimodal activity. During the interview, the program representative emphasized that the implementation of multimodality is "just in its inception." While no faculty member "specializes in that area of study," the program representative believes they can no longer "retreat from" multimodality for two reasons: the increasing importance of being able to use digital technologies to create multimodal texts within and for the professional sphere, and the way multimodality reflects the field's current understanding of writing and literacy. Given multimodality's presence and significance in the professional sphere and to the field, the program representative said "there would be guilty consciences all around" if they ignored multimodality within the major.

The undergraduate major program in writing and rhetoric with medium multimodal activity—offered at the Master's/L institution in the South—is one of two majors, along with literature, offered within the Department of Literature, Writing, and Rhetoric.[2] This program, which was established in 1987, has between one hundred and two hundred majors at a given time. For this case study, unlike the prior one, I interviewed two people: the program representative who participated in my 2013 survey, and a faculty member, whom I refer to below as the faculty respondent, who teaches multimodality within the major. As noted by the program representative, the department made a commitment to implementing multimodality within the first-year writing program, an emphasis that then extended vertically into the major. However, when asked how prominent he considers multimodality to be within the major, the faculty respondent said, "Across the degree, multimodal has a presence, but I would say not an overwhelming strong one." Nonetheless, multimodality is an emphasis within this major, a result of curricular changes made between 2008 and 2009 based on three factors: responsible professional preparation, responsible civic preparation, and student feedback.

As of my interview, the faculty members are pleased with the curricular changes and with the way multimodality is implemented within the undergraduate major program. That said, the program representative admitted that it took them a long time to get to this point, as "not every faculty member [felt] comfortable about assigning or assessing multimodal [texts]." In addition, many students initially resist multimodality. As the faculty respondent said, "What I keep hearing repeatedly in student comments is, 'I'm a writing major; why am I having to learn this?'" Although he replies to such skepticism rather similarly—rebutting that, as writers, students need to position themselves as communicators to "think beyond just words as writing," "find the best way to fit the situation," and thus not think of writing and multimodality as dichotomous—he nonetheless admitted that helping students see the value of multimodality is "an ongoing battle."

The undergraduate major program in writing and rhetoric with high multimodal activity—offered at the DRU institution in the Midwest—is situated within an independent writing and rhetoric department. The major in writing and rhetoric, which has between fifty and one hundred students, offers three specializations: writing for the professions, writing for new media, and writing as a discipline.[3] While multimodality runs through all three specializations, I focused primarily on the specialization in writing for new media, as it contained the highest level of multimodal activity. Once again, I interviewed two people for this case study: the program representative who responded to my survey and a faculty member and then chair of the department who teaches multimodality and oversees the writing for new media specialization, whom I refer to below as the program chair.

The writing and rhetoric major was launched in 2008 and, according to the program representative, multimodality is "a concept that's woven throughout [the] program and all of [the] courses." In fact, "the concept of multimodality was something that came up from the beginning of the development of the major," he said. Similar to the major with low multimodal activity, the faculty members in this program also feel compelled to include multimodality because the concept reflects how the field now thinks about writing, literacy, and the tools we use to compose. And as is the case for the major programs with low and medium multimodal activity, the faculty members in this program also understand the importance of multimodality to the evolving marketplace.

Although multimodality is emphasized throughout the major, and especially within the specialization for writing for new media, the program representative indicated he is still displeased with the amount of attention given to multimodality, a theme we see across all three programs. "I think at this point it's underserved," he admitted. Although all nine of the program's faculty members implement multimodality in some fashion, the specialization that implements multimodality the most relies too heavily on one faculty member, who as noted above was also serving as the program chair. In short, the labor for this specialization is not well distributed. The fact that their "numbers are growing" in that specialization compounds matters further. As a result, the program representative hopes that they'll make "one or two, maybe three new hires in new media over the next five to six years."

Going forward, and given this programmatic context, I detail how these major programs define, teach, assess, and support multimodality and, in doing so, highlight and unpack the instances of overlap and disparity.

Defining Multimodality

Multimodality is in some ways a problematic term because it is often perceived in opposition and superior to alphabetic writing; moreover, some in the field consider it an empty signifier, whereas others tend to use interchangeably, and in many cases privilege, terms like *multimedia* and *new media*. However, those interviewed in the case studies exhibited a rather sophisticated understanding of multimodality. For example, the program representative for the undergraduate major with low multimodal activity displayed a nuanced understanding of the term informed by not only theory and scholarship in the field—in particular, the work of Shipka—but also his experiences at Ohio State's Digital Media and Composition (DMAC) Institute. "I much prefer thinking along the lines that Jody Shipka does," he said. "What we're talking about when we talk about multimodality is modalities that get beyond alphabetic print. So that could be, in Shipka's case, ballet slippers." Here, the program representative recognized that multimodality has existed as a phenomenon prior to, and therefore does not always need to be linked to, the digital. In addition, and despite describing himself as "just good enough" to teach multimodality, the program representative has nonetheless been able to define and explain multimodality enough to persuade other faculty members that the concept is a way of framing and understanding writing that is worth implementing into the curriculum. Thus, the program representative is both an anomaly and an advocate: without his willingness to put in the additional work as well as his continued insistence that multimodality necessitates a place in the curriculum, multimodality's presence would perhaps be nonexistent within this major.

The program representative for the major with medium multimodal activity pointed to an assumed definition: that *multimodality* refers to using a combination of modes to communicate. As she said, "When we talk about multimodality, we're talking about modes of communication in addition to . . . alphabetic words. So, aural, images, design, color—all of those things." This assumed definition also contains a bit of nuance. When asked if faculty members in this program use other terms, such as *multimedia* and *new media*, she said, "We probably tend to separate modes from media. . . . I think we suggest new media in terms of digital technologies and digital media, and the idea that that fosters multimodality in composing." In addition, the program chair for the undergraduate major program with high multimodal activity said he makes a concerted effort in class to differentiate *multimodality*—the "crossing" of modes to create a text—from terms such as *multimedia* (for him, texts and technologies that contain multiple media) and *new media* (online interaction between producer and consumer). According to the program chair, an important distinction is that *multimodality* is attentive to process while *multimedia* and *new media* describe products and our engagement with them.

However, the ways in which the interviewees understood the term sometimes conflicted with the ways they used the term in practice. For instance, the program representative for the major with low multimodal activity said he'll often avoid using the term *multimodality* in curricular discussions "because nobody knows what it is immediately." Despite acting as the vanguard for the implementation of multimodality, the faculty respondent for the major with medium multimodal activity said he rarely, if ever, uses the term in class with students and will only use it when addressing those in the field, opting instead to use terms such as *multimedia*, *interactive writing*, *new media*, or *emerging media* when addressing people outside the field. Even the program chair for the major with high multimodal activity, who devotes time to distinguishing *multimodality* from other terms, acknowledged that he will use *multimedia* more than *multimodality* during curricular discussions with colleagues.

The inconsistent ways in which *multimodality* is used, despite the rather informed ways in which it is understood individually, substantiate Claire Lauer's claim that the use of a given term is based less on difference in definition and more upon the context and the audience to whom the discussion is being directed ("Contending" 226). This trend also indicates that, while the practice of multimodality is being implemented within the curriculum, such implementation is often latent: it's not framed explicitly as multimodality, and it's not always informed by the theory of the field.

Teaching Multimodality

While the term *multimodality* was at times used inconsistently during my interviews, the teaching of multimodality across these three undergraduate major programs in writing and rhetoric does reveal some consistency. For example, those who teach multimodality—though they don't draw from a consistent set of terms, concepts, or readings and therefore don't enact a similarly theorized pedagogy—do nonetheless enact a model of analysis informed by Diana George before production, with analysis both serving the purpose of imitation and being rooted in notions of audience and genre.[4] For instance, the program representative for the major with low multimodal activity said he tends to bring in and use examples that are similar to what students will be creating. As such, when he does have students analyze texts, he frames the exercise around production rather than reception; that is, the ensuing analysis is not intended to strengthen reading comprehension but rather to prepare students to be effective producers. The program representative and the program chair for the major with high multimodal activity also follow the analysis-first, production-second pedagogical model. As the program representative said, students "look at and analyze the things that [they]'re going to be doing."

The case studies also indicate that the visual is the mode that receives the most pedagogical attention, and in many ways this may be symptomatic of the emergence over the last three decades of the subfield of visual rhetoric. In other words, our field has rigorously attended to the visual—in particular, the static image—in ways we haven't yet for other nonalphabetic modes.[5] For the major programs with low and medium multimodal activity, the visual acts as an anchor for how teachers approach and teach multimodal composing. The program representative for the major with low multimodal activity said he emphasizes the visual more because "it's dominant," "the demand for it is high," and "there's a great deal to learn about it." The program representative for the major with medium multimodal activity said that they tend to talk more about "visual rhetoric in composition, which then gets [them] to, or at least a part of, multimodality." Moreover, the attention given to the visual and to multimodality as a whole in this program is grounded more so in the concept of document design than in static or moving images. In other words, rather than refer to document design as a separate mode, what Gunther Kress refers to as "layout," the major with medium multimodal activity positions the visual as a capacious term encompassing three modes: static image, moving image, and, most important to them, layout.

The major with high multimodal activity appears to emphasize other modes in addition to the written word equally. The program representative said that his treatment of modes in class is rather similar, as he doesn't "want students to favor one over the other." In referring to his treatment of modes, the program chair said, "I try to mix them up. I probably lean more definitely toward video. But ideally, I would like to see it more balanced between video, static images, audio." Also worth noting is that the major with high multimodal activity was the only one that specifically mentioned audio, a mode that is too frequently overlooked and undertreated according to recent scholarship in multimodality (e.g., Alexander and Rhodes; Halbritter; Selfe, "Movement"). Thus, one defining feature of an undergraduate major program with robust multimodal instruction is that the pedagogy is inclusive of and attentive to multiple modes rather than just the visual as static image or layout. Furthermore, the coverage of modes should ideally invoke Aristotelian adaptability: that is, we should think in terms of the available modes of persuasion by considering which modes are most appropriate given social practices and the rhetorical situation.

Assessing Multimodal Texts

The collective ways in which these three undergraduate major programs assess student-created multimodal texts reveal two trends: rubrics are only used to assess multimodal texts within the major program with high multimodal activity, and the assessment of multimodal texts typically involves a required reflective component. Both the program representative and the program chair for the major with high multimodal activity said they design a different rubric to evaluate each multimodal assignment. The program representative for the major with low multimodal activity, on the other hand, said he doesn't use rubrics because they're "too confining." Instead, he, as does the faculty respondent for the major with medium multimodal activity, tends to isolate and utilize a set of criteria that are emphasized during in-class instruction. That said, the program representative for the major with low multimodal activity did admit that the criteria become more difficult to define for multimodal texts because the assessment isn't being applied to one mode (i.e., the alphabetic) but rather to multiple modes and the meaning produced via the modes' collaboration.

Whether or not they use a rubric, all five interviewees said they require students to create a reflective text that accompanies their multimodal projects. The representatives from the programs with low and medium multimodal activity said that students create a reflective text that articulates their process. The representative for the major with low multimodal activity called the reflective piece "a learning statement." His reasons for assigning it are as follows:

> I'm very much looking at learning, and the way that I get at learning apart from the document itself . . . is [through] some kind of reflective work. . . . How did this come to be, what did we learn while we did it, what should an assessing reader know about this that might not show up in the document but that might be important to know, those kinds of things. And so that commentary that students can provide becomes really, really essential.

The faculty respondent for the major with medium multimodal activity requires a reflective text for similar reasons: as he said, "I need to understand their thought process [in order] to understand what decisions they made along the way." This written reflective account of the students' processes gives him "an insight into what their thinking was that can help [him] out." This focus on process, and not just the finished multimodal product, reflects our field's commitment to teaching writing as a process but at the same time reveals our inexperience assessing modes beyond the alphabetic—especially as it concerns issues of design and layout. As the faculty respondent noted, many of the faculty members are trying to figure out how to evaluate design as a separate component but in ways that don't perpetuate the false binary between form and content. The concern about design in this major is also a product of the visual receiving more attention than other modes. Put another way, the way in which the implementation of multimodality privileges the visual generates additional anxiety over how to assess the visual as a mode in the context of other modes.

These reflective texts also signal to students that their own inexperience in deliberately composing with multiple modes is to be expected and can be mitigated by good intentions. For instance, the program representative for the major with low multimodal activity acknowledged that he does tend to temper his own expectations when assessing multimodal compositions because of such compositions' inherent complexity, and he suggested that "our assessment needs to account for that complexity." Consequently, he argued that the assessment of multimodal texts must refrain from discouraging students' exploration of multimodality.

However, for the major with high multimodal activity, students create a reflective text that serves two purposes: it's an account of process but also a defense of rhetorical choices. As the program representative said, students are "assessed based on their rhetorical choices." As such, students "reflect on what they did; they talk about the choices that they made, why they did what they did." And per the program chair, "[W]hat ends up being most important [in terms of assessment] is the way that [students] can articulate their choices of design and [analyze their] final project [regarding] what its strengths and weaknesses are." In other words, students' ability to articulate and, more important, defend the choices they've made tends to be just as valuable as the quality of the final project. Similar to the program representative for the major with low multimodal activity, the program chair for the major with high multimodal activity perceives the reflection and defense as a means to address the difficulty of consciously composing multimodally. "It's a little unfair to judge the quality of graphic design when they come into the class at such different levels," he said, so putting additional stock into the accompanying reflective piece can help level "the playing field a little bit." In short, both faculty members are concerned more with the rhetorical reasoning behind choices of design than with the aesthetic quality of the design. And here, students move beyond the idea of process, beyond just what they did, and perhaps what they learned, and toward the notion of defense—toward *why* they did what they did. The latter speaks to a sense of rhetorical awareness and efficacy that a simple account of process does not. That said, these reflections ultimately provide teachers with a supporting text that is familiar to them—a primarily alphabetic one—which might also be an impetus in assigning the reflections alongside overtly multimodal texts.

Supporting Multimodality

To be sure, the available support will greatly affect the degree to which an undergraduate major program can implement multimodality. In these case studies, I approached support in two ways: the support available for teachers implementing multimodality, and the support available for students creating multimodal texts. Overall, the lack of support for multimodal composing is a conspicuous constraint that influences the extent to which multimodality is implemented into the undergraduate major program with low multimodal activity: lack of support impedes faculty interest and buy-in on one end, and it limits the tools available for students to mix modes and create multimodal texts on the other. For example, the major has access to very few computer classrooms; as the program representative said, "Here, it's kind of a headache to schedule a computer lab classroom for a semester. You kind of need a note from God." Exacerbating matters is the unreliable Wi-Fi, which prevents students from participating in the bring-your-own-technology model. However, even if the Wi-Fi were more reliable and accessible, the idea of students bringing their laptops to class is, according to the program representative, out of step with the current institutional culture. As he said, "My impression has been that probably about 80% of the faculty on campus are the kind of faculty who, if a student showed up and opened a laptop, they would give the student a dirty look." In short, this program in particular and the institution as a whole neither recognize nor reward multimodality, and as a result, per the program representative, "the sleeping dog just lies."

While the technological access provided in class is vastly superior for the major with medium multimodal activity (any teacher who wants a computer-assisted classroom is usually able to attain one), every course in the major with high multimodal activity is taught in a computer-assisted classroom or in a room that has available and reliable Wi-Fi. Moreover, the program chair for the major with high multimodal activity is looking to add to students' already impressive technological access by purchasing four Chromebook carts, which together could serve four classrooms at once and for less than the price it costs to create and sustain one computer-assisted classroom. The university also offers additional technology support through the Student Technology Center (STC). Located in the library, the STC "offers full support for students who've been working on video projects, audio projects, any kind of computer project," the program chair said. Moreover, the STC allows students to check out and use various technologies within the library, such as video cameras, cameras, and iPads.

However, while the major with high multimodal activity offers more in- and out-of-class access to technology, none of the three undergraduate major programs offer support in terms of professional development workshops about multimodality for faculty members. The program representative for the major with low multimodal activity outlined his ideal model, which involves distributed workshops taught by various faculty members, depending on expertise. The majors with medium and high multimodal activity offer workshops on multimodality, but both target adjuncts and contingent faculty members teaching first-year composition, as multimodality has become a staple for each department's first-year composition program. The common reason why professional development workshops on multimodality aren't offered to faculty members who staff the major is the prevailing assumption that those who teach in the major don't need the additional support. But as I argue below, this mentality perpetuates the uneven distribution of labor regarding the ways multimodality is implemented.

A final form of support for students creating multimodal texts, one present across all three major programs, includes providing them an outlet to distribute their work beyond the walls of the classroom. Students in the major with low multimodal activity can participate in a campus-wide event celebrating student research that has been occurring for the past four years. The program representative hopes that, someday, the major can hold its own signature showcase event. Likewise, those teaching in the major with medium multimodal activity encourage their students to participate in the university's symposium showcase of undergraduate research and creative projects. In so doing, their students "will do either a poster presentation or a conference presentation using lots of multimodal [composing]," said the program representative. The major with high multimodal activity had a similar showcase event. Unfortunately, this event has been discontinued due to lack of funding and institutional support. The showcase would "chew up a great deal of department time and department resources, but it was not a department event. It was a university event," said the program representative. Eventually, the faculty members decided to boycott the event to "test the university to see if they would rightfully compensate [the department] for keeping it going." As of now, the university has yet to offer any compensation, and so the event no longer exists. "It's a shame," the program representative lamented. "That really cool event went away because the university wanted us to do it for free," and it was no longer practical or feasible to do so. For all three institutions, though, the showcase event is and was institutional, not departmental.

While the major with low multimodal activity is hamstrung by its lack of support, the majors with medium and high multimodal activity are relatively pleased with the support available to them. Members of both majors acknowledged that they could always have more, but the program chair for the major with high multimodal activity quickly added that "it's actually good that there's a little tension because . . . it's easy to go overboard with the technology, and then it gets underutilized." In other words, the program chair is well aware that technology has a short life span, one that only seems to shrink. As a result, he believes faculty members and administrators need to think carefully about what technology to invest in and implement in the classroom, considering limited finances; they must "make sure that it's really going to be used and used appropriately." As he said, "Sometimes, it's better to use that money for professional development or other types of support for students."

Additional Trends

In closing, I want to highlight two additional trends across these three case studies. First, there are three primary reasons why multimodality is implemented within the curriculum: professional preparation, civic preparation and the culture at large, and the current status of the field. Interestingly, these three motivating factors align with Rebecca Moore Howard's three objectives for the advanced undergraduate writing curriculum. As she says in the introduction to *Coming of Age*, the advanced undergraduate writing curriculum should "prepare students for careers as writers," "prepare students for highly rhetorical participation in public life," and provide students with "a historical and theoretical awareness of writing as a discipline" (xv). Thus, in making space for multimodality—or in acknowledging that all writing is multimodal—we don't need to deviate from the goals we envisioned for ourselves prior to the multimodal turn.

Second, the institution and the department heavily influence the degree to which multimodality is implemented, and the distribution of labor regarding how multimodality is implemented is imbalanced despite institutional and departmental support. In other words, a select few individuals shoulder most of the responsibility regarding the implementation of multimodality. For instance, the program representative for the major with low multimodal activity is the only one who "teaches multimodal composing as, per se, multimodal composing." Without his continued insistence that multimodality demands a place within the curriculum, multimodality would most likely not receive any programmatic attention. Furthermore, for the majors with medium and high multimodal activity, a handful of people are responsible for implementing multimodality despite increased interest and buy-in among faculty members. For the major with medium multimodal activity, the faculty respondent and a few other recently hired faculty members bear most of the work, and as the program representative for the major with high multimodal activity said, the program chair is "the primary professor" for courses that offer instruction in multimodality.

The imbalance of labor regarding the implementation of multimodality parallels Cynthia Selfe's argument in "Technology and Literacy: A Story about the Perils of Not Paying Attention." Here, Selfe claims that we conveniently split ourselves into two camps: those who teach technology and those who do not. Those in the latter camp tend to absolve themselves of issues connected to technology (412–13). Multimodality, although present before the emergence of the digital, is still very much linked to technology. As Shipka says, the field still tends "to treat multimodality as a relatively new phenomenon—and one that . . . is too often and too narrowly associated with computer technologies and the production of digitized texts" (12). Although Selfe's CCCC Chair's Address was delivered twenty years ago, and although the work the field does is inextricably linked to the technologies that people use to create meaning, we still relegate technology to a small number of people. I know this firsthand. The continued relegation of technology has now resulted in multimodality being framed and treated as the work of "technology people" even though the field at large now recognizes multimodality, as Kress says, "as the normal state of human communication" (1).

To be sure, whenever we think about developing or revising curricula, we must always be cognizant of and sensitive to the local context; with that, we must also consider the goals and outcomes of our programs and the students we serve. Nonetheless, in looking across these case studies, we can see rather clearly that a curricular shift to incorporate and emphasize multimodal composing requires not only faculty expertise and buy-in but also multiple forms of departmental and institutional support. The importance and recognition of multimodality is only going to increase as we move further into the twenty-first century, so as we (continue to) redesign our curricula to respond to the demands of multimodality, we must think critically about how to do so in ways that are effective, ethical, and sustainable.

Notes

1. This department also offers minors in English writing and in literature and a master's degree in English.

2. This department also offers four minors: English literature, English writing and rhetoric, journalism, and women's studies.

3. This department also offers a minor in writing and rhetoric.

4. Also interesting is that both interviewees for the major program with medium multimodal activity and the program representative for the major program with high multimodal activity all said that one of the multimodal projects they assign is a remediation of prior work. In other words, the theory of remediation (Bolter and Grusin), given its connections to mass media, appears to mirror phenomena happening in the culture at large, which gives students a lens to understand that culture in ways that Gunther Kress's work doesn't. In short, these teachers singled out the theory of remediation as a fruitful lens in helping students transition to multimodal composing, whereas Kress was mostly absent from their discussions.

5. Even though we've devoted much scholarly attention to the visual, a longstanding critique of the subfield of visual rhetoric, one reiterated by the program representative for the major with low multimodal activity, is that the academic focus is grounded more in how to analyze and interpret visuals than in how to create visuals effectively. That is, there's a perceived imbalance that favors analysis over creation.

Works Cited

Alexander, Jonathan, and Jacqueline Rhodes. *On Multimodality: New Media in Composition Studies*. Conference on College Composition and Communication / NCTE, 2014.

Anderson, Daniel, et al. "Integrating Multimodality into Composition Curricula: Survey Methodology and Results from a CCCC Research Grant." *Composition Studies*, vol. 34, no. 2, 2006, pp. 59–84.

Balzhiser, Deborah, and Susan H. McLeod. "The Undergraduate Writing Major: What Is It? What Should It Be?" *College Composition and Communication*, vol. 61, no. 3, Feb. 2010, pp. 415–33.

Bolter, Jay David, and Richard Grusin. *Remediation: Understanding New Media*. MIT P, 1999.

George, Diana. "From Analysis to Design: Visual Communication in the Teaching of Writing." *College Composition and Communication*, vol. 54, no. 1, Sept. 2002, pp. 11–39.

Giberson, Greg A., and Thomas A. Moriarty, editors. *What We Are Becoming: Developments in Undergraduate Writing Majors*. Utah State UP, 2010.

Giberson, Greg, et al., editors. *Writing Majors: Eighteen Program Profiles*. Utah State UP, 2015.

Halbritter, Bump. *Mics, Cameras, Symbolic Action: Audio-visual Rhetoric for Writing Teachers*. Parlor Press, 2012.

Howard, Rebecca Moore. "Introduction: History, Politics, Pedagogy, and Advanced Writing." *Coming of Age: The Advanced Writing Curriculum*, edited by Linda K. Shamoon et al., Boynton/Cook, 2000, pp. xiii–xxii.

Kress, Gunther. *Multimodality: A Social Semiotic Approach to Contemporary Communication*. Routledge, 2010.

Lauer, Claire. "Contending with Terms: 'Multimodal' and 'Multimedia' in the Academic and Public Spheres." *Computers and Composition*, vol. 26, no. 4, Dec. 2009, pp. 225–39.

———. "What's in a Name? The Anatomy of Defining New/Multi/Modal/Digital/Media Texts." *Kairos*, vol. 17, no. 1, 2012, kairos.technorhetoric.net/17.1/inventio/lauer/index.html.

Lee, Rory. "Surveying the Available Modes of Persuasion." *Designing and Implementing Multimodal Curricula and Programs*, edited by J. C. Lee and Santosh Khadka, Routledge, 2018, pp. 89–110.

Lutkewitte, Claire, editor. *Multimodal Composition: A Critical Sourcebook*. Bedford/St. Martin's, 2013.

Morrison, Andrew, editor. *Inside Multimodal Composition*. Hampton Press, 2011.

Palmeri, Jason. *Remixing Composition: A History of Multimodal Writing Pedagogy*. Southern Illinois UP / NCTE, 2012.

Selfe, Cynthia L. "The Movement of Air, the Breath of Meaning: Aurality and Multimodal Composing." *College Composition and Communication*, vol. 60, no. 4, June 2009, pp. 616–63.

———. "Technology and Literacy: A Story about the Perils of Not Paying Attention." *College Composition and Communication*, vol. 50, no. 3, Feb. 1999, pp. 411–36.

Sheridan, David M., et al. *The Available Means of Persuasion: Mapping a Theory and Pedagogy of Multimodal Public Rhetoric*. Parlor Press, 2012.

Shipka, Jody. *Toward a Composition Made Whole*. U of Pittsburgh P, 2011.

Weisser, Christian, and Laurie Grobman. "Undergraduate Writing Majors and the Rhetoric of Professionalism." *Composition Studies*, vol. 40, no. 1, Spring 2012, pp. 39–59.

The Writing Major. Special issue of *Composition Studies*, vol. 35, no. 1, Spring 2007.

Part Four

Modality and Disciplinarity

Following Directions, Responding to Shifts, Shaking Foundations: Multimodal Composition within and across Writing Programs

Beth Brunk-Chavez

When my son, Jackson, was in ninth grade, in 2016–17, he participated in a program that required students to present projects in various media across four subjects: science, math, language arts, and history. The students presented research and arguments in *Prezi* and *PowerPoint* presentations, videos, plays, posters, models, art, architectural designs, and, yes, academic essays complete with MLA citations. Many times the audience was the teachers, but sometimes the audience was the students' peers, community members, school leadership, and sixth graders.

Many of these projects were collaborative. One night, I observed Jackson and his group members writing the script for a biology video about evolution and adaptation. On his school-issued laptop, Jackson had open the class learning management system (LMS), a digital textbook, the Google Doc that he and his group members were writing on in different colors, and several *Google* search tabs. He was chatting on *Google*, too, with the group members who were contributing to the Google Doc at that moment and texting with a group member who was on a bus coming home from a football game across town.

At the end of the evening, one of the group members volunteered to upload the Google Doc to the LMS so their teacher could provide feedback (feedback was often in video form) and another volunteered to print the document to bring to class for workshopping the next day. Later that week, after a round of revisions to the script, the group met before and after school to film their video in the school's green-screen room. The group used the Australian Outback as a theme to explain the biology concepts, and the video is complete with props, costumes, digital backgrounds, ninth-grade humor, and commendable attempts at Australian accents. The group uploaded their film to *YouTube* and shared the link with the teacher through their class LMS. They also presented the film in class and received immediate, oral feedback from the teacher and their classmates.

When I asked what he learned from this project, Jackson talked about content from his teacher, his textbook, and his group's research. From my perspective, however, the process was equally, if not more, valuable than the content. To design, develop, and deliver this multimodal biology project, he and his classmates engaged in activities that reflected planning, agility, flexibility, creativity, design thinking, technological experimentation, collaboration, and an engagement with subject matter that I generally had not seen with previous school projects. I acknowledge that Jackson's experience in a self-selected program at a relatively affluent high school is not indicative of all high school students' experiences. However, I also suspect it is not all that uncommon.

Kathleen Blake Yancey's "Made Not Only in Words: Composition in a New Key" was delivered at the Conference on College Composition and Communication in 2004—well over a decade ago. In the address, which she describes as a "multi-genred and mediated text that would embody and illustrate the claims of the talk" (299), Yancey argues that literacy was "in the midst of a tectonic change" (298). In retrospect, her point is well taken that "[n]ever before has the proliferation of writings outside the academy so counterpointed the compositions inside" (298). She calls upon turn-of-the-twentieth-century composition scholars and teachers to recognize that students have "the ability to write for purposes that are unconstrained and audiences that are nearly unlimited" (321). Five years later, in 2009, Yancey widens her audience to literacy teachers of all levels in her *Writing in the Twenty-First Century* report for the National Council of Teachers of English to demonstrate that students not only have the ability to write for unconstrained purposes and to wide-ranging audiences but also that they are taking full advantage of that ability. Yancey's report praises students for a clever and strategic networking strategy through *Facebook* that encouraged students taking AP tests to write "THIS IS SPARTA" anywhere in the test and then cross out the insertion so it wouldn't count against their score (5–6). She also applauds sixteen-year-old Tiffany Monk, who took photos and wrote e-mails asking first responders to rescue residents in her flooded trailer park in Florida after Tropical Storm Fay in 2008. As Yancey states, Monk was able to save her community members because "she knew how to compose in a twenty-first century way; and because she knew her audience" (5).

These examples of high school students employing multiple modes of composition for educational, entertaining, and lifesaving purposes are precursors to the power of networking and multimodal composition that the students of Marjory Stoneman Douglas High School in Parkland, Florida, demonstrated in early 2018. The Marjory Stoneman Douglas students' compositions—which document the horrific events of a school shooting and also lobby for changes to gun legislation—cross many modes: verbal, written, video, sound, silence, and multiple intersections and combinations of these. Their messages are delivered through *Twitter*, *Instagram*, *Snapchat*, *Facebook*, blogs, videos, live events, televised speeches, books, and so on. Their powerful voices have collectively created and contributed to the Never Again and Enough Is Enough movements and honor those who were killed. While it is too soon to measure the impact in legislative changes, these students' amplified voices brought attention to their experiences, opinions, and abilities in a way that had not been witnessed to date. Ten years after Tiffany Monk's response to a natural disaster, high school students again demonstrated their ability to compose effectively for twenty-first-century audiences.

When high school graduates enroll in college-level composition courses, they bring this rhetorical agility with them and may experience the counterpoints that Yancey mentions in 2004 ("Made"). Recognizing this in 2012, Duane Roen, then president of the Council of Writing Program Administrators, asked twelve WPAs and faculty members to participate in an Outcomes Statement (known as the WPA OS) revision task force. The charge was to determine if it was appropriate to update the OS, which had most recently been updated in 2008, in light of the field's and students' developments in multimodal, multimedia, and digital writing. The group convened and determined that it was, in fact, appropriate to revise the OS, and collected data from composition faculty members and administrators via surveys, conference workshops, and conference presentations. The feedback overwhelmingly confirmed that the OS should do more to define "composing as a multimodal activity" given the concerns that students "were becoming consumers and producers of digital media without having much opportunity [in composition courses] to reflect critically and capitalize on 'affordances' that digital media provide" (Dryer et al. 131–32).

The two previous versions of the OS did not include a definition of *writing*, suggesting, perhaps, that writing was readily identifiable and somewhat static. The 3.0 version, however, understands this to be a significant omission and includes a definition of *composing* that incorporates multimodal activities:

> [C]omposing refers broadly to complex writing processes that are increasingly reliant on the use of digital technologies. Writers also attend to elements of design, incorporating images and graphical elements into texts intended for screens as well as printed pages. Writers' composing activities have always been shaped by the technologies available to them, and digital technologies are changing writers' relationships to their texts and audiences in evolving ways. (Dryer et al. 138)

The inclusion of this dynamic definition of composing is coupled with the decision to integrate the "composing in electronic environments" plank throughout the revised OS. This plank, which was included in the 2008 version of the OS, recommends that students in composition classes should have the experience of engaging with "electronic environments" throughout their writing processes, of locating and using "research material collected from a variety of electronic sources," and of "understand[ing] and exploit[ing] the differences in the rhetorical strategies and in the affordances available for both print and electronic composing processes and texts" (Council of Writing Program Administrators 3). While it was a significant acknowledgement to add this plank in the 2008 version, the committee agreed in 2012 that maintaining electronic environments as an individual plank was counterintuitive to the ways we compose. The separate plank suggested that composing in electronic environments was something set apart from regular writing and composing and therefore a supplement to writing courses, something to be added to an already full curriculum. The 2012 revision, which was approved by the council in 2014, integrated the elements of that plank, along with several updates into each of the other four planks ("WPA Outcomes Statement"). In other words, each of the planks—rhetorical knowledge; critical thinking, reading, and composing; processes; and knowledge and conventions—should not, much less cannot, be separated from the digital and multimodal environments in which writing is composed and circulated. Yancey's tectonic changes were reflected in the 2008 version and then integrated in the 2012 revision.

As this edited collection has demonstrated, the composition field has spent considerable energy historicizing and theorizing multimodal composition and illustrating how instructors are incorporating multimodal projects and processes into their classes. Jason Palmeri draws upon several decades of composition scholarship and pedagogy that include visual and performing arts, nonverbal mental imagery, auditory forms, slideshows, collages, photography, and filmmaking to make the case that "composition has always already been multimodal" (21). Tracey Bowen and Carl Whithaus describe their edited collection *Multimodal Literacies and Emerging Genres* as "demonstrat[ing] how faculty and students are already exploring 'what else is possible'" (1), with its chapter authors "report[ing] on a range of classroom and programmatic practices where multimodal forms of writing are reshaping what is possible in college and university writing courses" (2). Bowen and Whithaus seek to highlight ways in which students are learning not only to develop multimodal projects but to also understand how both the students and the projects "work within social spaces" (2). Bowen and Whithaus's collection features a wide range of multimodal projects composed and presented in environments as complex as *Second Life* or as simple as *PowerPoint*, essays that integrate both text and images, storyboards, brochures, and even projects that incorporate found objects such as trash cans.

Drawing on the premise that "free online video may turn out to be as significant a media development as the arrival of print" (Anderson, qtd. in Arroyo 1), Sarah Arroyo's *Participatory Composition: Video Culture, Writing, and Electracy* builds connections between an online culture that constantly shares and seeks participation and collaboration to the composing that students can do in their coursework. Arroyo not only builds the theory of electracy but also includes pedagogical directions, student projects, and her own work in participatory composition. In *Digital Griots: African American Rhetoric in a Multimedia Age*, Adam Banks identifies composition's "repositioning that values cultural diversity and interrogates more deeply the social contexts in which writing occurs [along with] more importance on multiliteracies and multimedia writing" (10) and develops a theoretical framework of mix, remix, and mixtape (7). While *Digital Griots* is not focused on student projects and pedagogical processes, Banks calls for composition instructors to establish

> a firm commitment to build from the truths and tropes of black experience in writing curricula, courses, assignments, evaluation, feedback, and teacher stance and delivery . . . [and to build] assignments that invite students not only to work across modalities but

> also to link those multiple modalities, individual assignments, and assignment cycles and [to critically examine] the power relations and material conditions inscribed in technological tools, networks, and discourses. (165)

These texts represent a small portion of recent scholarship that acknowledges students' experience and expertise, addresses Yancey's ongoing call for us to recognize and build upon students' multimodal ways of communicating, and reflects the revisions to the WPA OS. My concern in this essay, however, is less about producing more scholarship that explains the significance of the tectonic change—and it is also less about publishing more accounts of how individual writing instructors are incorporating multimodal projects into their curricula. Rather, the concerns articulated in the remainder of this essay are focused more on how these changes can be translated across writing programs so that all students have "the opportunity to reflect critically and capitalize on 'affordances' that digital media provide" (Dryer et al. 132).

To wit, significant reservations were voiced about the revisions to the WPA OS both in the surveys and at the Writing Program Administrators conference and the Conference on College Composition and Communication, where the task force presented both before and after the OS was approved. The more common concerns were related to issues of time (as in: it is not possible to add more content and requirements onto an already full writing curriculum), access (as in: if our institution doesn't provide access to a computer classroom, how could we possibly teach our students how to compose this way?), and expertise (as in: I'm now expected to know how to use these technologies so that I can teach students how to use them too?). These are not insignificant concerns. But rather than roadblocks, the task force saw these concerns as an opportunity to understand how writing instructors may feel constrained against assigning, teaching, and assessing multimodal projects and to consider how faculty members might work to overcome them.

Additionally, these concerns remind us to consider and acknowledge the degrees of variance and diversity across institutions. While some of us may enjoy the support of campus administrators, have access to state-of-the-art computer classrooms or labs, work with faculty members who are technologically innovative and savvy, and engage with students who come to class with experience composing in multiple media for wide-ranging audiences, this may not be the case for all of us. What if the classrooms students sit in are not conducive to multimodal instruction? What if the faculty members who teach the classes are not the least bit engaged and interested in multimodal composition? What if the faculty members do not feel prepared to teach multimodal projects and what if the students are not as technologically sophisticated as we expect them to be? I explore responses to these questions in the remainder of this essay.

Curriculum

Many instructors and writing programs have found it necessary to argue to department chairs, deans, or faculty members across the university that incorporating multimodal projects does not change the outcomes of composition courses; that such projects simply provide students with alternative modes for communicating. In other words: different projects, same outcomes. However, several scholars have recently encouraged us to consider a more nuanced approach to incorporating multimodal projects in composition courses. While Palmeri reminds us not to overlook the fact that "alphabetic writing remains a valued form of composing that we are institutionally and professionally mandated to teach" (8), Jonathan Alexander and Jacqueline Rhodes note, as cited also by Pegeen Reichert Powell in the introduction to this collection, that "composition studies has found itself at a crossroads" (3). Alexander and Rhodes suggest that while the field has embraced the incorporation of new media into writing curriculum, this shift may fall short as the rhetorical affordances, richness, and diversity of these media are constrained "by mak[ing] them do the work of 'writing'" given our discipline's grounding in and privileging of text- and print-based composition (17).

Similarly, as Jennifer Falcon asks in her unpublished dissertation: Is it enough for composition faculty members to add multimodal projects to the curriculum as a remediation of a written research paper, for example? Or should the composition curriculum be rethought from start to finish? She states:

> Multimodal composition is more than using specific digital platforms and software to compose. The practice is more important than the platform, but if the practice of composing by mixing modes is only viewed as a means to include more technology in the classroom,

> then multimodal composition will not evolve in a nuanced and productive manner. Rather, it will be subject, and ultimately stagnant, to whatever is the next new technology.

Thus, both Alexander and Rhodes and Falcon identify tensions between the acceptance of multimodal projects and the implementation of them within composition classes. Avoiding the checkbox mentality of adding multimodal projects or forcing multimodal projects to do the work of writing requires a significant investment into rethinking nearly every aspect of the curriculum, including how it is taught and assessed.

When implementing such a change across a writing program, writing program administrators should seek opportunities to procure institutional resources to convene a group of faculty members who will read scholarship, including the WPA OS, and collaborate to determine the extent to which the program's curriculum necessitates a redesign, the extent to which individual faculty members will be required or encouraged to teach multimodality, and the extent to which instructors have the flexibility to make choices about what is taught in their individual courses. Particularly for programs without a history of teaching multimodal projects and digital writing processes, new textbooks should be reviewed, and assignments and scaffolding for those assignments need to be generated. This should not be a quick or one-time process; the program should seek to revise often by collecting both instructor and student feedback and making adjustments where appropriate.

Pedagogy and Faculty Preparation

As Bowen and Whithaus point out, it is not enough to implement new assignments; we must also look to make wholesale revisions in our pedagogy and students' composing processes when incorporating multimodal projects in composition courses. However, closely related to the perceived disconnect between the field's scholarship and the educational experiences our students have is the demographic of instructors teaching in writing programs, particularly at the first-year level. Too often, we write articles to and for those who are like-minded, who are engaged in reading the scholarship published in our edited collections, books, and journals. We present at conferences to scholars and instructors who attend the sessions because they are willing and able to revise their curriculum, to add something new, and to leave behind assignments that have become outdated. However, Peter Smagorinsky notes in his 2009 report on the NCTE Research Forum that teacher retention "is a major issue in first-year composition programs where courses are taught by an unstable cadre of graduate students and part-time or contingent faculty who are often employed as much for their availability as their proven effectiveness" (qtd. in "Symposium" 148). More recently, in "It Matters a Lot Who Teaches Introductory Courses. Here's Why," Beckie Supiano reports on recent studies at community and four-year colleges that find that assigning less-experienced instructors to teach introductory courses "could have negative consequences for students." One reason for this is the unstable cadres' disconnect from research in the field they are teaching.

Similarly, Cynthia Selfe notes in a 2004 essay that courses that incorporate multimodal, new-media projects in meaningful ways "are frequently taught by new media experts on whom the rest of the composition faculty—unsure about their own expertise or responsibilities to new media—confer the departmental responsibilities of dealing with emerging literacies" (56). In her contribution to this volume, Stephanie Vie indicates that multiple factors contribute to how likely faculty members are to incorporate social media, and these factors apply to the teaching of multimodal projects as well. First, "faculty members' orientations toward technology in general and social media specifically play key roles" in whether they will incorporate social media writing into composition courses. Several instructors in Vie's study mention that teaching students to write with and in social media contexts is not appropriate to composition courses because doing so would reduce time spent on words, would not prepare students for academic or workplace writing projects, and is not actual writing with emphasis on a writing process. Vie additionally finds that "positionality in the hierarchy of academia—as well as narratives about others' experiences [both positive and negative] within those hierarchies—hold considerable weight for faculty members when they decide whether or not to rely on social media in their pedagogy." These and other justifications against incorporating multimodal writing processes into a curriculum contribute to the scenario in which the lucky few students who enroll in the new-media expert's class—sometimes deliberately, often by chance—leave the class with the experience of learning about and developing multimedia projects. The remainder of the student population misses out on these learning opportunities.

Clearly, there are no simple resolutions to these scenarios. However, writing program administrators may have the opportunity to address such gaps through professional development, collaborative annual performance reviews, and other practices intended to develop "proactive cultures of teaching" (Doe 116). Administrators who are interested in incorporating multimodal projects program-wide must invest in professional development of all instructors at every level in the program. A significant redesign of my own institution's first-year composition program in 2009, to include the integration of multimodal projects, was made successful by offering engaging and intersecting professional development opportunities. Rather than focusing exclusively on the novice instructors—the graduate students—the regularly scheduled workshops also involved seasoned lecturers and contingent faculty members who were invited to lead sessions and serve as mentors. As I note elsewhere, when writing program administrators encounter constraints such as schedules or instructor resistance, "reminding ourselves that improved teaching quality often leads to increased student learning invites us to locate areas where meaningful faculty and instructional development are required" (Brunk-Chavez 153).

Diverse Students

The examples of the Parkland, Florida, high school students and my son, Jackson, run the risk of characterizing soon-to-be college students as young, media-savvy people eager to engage with a variety of technologies. As Kristine Blair and Cheryl Hoy state, "Writing instructors' depictions of undergraduate student writers . . . often presume students to be traditional 18–22-year-olds" (qtd in Reid) and thus characterize them as the (now often challenged) digital native. However, many of us teach at urban, commuter, regional universities or community colleges with a diverse student demographic. Perhaps these composition students did not enroll straight from high school, have not had significant high school experiences with multimodal projects, or have returned to college after a short break or after twenty years away.

Lynn Reid suggests that too much "emphasis on *age-based* concerns rather than the challenges that working with technology might pose for *any* user reinforces the misconception that age is the most significant determinant of a person's proficiency with digital tools." Instead of ignoring these challenges and forging ahead, or instead of adapting assignments to give in to anxieties around technology, Reid finds that "there is clear evidence to suggest that acknowledging the anxieties that returning adult [or any] students might bring to the classroom has the potential to impact their learning in significant and empowering ways." Reid provides several steps that move students from what Stuart Selber calls "computer-mediated users" to "empowered users" when completing multimodal projects (46). These steps include providing a context for the significance of multimodal projects, motivating students by establishing a positive environment that encourages students to collaborate and learn together rather than feel like they are on their own to figure things out, and developing connections between the projects and students' values and experiences. These steps are relevant for all students, whether we perceive them to be digital natives or digital immigrants, as Reid says, to create an "inclusive learning environment" and a "student-centered classroom."

Space and Access

In addition to students' experiences with technologies for the purpose of developing multimodal projects, another consideration is their access to the technologies for educational purposes. As James Purdy and Dànielle Nicole DeVoss point out in their introduction to *Making Space: Writing Instruction, Infrastructure, and Multiliteracies*, in the last couple decades, "the infrastructures of writing have captured the attention of writing studies scholars, researchers, and teachers." Purdy and DeVoss note that attention to computer labs "opened the door for larger disciplinary conversations about the relationship between space and writing." Practically speaking, this is what some instructors addressed when they asked the WPA OS committee how instructors could be expected to teach multimedia projects when they didn't have the appropriate classroom space in which to do it. How does an instructor teach students to develop multimodal projects when class is held in a traditional classroom with limited or no access to technologies? When revising the curriculum and preparing instructors to teach it, these are important considerations. Can students bring technologies—laptops or smartphones—to class? Can class be held in a computer lab on campus? Can the assignments be taught in such a way that access to technologies during class time is not a requirement?

However, concerns of access aren't focused solely on appropriate software with audio- and video-capturing and editing capabilities. As Todd Ruecker and I report in "Digital Writing Spaces across Institutions on the U.S.-Mexico Border," we agree with other scholars (Banks, *Race*; Selfe; DeVoss et al.) that "the presence and use of technology in institutional learning spaces is more complex than the number of computers available to students and the frequency of computer use." It is not enough to have access to a classroom full of computers if the instructor and students do not engage pedagogically and strategically about how to use the computers to students' benefit. Beyond basic skills instruction, such engagement may include whole-group or individual analysis of multimodal projects, guided training on how to use software—by the instructor, a campus computer technician, or a class member who has expertise—collaborative work between students to develop their projects, the sharing of drafts or final versions for feedback, and so on. Additionally, in their 1994 article, Cynthia Selfe and Richard Selfe recommend encouraging faculty and students to bring awareness to the racial, gendered, and class politics that are embedded within technologies and "re-design/re-reimage/re-create interfaces that attempt to avoid disabling and devaluating non-white, non-English background students, and women" (495). Again, it cannot be assumed that all instructors will know how to engage critically with the technologies and use them effectively the first few times they teach a multimodal composition curriculum. Professional development workshops and mentoring provide good opportunities for sharing and modeling effective practices.

Finally, a conversation yet to be fully developed in our scholarship is the consideration of multimodal composition projects that students are assigned and complete in virtual spaces or online courses. I argue that students enrolled in online classes should not have different expectations and outcomes than those enrolled in the face-to-face counterparts. Those of us who have taught online know that notifying students of the technological requirements and providing ample and clear instructions are essential to students' success. Providing instruction for a multimodal project may present challenges for instructors who aren't able to offer information and feedback in a just-in-time-teaching format. As noted above, providing a supportive environment where students can collaborate with each other and frequently ask questions can mitigate many of the challenges. In addition to determining how students will complete multimodal projects, instructors must also consider how students will be expected to submit projects not only for evaluation but also to share with their classmates. How will classmates be expected to respond to one another? In what modes will the instructor provide feedback? Working with instructional designers, when available, will help instructors address these questions and develop an effective online class. While the faculty member is the expert of the curriculum, the designer can assist with content presentation, process, interaction, and ADA compliance. Faculty members may also be able to collaborate with library and technical support staff to provide resources, online workshops, or webinars to assist students when needed. Finally, once a multimodal composition online course has been successfully developed, faculty members might share components of the course, or the course in its entirety, with other instructors in the program to build on what is already working effectively.

As a former writing program administrator, I realize that the considerations I addressed above come in addition to local matters that are sometimes more pressing, such as managing class size, hiring instructors, responding to student concerns, selecting textbooks, negotiating space, filing assessment reports, fielding departmental requests (and politics), and so on. The considerations above also remind us not to assume that multimodal composition—or any aspect of composition, for that matter—pedagogical approaches, faculty members, students, and spaces are the same, or even similar, across institutions. There are multiple, dynamic variables to attend to when selecting and applying theories, developing curricula and assessments, preparing faculty members, understanding and encouraging students, and contending with and designing learning spaces. This is a lot to negotiate. Additionally, as stated in its introduction, while the WPA OS "articulates what composition teachers nationwide have learned from practice, research, and theory," in spite of its strengths, the statement has no authority to set standards across programs nor to determine now to measure students' achievements. Those tasks have "deliberately been left to local writing programs and their institutions" ("WPA Outcomes Statement"). In other words, the WPA OS can be used as a guide for those programs and instructors who choose to use it, but it can also just as easily be ignored, if, in fact, instructors of composition are even aware of it.

However, beyond these significant and complex opportunities and constraints, I conclude this essay by encouraging us to additionally consider our roles in the larger university and educational context and how multimodal composition may have an impact. To put in perspective the resistance we may face at the level of instructors, programs, and institutions, Michael Crow and William Dabars's *Designing the New American University* tells us that "[r]esistance to reform is common enough in any sector of human endeavor, but it seems particularly endemic to academe." They quote F. M. Cornford, who in 1908 satirically advised young faculty members that "the basic rule of faculty governance is, 'Nothing should ever be done for the first time'" (126). Crow and Dabars provide multiple examples to demonstrate that "universities are moving too slowly to accommodate the pace of transformation in the structure of knowledge" (24) in part because of "structural inertia" that "tends to favor incremental adjustments" (125). This sluggishness may also be due to our "academic wrist watches [that] mark time in increments of quarters or semesters. . . . Faculty committees tend to deliberate while shifts in policy, culture, and technology flash by at warp speed" (182). In other words, universities collectively become too comfortable in the way we have always done things, and we take too much time to deliberate on whether and how to make adjustments in our courses and curriculum. By no means has our field been stagnant; in some ways, I'd say that our academic wristwatch ticks a bit faster than other disciplines' timekeepers do. Yet, I believe we can do more.

In *The New Education: How to Revolutionize the University to Prepare Students for a World in Flux*, Cathy Davidson encourages administrators, faculty, students, parents, and the public to think transformationally about higher education opportunities. In part, she encourages faculty members to develop and teach a curriculum that enables students to become "digitally literate—so that they understand, gain insight into, and maybe even exert more control over the technologies that have changed and sometimes dominated our lives and will do so even more in the future" (80). She tells us something we know but somehow can't entirely break away from, that "[s]tudents learn to write essays that only they and their professor will be reading, in a form and format that are rarely used beyond the classroom," and points to Andrea Lunsford's Stanford Study of Writing to demonstrate the importance of "bolster[ing] students' already strong sense of *kairos*" by encouraging them to "define and address an audience beyond her, beyond the classroom" (93). In a time where an "audience can speak back to you, regardless of your status and power," Davidson asks, "Why aren't we educating for an era in which the skills of connecting and constructing are more important than ever?" (110). While such questions are fair, they certainly are not new ones, as the brief history in this essay—and throughout this collection—shows. Nor are such questions directed entirely at writing studies, but we certainly do bear responsibility in considering responses to queries such as Davidson's "What forms of higher education are possible now?" (229).

To this question I might add: How does the inclusion of multimodal composition influence transformational directions for composition courses? Is there a way to blend our students' experiences, the calls we have heard from the field, the integration of multimodal writing into the WPA OS, and the scholarship our field has developed to genuinely transform what we do? Can we, as Davidson suggests, unbundle and rebundle education for writing students, realizing that it is "not possible to redesign one aspect" of our work but that "everything [should be] remade at the same time" (121)? Are we left to rebuild after the tectonic change? Or are we, ourselves, the force that brings about the shift?

Works Cited

Alexander, Jonathan, and Jacqueline Rhodes. *On Multimodality: New Media in Composition Studies*. Conference on College Composition and Communication / NCTE, 2014.

Arroyo, Sarah J. *Participatory Composition: Video Culture, Writing, and Electracy*. Southern Illinois UP, 2013.

Banks, Adam J. *Digital Griots: African American Rhetoric in a Multimedia Age*. Southern Illinois UP, 2011.

———. *Race, Rhetoric, and Technology: Searching for Higher Ground*. NCTE, 2006.

Bowen, Tracey, and Carl Whithaus, editors. *Multimodal Literacies and Emerging Genres*. U of Pittsburgh P, 2013.

Brunk-Chavez, Beth. "Embracing Our Expertise through Faculty and Instructional Development." *WPA: Writing Program Administration*, vol. 34, no. 1, Fall 2010, pp. 152–55.

Council of Writing Program Administrators. "WPA Outcomes Statement for First-Year Composition." July 2008. *State of Indiana*, www.in.gov/che/files/

WPA_Outcomes_Statement_for_First-Year_Composition.pdf. Accessed 22 Apr. 2018.

Crow, Michael M., and William B. Dabars. *Designing the New American University*. Johns Hopkins UP, 2015.

Davidson, Cathy N. *The New Education: How to Revolutionize the University to Prepare Students for a World in Flux*. Basic Books, 2017.

DeVoss, Dànielle Nicole, et al. "Infrastructure and Composing: The *When* of New-Media Writing." *College Composition and Communication*, vol. 57, no. 1, Sept. 2005, pp. 14–44.

Doe, Sue. "Response to 'A Symposium on Fostering Teacher Quality.'" *WPA: Writing Program Administration*, vol. 34, no. 2, Spring 2011, pp. 115–18.

Dryer, Dylan B., et al. "Revising FYC Outcomes for a Multimodal, Digitally Composed World: The WPA Outcomes Statement for First-Year Composition (Version 3.0)." *WPA: Writing Program Administration*, vol. 38, no. 1, Fall 2014, pp. 129–43.

Falcon, Jennifer Andrea. *Rethinking Multimodality in First-Year Composition: Applying Theories of Digital Rhetoric, Procedural Rhetoric, and Electracy to Multimodal Assignments*. 2018. U of Texas at El Paso, PhD dissertation.

Palmeri, Jason. *Remixing Composition: A History of Multimodal Writing Pedagogy*. Southern Illinois UP / NCTE, 2012.

Purdy, James P., and Dànielle Nicole DeVoss. "Making Space to Theorize and Situate Space Making: An Introduction." *Making Space: Writing Instruction, Infrastructure, and Multiliteracies*, edited by Purdy and DeVoss, U of Michigan P, www.digitalrhetoriccollaborative.org/makingspace/introduction.html. Accessed 22 Mar. 2018.

Reid, Lynn. "Returning Adults in the Multimodal Classroom." *Showcasing the Best of CIWIC/DMAC: Approaches to Teaching and Learning in Digital Environments*, no. 1, 2015, www.dmacinstitute.com/showcase/issues/no1/reid-returning-adults.

Ruecker, Todd, and Beth Brunk-Chavez. "Digital Writing Spaces across Institutions on the U.S.-Mexico Border." *Making Space: Writing Instruction, Infrastructure, and Multiliteracies*, edited by James P. Purdy and Dànielle Nicole DeVoss, U of Michigan P, www.digitalrhetoriccollaborative.org/makingspace/ch11a.html. Accessed 27 Mar. 2018.

Selber, Stuart A. *Multiliteracies for a Digital Age*. Southern Illinois UP, 2004.

Selfe, Cynthia L. "Students Who Teach Us: A Case Study of a New Media Text Designer." *Writing New Media: Theory and Applications for Expanding the*

Teaching of Composition, edited by Anne Frances Wysocki et al., Utah State UP, 2004, pp. 43–66.

Selfe, Cynthia L., and Richard J. Selfe, Jr. "The Politics of the Interface: Power and its Exercise in Electronic Contact Zones." *College Composition and Communication*, vol. 45, no. 4, Dec. 1994, pp. 480–504.

Supiano, Beckie. "It Matters a Lot Who Teaches Introductory Courses. Here's Why." *The Chronicle of Higher Education*, 15 Apr. 2018, www.chronicle.com/article/It-Matters-a-Lot-Who-Teaches/243125.

"A Symposium of Fostering Teaching Quality." *Writing Program Administration*, vol. 34, no. 1, 2010, pp. 148–65.

"WPA Outcomes Statement for First-Year Composition (3.0)." *Council of Writing Program Administrators*, 17 July 2014, wpacouncil.org/positions/outcomes.html.

Yancey, Kathleen Blake. "Made Not Only in Words: Composition in a New Key." *College Composition and Communication*, vol. 56, no. 2, Dec. 2004, pp. 297–328.

———. *Writing in the Twenty-First Century: A Report from the National Council of Teachers of English*. NCTE, 2009, www.ncte.org/library/NCTEFiles/Press/Yancey_final.pdf.

Reclaiming Composition: A Twenty-First-Century Interdisciplinary Imperative

Derek Owens and Tara Roeder

As other essays in this collection demonstrate, to consider alphabetic literacy as belonging to the past and to consider digital image, video, and sound as belonging to the future is to entertain a false binary. However, we argue that the term *writing studies* (coined as a way to expand the purview of composition beyond the first-year writing classroom) privileges traditional alphabetic print at the expense of other strategies and modes of meaning-making. Considering the wide variety of practices and technologies our students engage with—designing Web sites, shooting and editing video, making handmade books, performing and recording spoken-word poetry—we propose that *composition and design* better captures what it is we do in the twenty-first century. We maintain that the multimodal turn in composition, combined with a growing interest in design thinking, signifies an increasingly cross-disciplinary field more than a self-contained discipline, and that such a field cannot be subsumed or co-opted by other disciplines, including English.

Print has always existed in collaboration with the visual and the aural. The designation *composition and design* calls for a shift in attitude and acceptance: a willingness to learn from our students and other colleagues about methodologies of composition that might be unfamiliar to us but that demand inclusion in our courses; an eagerness to construct classroom environments and curricula in which multiple and hybrid forms of composing circulate; and an openness to courses designed as fluid studio workshops in which students and faculty members alike experiment with different compositional strategies, technologies, and forms.

In this essay we look at how the term *writing studies* surfaced as a replacement for *composition*, trace the growing impact of design thinking and the multimodal turn as foundational shifts that are more representative of our work than the label *writing studies*, and ultimately argue that composition and design's increasingly cross-disciplinary nature productively challenges the departmental silo model that has so often hampered our field's institutional positioning.

When *Writing Studies* Replaced *Composition*

At some point early in the twenty-first century *composition* became *writing studies*. Looking back, the shift was probably inevitable; it was only several decades earlier that English as a discipline had, like other fields, added the now ubiquitous *studies* to its name. But this not-insignificant shift in terminology, which was never simply the addition of a word but the replacement of *composition* with *writing*, has taken place with little commentary or self-reflective analysis. Now that *writing studies* has crept into our lexicon, pushing aside the older *composition*, a review of the literature can piece together an etymology of sorts, tracing when and why the term began to surface.

One of the earliest appearances of writing studies as a concept is found in a 1993 presentation at CCCC by Shirley K. Rose, "Metaphors for Creating a Department of Writing," an account of when six faculty members who taught academic skills attempted to create a department of rhetoric and writing studies, and the department of English and comparative literature opposed the change. Rose's presentation never defines writing studies; rather, her focus is to analyze her English colleagues' resistance as a reflection of feelings of emotional loss, deprivation, diminishment, and even violence and brutalization. Six years later Richard Boyd published "Reading Student Resistance: The Case of the Missing Other," which begins with this sentence: "Teachers and scholars working in the field of composition and writing studies have long been interested in what has typically been characterized as student 'resistance'" (589). It is the only time the phrase "composition and writing studies" is used, implying that writing studies is both separate yet also connected to composition. A year later, Katherine Haake introduced the term *creative writing studies* in *What Our Speech Disrupts: Feminism and Creative Writing Studies*, and while here there is no explicit reasoning for the addition of *studies*, in 2009 Tim Mayers made a case for further professionalizing creative writing by tacking *studies* onto the term in "One Simple Word: From Creative Writing to Creative Writing Studies."

While the term *writing studies* makes some tentative appearances throughout the 1990s, it picks up momentum early in the twenty-first century. In various articles the term gets invoked as a matter of fact, as if it had already been well established (Davis); elsewhere, the term is connected to *writing majors* in opposition to English studies and English majors (Delli Carpini). In a 2006 issue of *College English* (vol. 69, no. 2) featuring several articles on the theme "What Should College English Be?," the term *rhetoric and writing studies* is used instead of *composition*, though in "Making the Case for Disciplinarity in Rhetoric, Composition, and Writing Studies: The Visibility Project," the authors refer at some times to "the disciplinarity" of writing and rhetoric studies, and elsewhere to "rhetoric and composition/writing studies" (Phelps and Ackerman). Gregory G. Colomb is even more ambivalent in "Franchising the Future," where he refers to "the future of rhetoric and composition (or writing studies or whatever label we use)" (11).

The shift from *composition* to *writing studies* has been largely opportunistic, an attempt to garner disciplinary leverage and respect within institutions (particularly from English departments) that had traditionally undermined or dismissed composition as not on the same intellectual playing field as other, more bona fide disciplines—"to improve the disciplinary status and professional respect for the work of writing teachers" and raise "writing studies' standing in the academy" (Heilker and Vandenberg, *Keywords* xv). Despite the fact that first-year composition remains the most widely taught course in colleges in the United States (or perhaps because of this fact), composition has always struggled against being identified as a service discipline, a marginalized skills-and-drills arena in contrast to disciplines that characterize themselves as more scholarly knowledge-making domains with historically established research methodologies. Complicating this is the widely held perception that composition is ultimately something all faculty members can inherently claim as their own: "it is a truism in rhetoric and composition that everyone thinks they know how to teach writing" (Skinnell 14).

It is early on in the twenty-first century when we begin to see a surge in calls for writing studies as an independent, autonomous field. Charles Bazerman's "The Case for Writing Studies as a Major Discipline," published in 2002, criticizes composition for its narrow scope and its preoccupation with pedagogy, particularly of the first-year writing course. He argues that composition finds itself

> best positioned to begin to put together the large, important, and multidimensional story of writing. We are the only profession that makes writing its central concern. . . . It is time for us to rise above the accidents of disciplinary history that have kept our truly significant subject only minimally visible and that have blinded us to the enormity of the material we have taken to instruct our students in. It is time to recognize that writing provides some of the fundamental mechanisms that make our world work, and it is time to assert that writing needs to be taken seriously along with the other major matters of inquiry supported by institutional structures. (33–34)

In hopes that his appeal will be taken seriously, Bazerman distinguishes between English studies as a forum for textual interpretation and writing studies' focus on the cultural production of writing. A similar position is shared by Susan Miller in the same volume. Miller goes so far as to view writing studies as a realm absent of the baggage she ascribes to composition:

> Writing studies places a nonevaluative spin on the more traditional label "composition studies," offering a way to describe the cultural work undertaken in any act of writing. By defining that work as the conjunction of a specific composing process and a resulting text, "writing studies" thus decisively promotes attention to the production of texts over their interpretation. (41)

It's no surprise that an article like Douglas Downs and Elizabeth Wardle's "Teaching about Writing, Righting Misconceptions: (Re)envisioning 'First-Year Composition' as 'Introduction to Writing Studies'" made an appearance five years later. Downs and Wardle privilege their version of writing studies to such an extent that they recast first-year writing as an introduction to scholarship written by compositionists—that is, what used to be called compositionists, since now they would be framed as writing-studies specialists. Their proposal to turn first-year writing courses into an entry-level seminar where students read "studies by Berkenkotter, Sommers, Perl, Flower and Hayes, Murray, Swales, Dawkins, Beason" (560) is an unapologetic bid to help establish writing studies majors: "a cornerstone course for writing studies majors beginning to take root across the country." Their parenthetical aside—

"(Having a major, of course, dramatically changes a field's standing in the academy)"—makes clear their objective is to use first-year writing curricula as a mechanism for attaining greater professional and institutional standing (554).

A less self-promotional stance that raises questions about the future of writing is found in Kathleen Blake Yancey's 2009 *Writing in the Twenty-First Century.* Yancey quotes John Trimbur's suggestion in 2003 that we design writing studies curricula that shift our focus from improving writing to writing as an object of study. Quoting Trimbur, Yancey writes, "When we say 'writing' . . . do we mean its participial form that refers to writing as an unfolding activity of composing or do we designate its noun form to refer to the material manifestations and consequences of writing as it circulates in the world?" (7). Yancey responds to Trimbur's question in this manner:

> This question, in posing *both* answers, points us beyond windowpane composition and beyond an obsessive attention to form and beyond writing as testing; it points us toward creating the fully articulated research base, the theories of composing, and the planned curriculum that have been missing from composition and its instruction for over a hundred years. (7–8)

She closes her essay by proposing three key tasks for professionals in the field. Interestingly, the first of them draws our attention to neither the participial nor the noun form of *writing* but rather returns us to *composition*: "Articulate the new models of composing developing right in front of our eyes" (7).

However one traces the evolution of how we define our field (this brief tour is only a cursory sketch of a nuanced trajectory), it seems clear that during the two decades between the publication of Paul Heilker and Peter Vandenberg's *Keywords in Composition Studies* in 1996 and the updated *Keywords in Writing Studies* in 2015, our field effectively retired the term *composition*, along with its windowpane pedagogical focus, with the presumed breadth and scope of the term *writing studies*. In their introduction to the updated *Keywords in Writing Studies*, Heilker and Vandenberg write that "[o]ne way to gauge the extent to which the study of writing can be considered a serious intellectual endeavor with full disciplinarity might be to look at how *writing studies* is being used to name or rename university departments, programs, and research centers" (xv).

Composition and Design

In recent years compositionists have invoked design as not just an essential component in our praxis but a central metaphor around which the field might be reconceptualized. As Richard Marback (whose influential article is addressed below) points out, perhaps the earliest call for design is "Process Paradigms in Design and Composition: Affinities and Directions," an overlooked essay by Charles Kostelnick published in 1989 that turns to design studies as a new means for theorizing process paradigms. Seven years later the New London Group proposed "a metalanguage of multiliteracies based on the concept of 'design'" (73). Inspired by the centrality of innovative design in the workplace, the authors promote not just "the grammars of languages" but those "of other semiotic systems such as film, photography, or gesture" (74). In furthering a "pedagogy of multiliteracies" they highlight the need to acknowledge six "metalanguages"—linguistic design, visual design, gestural design, spatial design, and audio design (83)—to be taught within the context of "situated practice": "immersion in meaningful practices within a community of learners who are capable of playing multiple and different roles based on their backgrounds and experiences" (85). Although the authors focused on linguistic design more than their other metalanguages (and despite a problematic vocabulary reliant upon goals of "mastery," "expert" teachers and "novice" students), the New London Group's "A Pedagogy of Multiliteracies: Designing Social Futures" marked a significant turn.

The New London Group's article appeared the same year Barbara Maria Stafford published a collection of articles claiming that "[t]oday's instructional landscape must inevitably evolve or die," advocating for transdisciplinary "*constructive* model[s] of education through vision" (3). Stafford's sentiment that "we need to disestablish the view of cognition as dominantly and aggressively linguistic" (7) is echoed in Gunther Kress's publication four years later, "Design and Transformation: New Theories of Meaning." Here Kress warns that "the single, exclusive and intensive focus on written language has dampened the full development of all kinds of human potentials" (qtd. in Marback W406). Two years later Diana George's "From Analysis to Design: Visual Communication in the Teaching of Writing," inspired in part by the New London Group, suggested that "[p]erhaps more than any other technology, desktop publishing has moved writing instruction into the world of design. . . . To talk of literacy instruction in terms of *design* means to ask writers to draw on available knowledge and, at the same time, transform that knowledge/those forms as we redesign" (26). A year after George's article, Mary E. Hocks's "Understanding Visual Rhetoric in Digital Writing Environments" appeared, in which she urges us to help students "enact their understanding of visual and digital rhetoric" through such methods as storyboarding for digital environments, mapping and drawing media elements for Web sites, and considering the use of color, graphics, spatial placement, and so on (650). Such "[d]esign projects require writers to look at successful models, to think deeply about audience, to design visual and verbal arguments together, and to actively construct new knowledge" (651–52).

To date, the most influential composition studies article promoting design is Marback's CCC article from 2009, "Embracing Wicked Problems: The Turn to Design in Composition Studies." Marback references design theorists while providing in-depth readings of the aforementioned articles by Kostelnick, the New London Group, Kress, George, and Hocks. His article opens with the claim that the "centrifugal forces of critique" that have influenced the field for decades, beginning with James Berlin's late-'80s social constructivism, are now "giving way to centripetal interest in design" (W398). Marback's uses of *wicked* comes from design theorist Horst W. J. Rittel, who uses the word to describe the type of perplexing design challenges that need to be tackled by out-of-the box, inventive thinkers. Marback's article introduces an exciting claim that composition needs, and in some ways is already engaged in, a paradigm shifting "turn to design" (W400), inspiring further scholarship that takes the metaphors of design (and wickedness) into new directions, such as Matthew Newcomb's arguments for sustainable design through "situational creativity" and Carrie S. Leverenz's call to teach writing as a design process that involves experimentation with prototypes.

As exciting as the implications for this "design turn" are, in some ways the current scholarship by compositionists turning toward design studies might not go far enough. Marback points in this direction when he critiques George for perpetuating text-based biases with her preoccupation with "visual argumentation" (W415) and her focus on "teaching the design of the visual in terms of the textual, using a vocabulary of claims and evidence that does not speak to the features of the visual that make it a distinctly pervasive and persuasive form of communicating meaning" (W411). Along with this reliance on textual vocabularies, we find circulating throughout some of these articles an overreliance on tropes of argumentation and critique, and a deemphasizing of student-centered construction in favor of a need to continually respond to outside audiences. When Marback invokes our need to "describe, teach, and then evaluate our responses to the relationship of image and word" (W406), the emphasis here is still on *reception*—responding not to works created by students but rather to those by (often hypothetical) designers. What's missing is an attention to *making*, the material end products fashioned by students who are also their own audience: working with a variety of nonalphabetic materials in an open, exploratory realm governed by the student's individual needs, passions, and interests. This preoccupation with solving problems and designing for the needs of outside audiences and clients—an understandable focus of the design firms where much of design thinking originates—can be problematic when displaced to composition courses like first-year writing where, we argue, students' goals ought to take center stage. Our concern is with how the discourse of design, at least how it is currently influencing composition, can seem to overemphasize critique and argument as the obvious endpoints. Exploratory making and experimentation—even when there is no explicit problem, per se, to be addressed, other than students' desire to become further immersed in their fascinations—are just as important as composing for and responding to outside recipients.

Ironically, Marback closes his argument that composition studies is now experiencing a design turn by putting on the brakes and urging colleagues to "tame the ambitions in any appeal to design" (W415). While he is understandably concerned about would-be design proponents who don't fully appreciate the cross-disciplinary imperatives involved, and who ultimately still wind up privileging the textual over the visual, we propose something more along the lines of an untamed learning environment where students are introduced to an overabundance of composing opportunities—the composition environment as an open exploratory space where students can experiment with photography, video, Web design, handmade books, textiles, performance, and so on. We wish to underscore Marback's conclusion when he declares that "[d]esigning is about making artifacts" (W418). And here is where compositionists inspired by design thinking can benefit from further consideration of key figures in the field who are advancing the multimodal turn—a turn that tends to be consistently more focused on student-based, experiential learning than on outside design challenges.

The first significant study in composition that would lead to the multimodal turn is Geoffrey Sirc's *English Composition as a Happening*.

Newcomb, in extending and refining Marback's turn to design, quotes Sirc's insistence that our goal should be for students to "[do] something unconventional, sublime, exciting" in our courses (596). Newcomb follows this, urging that "[d]esign in composition should not take only a technical direction but should allow a more experimental and innovative approach, with new creative passions involved, for many forms of written composition" (598)—not just for written composition, but other modes of construction as well. Certainly we disagree with Newcomb when he writes: "What does design do? It brings an aesthetic element to composition that has a more situational or rhetorical basis, and less of the individualistic focus that can come with creative writing in composition" (606). For too long the personal, the individualistic, the expressive have been unfairly assumed to be uncritical, solipsistic, and socially disengaged (see Roeder and Gatto). And yet we do share Newcomb's enthusiasm in the closing of his essay when he invokes "multiwriting," the concept introduced by Robert Davis and Mark Shadle, early proponents of the multimodal, multimedia turn.

Other foundational works for expanding composition to include multimodal, multigenre, and multimedia enactments are to be found from scholars like Jody Shipka, Jason Palmeri, and Nancy Mack. Shipka (a former student of Sirc's) explores the multimodal dimensions of composition in *Toward a Composition Made Whole*; examples of relevant student work are showcased on her Web site (remediatethis.com/student/index.html). Mack's *Engaging Writers with Multigenre Research Projects* is a necessary companion to Shipka's work, as is Palmeri's *Remixing Composition: A History of Multimodal Writing Pedagogy*, which concludes as follows:

> Ultimately, if we seek to value the diverse embodied knowledges of *all* students and teachers in the field of composition, we must embrace a capacious vision of multimodal pedagogy that includes both digital and nondigital forms of communication: live oratory and digital audio documentary; quilting and video gaming; paper-based scrapbooking and digital storytelling; protest chanting and activist video making. (160)

The intersection of design and multimodality privileges exploration, discovery, and surprise, and not just the solving of problems presented to students by their instructors. It calls for learning environments where students can interact with all manner of media and within a context that rewards risk-taking in open studio workshops where projects revolve around students' interests, passions, cultures, and histories. It emphasizes critically expressive, creative practice—entertaining genres and media in a safe, flexible space where play, making, and invention regularly occur.

In our courses, for example, students design their own projects in a variety of forms and using a variety of media. Our courses are workshop-based, collaborative, and generative spaces where students have produced everything from cookbooks to documentaries, Web sites to podcasts, performances to comic books. Students have created video presentations composed and edited on their cameras, designed chapbooks of prose poetry mingling with photography, and constructed mixed-media journals using acrylics, collage, and textiles.[1] By privileging the design, making, and response to work in multiple modes, we value the composition course as a site for experimentation as we ourselves experiment with the implications of teaching *composing* in an expansive, more inclusive environment.

Future Implications

Whether one characterizes these expansive shifts in the field as the turn toward design, or the multimodal turn, or some combination of both, it should be clear that the cross-disciplinary nature of composition as a field is misunderstood if we insist on framing it within the parameters of *writing* studies. Nor does composition, viewed in this light, have any inherent or obligatory connection to English studies (if anything, composition would have as much if not more in common with curricula in departments of art and design, of film, television, video, and especially numerous new programs in design studies [see Gardner]). As composition continues to expand its focus to include modes of composing beyond writing, acknowledging that the alphabetic is not inherently composition's center but just one of many modalities relevant to acts of composing, our field cannot help but continually seek to rearticulate its role within the academy.

Not that this will be easy. Even for programs that wish to establish a self-contained writing discipline instead of the more expansive terrain necessitated by multimodality and design, maintaining institutional autonomy ought never be taken for granted. Writing program administrators and faculty members who teach writing would be wise to bear in mind Scott Stevens's cautionary reminder: "no writing program, no matter how successful, stands invulnerable to being jacked" (29). In just several decades there has been a surge in various iterations of writing studies programs and in new majors, minors, and certificate recipients. The CCCC Committee on the Major in Writing and Rhetoric's spring 2016 report counts 141 undergraduate majors in writing or rhetoric, either in English departments with dedicated writing tracks or separate departments of writing ("Committee"). As the number of students majoring in writing has gone up, however, English majors are in decline, a widely documented trend (Flaherty). Douglas Hesse, for instance, cites how "Yale University saw its number of English majors drop almost by half from 2002 to 2008, while the writing program at Rowan University increased ten-fold over that same period" (14). English departments have long taken for granted an institutional power stemming from their ownership of first-year writing courses that, because of the course's cornerstone status in core and general education curricula, lends those departments considerable influence. Within the current climate such departments might well dig in their heels with renewed energy to control and colonize writing programs—programs they may not have designed or wished to teach in but that offer considerable departmental gain.

Nor will composition necessarily have an easy time reestablishing itself as an inherently cross-disciplinary site within institutional landscapes still largely resistant to interdisciplinarity. Those of us drawn to these new turns and forces that are reshaping our field, and who eagerly embrace video, sound, drawing, performance, and other modes of composing as we continue to unpack the implications of design and multimodality on our work, can't naively expect other departments that implicitly declare ownership over these domains to automatically embrace our efforts.

And yet, as composition is well on its way to being recognized as a field of composing in the broadest sense of the term, the prospects are both energizing and challenging. Digital technologies will only continue to advance, rapidly and unexpectedly, making it easier for students (and ourselves) to compose with image, sound, text, and motion using widely accessible tools and materials. As our courses increasingly mirror studio workshop environments where we surprise ourselves with new making methodologies and the artifacts they engender, we can expect composition and design to evolve, in perhaps bold and unanticipated ways, further establishing itself as a uniquely creative and interdisciplinary realm.

Note

1. The implications for assessment in such an environment deserve their own essay, but we might evaluate students on their commitment to regular production and experimentation along with sustained peer response. Students might also design their own rubrics for various projects.

Works Cited

Bazerman, Charles. "The Case for Writing Studies as a Major Discipline." Olsen, pp. 32–38.

Boyd, Richard. "Reading Student Resistance: The Case of the Missing Other." *JAC*, vol. 19, no. 4, 1999, pp. 589–605.

Colomb, Gregory G. "Franchising the Future." *College Composition and Communication*, vol. 62, no. 1, Sept. 2010, pp. 11–30.

"Committee on the Major in Writing and Rhetoric." *Conference on College Composition and Communication*, Mar. 2016, www.ncte.org/cccc/committees/majorrhetcomp.

Davis, Diane D. "Finitude's Clamor; or, Notes toward a Communitarian Literacy." *College Composition and Communication*, vol. 53, no. 1, Sept. 2001, pp. 119–45.

Davis, Robert L., and Mark F. Shadle. *Teaching Multiwriting: Researching and Composing with Multiple Genres, Media, Disciplines, and Cultures*. Southern Illinois UP, 2007.

Delli Carpini, Dominic. "Re-writing the Humanities: The Writing Major's Effect upon Undergraduate Studies in English Departments." *Composition Studies*, vol. 35, no. 1, Spring 2007, pp. 15–36.

Downs, Douglas, and Elizabeth Wardle. "Teaching about Writing, Righting Misconceptions: (Re)envisioning 'First-Year Composition' as 'Introduction to Writing Studies.'" *College Composition and Communication*, vol. 58, no. 4, June 2007, pp. 552–84.

Flaherty, Colleen. "Major Exodus." *Inside Higher Ed*, 26 Jan. 2015, www.insidehighered.com/news/2015/01/26/where-have-all-english-majors-gone.

Gardner, Lee. "Can Design Thinking Redesign Higher Ed?" *The Chronicle of Higher Education*, 10 Sept. 2017, www.chronicle.com/article/Can-Design-Thinking-Redesign/241126.

George, Diana. "From Analysis to Design: Visual Communication in the Teaching of Writing." *College Composition and Communication*, vol. 54, no. 1, Sept. 2002, pp. 11–39.

Haake, Katharine. *What Our Speech Disrupts: Feminism and Creative Writing Studies*. NCTE, 2000.

Heilker, Paul, and Peter Vandenberg, editors. *Keywords in Composition Studies*. Boynton/Cook, 1996.

———. *Keywords in Writing Studies*. Utah State UP, 2015.

Hesse, Douglas. "Who Speaks for Writing? Expertise, Ownership, and Stewardship." Rich and Lay, pp. 9–22.

Hocks, Mary E. "Understanding Visual Rhetoric in Digital Writing Environments." *College Composition and Communication*, vol. 54, no. 4, June 2003, pp. 629–56.

Kostelnick, Charles. "Process Paradigms in Design and Composition: Affinities and Directions." *College Composition and Communication*, vol. 40, no. 3, Oct. 1989, pp. 267–81.

Kress, Gunther. "Design and Transformation: New Theories of Meaning." *Multiliteracies: Literacy Learning and the Design of Social Futures*, edited by Bill Cope and Mary Kalantzis, Routledge, 2000, pp. 153–61.

Leverenz, Carrie S. "Design Thinking and the Wicked Problem of Teaching Writing." *Computers and Composition*, vol. 33, Sept. 2014, pp. 1–12.

Mack, Nancy. *Engaging Writers with Multigenre Research Projects: A Teacher's Guide*. Teachers College P, 2015.

Marback, Richard. "Embracing Wicked Problems: The Turn to Design in Composition Studies." *College Composition and Communication*, vol. 61, no. 2, Dec. 2009, pp. W397–W419.

Mayers, Tim. "One Simple Word: From Creative Writing to Creative Writing Studies." *College English*, vol. 71, no. 3, Jan. 2009, pp. 217–28.

Miller, Susan. "Writing Studies as a Mode of Inquiry." Olsen, pp. 41–54.

Newcomb, Matthew. "Sustainability as a Design Principle for Composition: Situational Creativity as a Habit of Mind." *College Composition and Communication*, vol. 63, no. 4, June 2012, pp. 593–615.

The New London Group. "A Pedagogy of Multiliteracies: Designing Social Futures." *Harvard Educational Review*, vol. 66, no. 1, Spring 1996, pp. 60–92.

Olsen, Gary A., editor. *Rhetoric and Composition as Intellectual Work*. Southern Illinois UP, 2002.

Palmeri, Jason. *Remixing Composition: A History of Multimodal Writing Pedagogy*. Southern Illinois UP / NCTE, 2012.

Phelps, Louise Wetherbee, and John M. Ackerman. "Making the Case for Disciplinarity in Rhetoric, Composition, and Writing Studies: The Visibility Project." *College Composition and Communication*, vol. 62, no. 1, Sept. 2010, pp. 180–215.

Rich, Jennifer, and Ethna D. Lay, editors. *Who Speaks for Writing: Stewardship in Writing Studies in the Twenty-First Century*. Peter Lang, 2012.

Roeder, Tara, and Roseanne Gatto, editors. *Critical Expressivism: Theory and Practice in the Composition Classroom*. WAC Clearinghouse / Parlor Press, 2015.

Rose, Shirley K. "Metaphors for Creating a Department of Writing." Conference on College Composition and Communication, 31 Mar.–3 Apr. 1993, San Diego, CA.

Shipka, Jody. *Toward a Composition Made Whole*. U of Pittsburgh P, 2011.

Sirc, Geoffrey. *English Composition as a Happening*. Utah State UP, 2002.

Skinnell, Ryan. *Conceding Composition: A Crooked History of Composition's Institutional Fortunes*. Utah State UP, 2016.

Stafford, Barbara Maria. *Good Looking: Essays on the Virtue of Images*. MIT P, 1996.

Stevens, Scott. "Who Stole Our Subject?" Rich and Lay, pp. 23–32.

Trimbur, John. "Changing the Question: Should Writing Be Studied?" *Composition Studies*, vol. 31, no. 1, Spring 2003, pp. 15–24.

Yancey, Kathleen Blake. *Writing in the Twenty-First Century: A Report from the National Council of Teachers of English*. NCTE, 2009, www.ncte.org/library/NCTEFiles/Press/Yancey_final.pdf.

Epilogue

John Trimbur

Writing Changes is a welcome sign that the sweeping generalities that greeted the arrival of multimodality in US college composition in the United States are now starting to subside. The contributors in this collection have for the most part avoided the breathless enthusiasm that cast the multimodality of digital culture as an epoch-changing break from the rearguard monomodality of alphabetic writing. This sense of exhilarating newness, it didn't take long for skeptics to see, posed some serious questions of historical interpretation and, unwittingly or not, aligned with high tech marketing strategies and the discourses of neoliberalism. As Bruce Horner notes in his essay for this collection, "Modality as Social Practice in Written Language," the idea that multimodality represents "the new, the better, the enriching, and even the liberating" has troubling affinities with neoliberalism's market mentality, especially with the aura of novelty, diversity, and disruptive innovation that disguises the commodification of new media by promising unprecedented personal powers to its users.

Traces of this millenarian sense of multimodality remain on composition's radar screen, to be sure. But the essays in this volume, I am happy to report, begin from a more measured and nuanced stance to examine multimodal text designs, the pedagogical possibilities of multimodal composing, and the theoretical premises and historical conditions on which the very notion of multimodality rests. If anything, as the volume's editor, Pegeen Reichert Powell, notes, the collection reflects a newly emergent consensus that rejects the idea that multimodality represents a break with the past, holding instead that "all writing is multimodal." The impulse that animates this collection is to sidestep the binaries—the old and new literacies, print and digital cultures, the logic of writing and the logic of the image—that inflected the early uptake of multimodality. The task instead is to sort through the blend of New London Group multiliteracies, new media theory, digital rhetorics, and Gunther Kress–style social semiotics that US college composition put together under the aegis of multimodality in the early 2000s.

In this sense, the catchphrase *all writing is multimodal* has joined the cavalcade of slogans—*process not product, writing is a social act, writing is never neutral*—that mark moments of high intensity in composition, when new sensibilities and conceptual frameworks emerge and consolidate. As Reichert Powell's introduction recognizes, however, while such slogans may seem at first glance to clarify the past, explain the present, and point to the future, the complications are quick to set in, unsettling what had seemed like a reasonable balance of attention to both new-media-age multimodal composing and the multimodal analysis of the production and reception of print texts. The problem is that even though all writing (or composing or design or textual labor or whatever you want to call it) amounts at the point of production, in the moment of poiesis, to a multimodal deployment of the available semiotic resources, there are instances that the slogan *all writing is multimodal* doesn't really help explain.

I am thinking in particular of cases when actual worldly conflicts take place between alphabetic writing and other systems of multimodal composition. This occurred, for example, as Damián Baca has pointed out, when Spanish invaders encountered the precolonial Mesoamerican writing systems that combined pictographs, hieroglyphs, and abstract signs in codices that made up a vast body of scientific, legal, and ceremonial knowledge. As the Franciscan friar Diego de Landa remarked, at least some of the Spanish were well aware that the Mesoamericans

> used certain characters . . . with which they wrote in their books about their antiquities and their sciences; with these, and with figures, and certain signs in the figures, they understood their matters, made them known, and taught them. We found a great number of books . . . and since they contained nothing but superstitions and falsehoods of the devil we burned them all, which they took most grievously, and which gave them great pain. (qtd. in Baca 236)

Notice here the close attention to native texts as a signifying system, with their "characters," "figures," and "signs in the figures," and the acknowledgement on Landa's part of the role of indigenous composition in the production and circulation of knowledge. For Landa, the issue is not literacy per se. He clearly acknowledges the capacity to produce written texts. It is instead the type of inscription employed, the hybrid nonalphabetic writing system that belongs, he says, in its strangeness to the "superstitions and falsehoods of the devil." Faced with an indigenous semiotics they had never seen before, the Spanish marked Mesoamerican writing as deviant—as a departure from the Eurocentric alphabetic norm, an offense to God, and, accordingly, the grounds for conquest and occupation.

Or consider the Protestant Reformation as a semiotic battle over rival sign systems. On one hand, the older Roman Catholicism was based on a multisensory multimodality, with its seasonal rituals, Latin liturgy, priestly vestments, incense, wine and communion wafers, choirs, the pageantry of solemn high masses, and so on. On the other hand, the upstart Protestants located the authority of God's word in the alphabetic literacy of the newly translated vernacular bibles of early European print culture. In contrast to what they considered the vanity and ostentatious display of Catholic churches, Protestant iconoclasts sought an austere style, as free as possible of sensory distractions, eliminating the pictorialism of statues, stations of the cross, and stained glass, sometimes sacking and burning Catholic churches to wipe out the tangible corruptions of the Papists that stood between the congregants and unmediated access to God's word in print.

The point is that alphabetic literacy looms in these two examples not so much as a practice you can easily slip into the all-writing-is-multimodal paradigm. More consequentially, the alphabet served as an icon of power and cultural domination, the normative underpinning of language ideologies dedicated to the eradication of alternative sign systems—and too often their users as well. The semiotic polarization that is so evident during the Spanish conquest and the Protestant Reformation involves blood and thunder, not just problematic conceptual binaries you can dissolve theoretically. Alphabetic writing systems, that is, secured their hegemonic place in early modern Europe and in the New World by establishing what Walter Mignolo calls a "locus of enunciation" (114–16), or rhetorical footing, seized in a war of positions and endowed through struggle, conquest, and occupation with power, normativity, and legitimacy.

The essays in *Writing Changes* are good at dismantling dichotomies, showing what Hannah Rule calls the "dynamic multimodality within the linguistic," as well as what Reichert Powell identifies as "the ways that alphabetic writing is intrinsic to producing and circulating new media." I am amazed by the range and variety of semiotic practices and artifacts the contributors analyze, including the ephemera of vernacular literacies (Cooper), the work of translation (Gonzales), medieval manuscripts (Davis and Mueller), search engine optimization schemes (Sheffield), augmented reality technology (Blevins), textbooks (Sarat-St. Peter and Allan), and social media (Vie). Interesting paradoxes turn up, such as the gap between an online badging system and the print texts students submit to gain badges (Paster and Reid). And there are compelling intellectual recoveries, such as T. W. Adorno's "Essay as Form" (Harris) and Edward Corbett's lexicon of style (Lutkewitte et al.). The overriding sense of the volume is nonbinary, emphasizing the interpenetration of signs, the nonisolability of modalities, the bricolage of remediation and remix, the textual labor that shows how all writing is multimodal.

What remains more faintly marked, however, and why I bring up the Spanish conquest and the Protestant Reformation, is the variable and shifting epistemic, cultural, and political authority ascribed to the realization of modalities. At times the text objects in the book appear oddly unmarked or uninflected, as though they don't appear in systems of value, economies of writing, or political states of exception. It's not that the contributors have failed to contextualize their materials; it's more that the discussions, for all their sophistication, tend toward the technical side and the poetics of making, with little emphasis on texts as vectors of conflict and little attention to the contending language ideologies, semiotic stratifications, and historical valences that modalities simultaneously index and enact. The examples I have offered—of the Spanish conquest and the Protestant Reformation—are, of course, dramatic, even hyperbolic, world-changing events. My point, however, is that the dynamics of semiotic authority and the contentiousness of sign systems they make so evident play out as well in mundane ways, in the ordinary composing situations and practices of school, work, popular culture, and public and counterpublic spheres of influence.

I want to interject here the grammatical meaning of modality as mood to underscore how modalities articulate variable hegemonic and counterhegemonic claims to secure consent to representations of reality. To my mind, the grammatical sense of modality is especially pertinent for the way it directs attention to what Ron Scollon and Suzie Wong Scollon call "a variety of stances that can be taken concerning the value of linguistic statements" (176)—the degree, that is, of certainty, contingency, identification, division, wish fulfillment, regret, and so on that determine the pragmatic force of a verbal statement. (This may be seen, for example, in the linguistic differences between saying *I am going, I must go, I may go, I should go*, and so on.) The usefulness of transferring the grammatical sense of modality to the concerns of this volume is to highlight how the variable deployment of modalities is deeply implicated in the ideological determination of truth-value, social weight, and cultural influence.

Modality, that is, operates across what Jan Blommaert calls "orders of indexicality"—"large stratified complexes in which some forms of semiosis are systematically perceived as valuable, others less valuable and some are not taken into account at all . . ." (38). From this angle, modality expresses degrees of epistemic authority within hierarchical systems that distribute unequally, according to rules of access put in place through protracted struggles, the capacity to determine the rhetorical and political frameworks that represent reality, in what domains, by whom, based on what social solidarities, and for what purposes.

One advantage of foregrounding this grammatical-ideological sense of modality is that it can help circumvent the view that multimodality consists of a set of tools, a repertoire of various affordances that somehow belong to the modes of communication themselves, as inherent properties that sign-makers then draw upon in the activity of composing. Such a model of composing, as Bruce Horner notes, evokes neoliberal ideologies of personal choice, of composers acquiring their means of production from a dazzling array of affordances made available through commodified modes of communication. In contrast to thinking of modalities as affordances that composers acquire from the market of signs to use freely as they see fit, the alternative is to see composers positioning their activity within sign systems that are already accented by history and contending human motives, prestructured by the orders of indexicality that locate modes of communication in variable relation to each other.

One of the promises of neoliberalism, as has been often noted, is to offer more freedom and more agency to individuals than any previous or alternative system. In this regard, thinking of multimodal composing as rhetorical positioning within a semiotic field appears more constrained and rule-bound, as opposed to the free choice exercised in the multimodal marketplace of affordances. The issue, however, is not the amount but the kind of agency involved: the difference between what Friedrich Engels in *Anti-Duhring* called freedom as the "insight into necessity" (105) and the illusory freedom of choice in an endless—and endlessly unfulfilling—cycle of consumption.

This difference comes across quite clearly, I think, in Bruce Horner's essay, when he argues for understanding modality "as practice rather than text-object element" and for making the aim of writing courses "not the production of particular kinds of text-objects (as in, this week one alphabetic print essay due; next week one multimodal composition due, with more points for more modes) but rather composers' and readers' increasingly conscious concern with modality as social practice." Horner recounts a telling classroom incident when most of his students, given the choice of experimenting with modality in revising an earlier essay, opted for the conventional default look of the manuscript page, rejecting the creativity of adding, say, video clips or images or jazzy graphic design, going instead with "Times 12-point font, double-spaced black ink on white background texts in conventional student essay manuscript layout."

Now, like a lot of writing teachers (see Joseph Harris's essay, for example), I have given students assignments that call on them to translate a print essay into another mode, such as a blog, a graphic essay (drawing on the conventions of comix), or a photo essay, and to write a commentary on the different affordances and their rhetorical effects. What Horner's essay makes me realize is that this is a studio exercise; it's practice with techniques and modes, useful in its way, but, even with the reflective piece, the assignment doesn't confront the critical evaluation of semiotic conventions as Horner's students did. There is a significant difference, that is, between the translation approach I've used (and taught many graduate instructors to use) and what Horner calls a "transmodal" approach. As Horner says, his students' decision to use standard print conventions in their revisions is

> evidence of pedagogical accomplishment insofar as even the default was critically considered and chosen rather than unwittingly followed. They were opting not for fewer features but, instead, those that a dominant ideology of multimodality has blinded us from recognizing as modal features. Thus, from a transmodal perspective,

> students can come to see the modal practices that currently constitute conventional writing which that ideology has kept hidden. And, from a transmodal perspective, modality is neither an unquestioned given (the default) nor even an array of choices but, instead, the always emerging outcome of their practices, and of those engaging with their compositions.

Horner's transmodal approach bolsters the grammatical-ideological sense of modality I have been trying to describe here, enabling us to ask, across modalities, why, say, numerical data—when compared to words—have acquired such authority as precise, value-free, and trustworthy elements of knowledge production (as in the expression *numbers don't lie*) in scientific findings, corporate metrics, government audits, or academic citation counts and impact factors. Or one could consider how the shift from black-and-white photography to color was a shift in the default coding orientation that signifies the truth-value of accurate depiction, the feeling of looking out the window, that what you see in the photograph is really there. The idea is not to assemble an unfolding procession of forms and technical innovations but to examine changing evaluations of the relative weight and value of words, images, numbers, styles of graphic design, and so on in the activity of composing—to see how black-and-white photography is not so much surpassed by color as recoded in the shifting order of indexicality to signify historical authenticity, documentary veracity, and nostalgic evocations of the past.

To my mind, the point is that you can't jump out of history—its conflicts and always changing conventions. To think of multimodal composing as "untamed" territory, with an "overabundance of composing opportunities," as Derek Owens and Tara Roeder urge us to do, reveals a desire for a composition class outside history, on an uncharted frontier that calls up images of American exceptionalism, with students as the innocents in the virgin land of semiosis, fleeing, like Huck Finn, civilized sign systems. To be fair, Owens and Roeder are right in the sense that the "untamed learning environment" they imagine is less colonized by teacher-talk, less occupied and settled by the discipline of standard analytical frameworks than alphabetic writing is. My experience teaching multimodality and the rhetoric of visual design is indeed that students are often more excited about the material, more willing to try new things, like reading theory from Roland Barthes or Kress and Theo van Leeuwen, than they might be in an old-fashioned literature or composition course. But, to me, this is a pedagogical gap quickly being filled by work in composition such as this collection rather than an inherent characteristic of new-media and new-composing assignments.

The upshot, I suppose, as Reichert Powell notes in her introduction, is that "the persistence of the writing-multimodality binary in our discourse, in the progress narrative we tell ourselves about the field, may be less about communication practices and more about the lack of a disciplinary center—or, at the very least, that at the center is simply a question of identity." No appeal to "threshold concepts" or dissolving old/new binaries is going to get us out of this fix. The questions of who we are and who the students are and what we imagine we might do together remain a social experiment determined not so much by the illusory phantom of disciplinarity or the overabundance of new technology but by how we make sense of the instability of knowledge production and the ever-changing histories of its textual forms.

Works Cited

Baca, Damián. "Rethinking Composition, Five Hundred Years Later." *JAC*, vol. 29, nos. 1–2, 2009, pp. 229–42.

Blommaert, Jan. *The Sociolinguistics of Globalization*. Cambridge UP, 2010.

Engels, Friedrich. *Anti-Duhring*. 1877. *Marx and Engels: Collected Works*, vol. 25, Lawrence and Wishart, 2010, pp. 1–309.

Mignolo, Walter D. *Local Histories / Global Designs: Coloniality, Subaltern Knowledges, and Border Thinking*. Princeton UP, 2000.

Scollon, Ron, and Suzie Wong Scollon. "Multimodality and Language: A Retrospective and Prospective View." *The Routledge Handbook of Multimodal Analysis*, edited by Carey Jewitt, Routledge, 2009, pp. 170–80.

Notes on Contributors

Elizabeth G. Allan is associate professor in the writing and rhetoric department at Oakland University. Her research interests include writing pedagogy and assessment, multimodal rhetorics in design disciplines, writing across the curriculum and writing in the disciplines, rhetorical ethnography, and the scholarship of teaching and learning. Her research has been published in, among others, *Pedagogy: Critical Approaches to Teaching Literature, Language, Composition, and Culture*; *Assessing Writing*; and *Across the Disciplines*.

Brenta Blevins is assistant professor of writing studies and digital studies at the University of Mary Washington. She teaches and researches multimodal and digital literacy, rhetoric, and pedagogy. Her publications address digital media and pedagogy, multimodality, and multiliteracy centers. In 2017 her dissertation, *From Corporeality to Virtual Reality: Theorizing Literacy, Bodies, and Technology in the Emerging Media of Virtual, Augmented, and Mixed Realities*, received honorable mention for the Hugh Burns Best Dissertation Award.

Beth Brunk-Chavez is dean of Extended University and professor of rhetoric and writing studies at the University of Texas at El Paso. She recently served as president of the University of Texas System Academy of Distinguished Teachers and is a 2009 recipient of the Regents' Outstanding Teaching Award. Her administrative work focuses on online degree programs and her research areas include writing program administration, writing assessment, digital composition, teaching with technologies, and multilanguage writers. She serves on the executive board of the Council of Writing Program Administration.

Sara Cooper is assistant professor of English at Murray State University, where she teaches graduate courses in curriculum, research methods, instructional technology, and writing studies. Her research focuses on disrupting binaries—between form and formula, convention and invention, scholarly and creative work—in secondary and postsecondary contexts toward increased rhetorical agency for marginalized student writers. While completing her doctorate at the University of Houston, she mentored teachers through the Writers in the Schools program.

Matthew Davis is associate professor of English at the University of Massachusetts, Boston, where he directs the Center on Media and Society. He is the coeditor of *Composition Studies*, and his work has appeared or is forthcoming in several edited collections and in *Computers and Composition* and *WAC Journal*, among others.

Laura Gonzales is assistant professor of digital writing and cultural rhetorics in the English department at the University of Florida. Her work focuses on highlighting the importance of linguistic diversity in professional and academic spaces. Gonzales is the author of *Sites of Translation: What Multilinguals Can Teach Us about Digital Writing and Rhetoric* (2018).

Joseph Harris teaches composition, creative nonfiction, and digital writing at the University of Delaware. He has also directed the first-year writing programs at the University of Pittsburgh and Duke University. His books include *A Teaching Subject: Composition since 1966*, *Rewriting: How to Do Things with Texts*, and *The Work of Teaching Writing: Learning from Fiction, Film, and Drama*.

Bruce Horner is endowed chair in rhetoric and composition at the University of Louisville, where he teaches courses in composition theory and pedagogy and in literacy studies. His recent books include *Rewriting Composition: Terms of Exchange* (2016); *Economies of Writing: Revaluations in Rhetoric and Composition* (2017), coedited with Brice Nordquist and Susan M. Ryan; and *Crossing Divides: Exploring Translingual Writing Pedagogies and Programs* (2017), coedited with Laura Tetreault and winner of the MLA Mina P. Shaughnessy Prize.

Rory Lee is assistant professor in rhetoric and composition at Ball State University, specializing in digital rhetoric, multimodality, digital literacies, undergraduate major programs in rhetoric and writing, and multiliteracy centers. He also teaches undergraduate and graduate courses that explore the intersections of digital rhetoric, technology, and culture. His research has appeared in *Kairos*, *Enculturation*, *Computers and Composition Online*, and other edited collections.

Claire Lutkewitte is associate professor of writing at Nova Southeastern University. She teaches courses in basic writing, writing with technologies, research methods, and teaching writing online. Lutkewitte's research interests include writing technologies, first-year composition pedagogy, writing centers, and graduate programs. In addition to articles for journals such as *Academic Exchange Quarterly* and *Writing Lab Newsletter*, she has published three books, including *Mobile Technologies and the Writing Classroom* (2016) and *Multimodal Composition: A Critical Sourcebook* (2013).

Alex Mueller is associate professor of English at the University of Massachusetts, Boston, and the author of *Translating Troy: Provincial Politics in Alliterative Romance* (2013), as well as articles on medieval manuscript culture, open-access publishing, and digital pedagogy. He is currently completing his second book, "Social Networking in the Scriptorium: A Prehistory of Digital Writing," an investigation of medieval rhetorical modes within online writing environments.

Derek Owens is professor of English at St. John's University. Information about his art, writing, and teaching can be found at www.derekowens.net.

Denise P. Paster is associate professor of English in composition and rhetoric at Coastal Carolina University, where she also directs the first-year writing program. Her interests include writing program administration, inquiry-based pedagogies, and teaching with emerging technologies. She published the textbook *Writing Moves* with coauthors Eleanor Kutz and Christian Pulver (2017) and writes with Alan J. Reid about the *Coastal Composition Commons*, a digital badging initiative at Coastal Carolina.

Pegeen Reichert Powell is professor of English and chair of the English and creative writing department at Columbia College Chicago. Reichert Powell is the author of *Retention and Resistance: Writing Instruction and Students Who Leave*, a study of the role of writing instruction in institutional retention efforts (2014). Her work on pedagogy, writing program administration, and critical discourse analysis has been published in several journals and edited collections.

Alan J. Reid is assistant professor of first-year writing and instructional technologies at Coastal Carolina University, where he teaches English and new media courses. He also works in the Center for Research and Reform in Education at Johns Hopkins University as an evaluation analyst.

Tara Roeder is associate professor of first-year writing at St. John's University in Queens, New York. She is coeditor of the collection *Critical Expressivism: Theory and Practice in the Composition Classroom* (2015).

Hannah J. Rule is assistant professor of English in rhetoric and composition at the University of South Carolina, where she teaches courses in composition studies, writing pedagogy, and writing process histories and theories. Her scholarship, focused on pedagogical questions relating to composing processes, freewriting, rhetorical grammar, embodiment, and materiality, appears in venues including *College Composition and Communication*, *Composition Studies*, *Composition Forum*, and in her book, *Situating Writing Processes* (2019).

Hilary A. Sarat-St. Peter is associate professor of professional writing at Columbia College Chicago. Much of her research examines the role of technical communication genres, such as online tutorials, in spreading terrorist tactics.

She has published works about the use of instructional materials and other resources for teaching and learning in the college writing classroom.

Jenna Pack Sheffield is assistant professor of English at the University of New Haven, where she directs the writing across the curriculum program and works as the assistant provost for curriculum innovation. Sheffield's research interests include professional and technical writing pedagogy, writing program administration, and computers and composition. Her research has appeared in *Computers and Composition International*, *Computers and Composition Online*, *WAC Journal*, and the *PraxisWiki* from *Kairos*, among others.

John Trimbur is professor in the Department of Writing, Literature, and Publishing at Emerson College. He has written extensively on cultural studies of literacy, multimodality, and the politics of language, including in the Richard Braddock Award–winning article "English Only and U.S. College Composition," coauthored with Bruce Horner. His most recent book is *Grassroots Literacy and the Written Record: A Textual History of Asbestos Activism in South Africa*.

Star Medzerian Vanguri is associate professor and associate chair in the Department of Writing and Communication at Nova Southeastern University. She teaches courses in writing and rhetoric, and her research interests include stylistics, onomastics, spatial rhetorics, and classroom writing assessment. She has published two edited collections: *Rhetorics of Names and Naming* (2016) and *The Centrality of Style* (with Mike Duncan, 2013). Her work has also appeared in *Rhetoric Review* and the *Journal of Writing Research*.

Stephanie Vie is professor of English and associate dean of Outreach College at the University of Hawai'i, Mānoa. She is coeditor of *Social Writing / Social Media* (2017) and has been interviewed internationally regarding social media, privacy, and the use of hashtags for digital activist efforts. Her work has been published in numerous collections and journals, including *Computers and Composition*, *Kairos*, and *First Monday*.